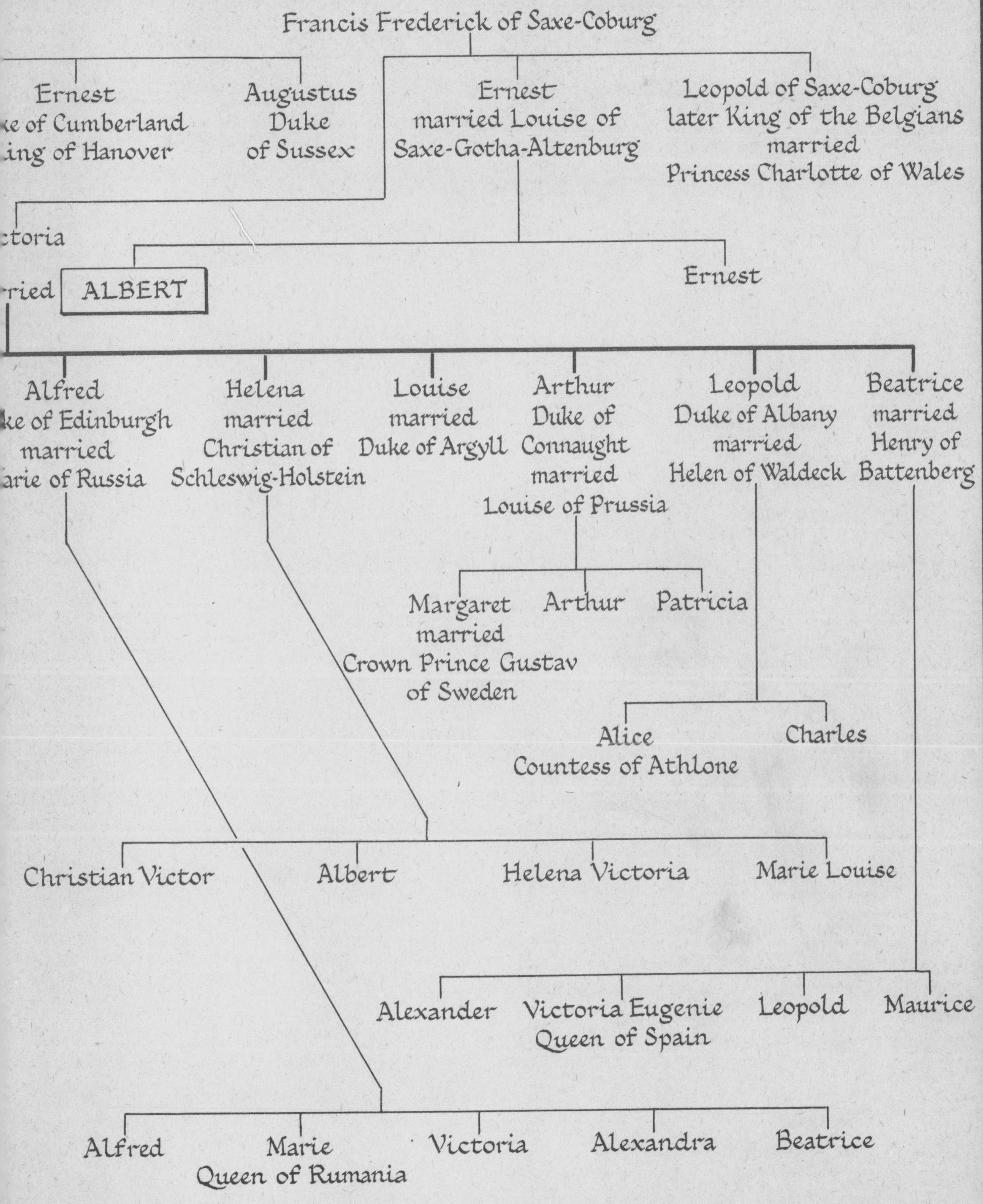

Francis Frederick of Saxe-Coburg

Ernest
Duke of Cumberland
King of Hanover

Augustus
Duke
of Sussex

Ernest
married Louise of
Saxe-Gotha-Altenburg

Leopold of Saxe-Coburg
later King of the Belgians
married
Princess Charlotte of Wales

Victoria

married | ALBERT |

Ernest

Alfred
Duke of Edinburgh
married
Marie of Russia

Helena
married
Christian of
Schleswig-Holstein

Louise
married
Duke of Argyll

Arthur
Duke of
Connaught
married
Louise of Prussia

Leopold
Duke of Albany
married
Helen of Waldeck

Beatrice
married
Henry of
Battenberg

Margaret
married
Crown Prince Gustav
of Sweden

Arthur

Patricia

Alice
Countess of Athlone

Charles

Christian Victor

Albert

Helena Victoria

Marie Louise

Alexander

Victoria Eugenie
Queen of Spain

Leopold

Maurice

Alfred

Marie
Queen of Rumania

Victoria

Alexandra

Beatrice

# VICTORIA R.

*A Biography with Four Hundred Illustrations
based on her Personal Photograph Albums*

*Books by Helmut and Alison Gernsheim:*

L. J. M. DAGUERRE

ROGER FENTON, PHOTOGRAPHER OF THE CRIMEAN WAR

THE HISTORY OF PHOTOGRAPHY

THOSE IMPOSSIBLE ENGLISH

*Books by Helmut Gernsheim:*

CHURCHILL: HIS LIFE IN PHOTOGRAPHS

LEWIS CARROLL—PHOTOGRAPHER

JULIA MARGARET CAMERON

MASTERPIECES OF VICTORIAN PHOTOGRAPHY

TWELFTH CENTURY PAINTINGS AT HARDHAM AND CLAYTON

NEW PHOTO VISION

THE MAN BEHIND THE CAMERA

FOCUS ON ARCHITECTURE AND SCULPTURE

BEAUTIFUL LONDON

Queen Victoria at the age of sixty-six.
*Photograph by Alexander Bassano, 1885.*

# VICTORIA R.

*A Biography with Four Hundred Illustrations
based on her Personal Photograph Albums*

BY

HELMUT AND ALISON GERNSHEIM

G. P. PUTNAM'S SONS    *New York*

*FIRST AMERICAN EDITION*

Library of Congress Catalog Card Number: 59–11013

*Printed in Great Britain by Jarrold and Sons Ltd, Norwich*

# PREFACE

THE main emphasis of our biography of Queen Victoria in word and picture is on her personal life—the woman rather than the sovereign—her relationship with her family and with her ministers, rather than politics.

The Queen's own words, better than ours, convey her feelings and opinions, her joys and sorrows, and for this reason we have frequently quoted from her own writings. Whenever her emotions were aroused, her forceful personality found an outlet in emphatic underlining. Queen Victoria's journal and letters form an indispensable source for every writer on her life and reign. We have been granted permission to include extracts from these; and Messrs. John Murray have allowed us to make use of the text printed in their valuable edition. We have also drawn upon Queen Victoria's letters in the Prussian archives, and unpublished extracts from her journals, relating to photography, have been kindly furnished by the Royal Archives at Windsor.

Our choice of the 400 illustrations from many thousands of portraits and pictures of events may require an explanation of our intentions. As in the case of every great public figure, there exist countless photographs of Queen Victoria and graphic illustrations of events connected with her life. As far as possible we have given preference to truthful if unflattering photographic portraits over imaginative representations. This, we are sure, is as Queen Victoria herself would have wished, for in later years she did not permit any artistic licence deviating from the truth. Comparatively few events, however, could be illustrated by photography during the greater part of her reign, on account of the rather long exposures necessary until fast gelatine dry plates made instantaneous exposures possible (out-of-doors) in the 1880s.

Before the days of the press photographer it was the Queen's habit to commission artists in watercolour to make sketches from life of royal occasions, and many of these are preserved in the souvenir albums at Windsor. They possess a quality of freshness and spontaneity lacking in the woodcut illustrations of the period. We have been privileged to include a selection of these, together with a number of contemporary portrait miniatures. For this, and for facilities generously extended for making use of Queen Victoria's photograph albums, and her own drawings and etchings, we wish to record our dutiful gratitude.

The following photographs have been obtained from other sources:

Bassano Ltd., frontispiece, 253, 267; British Railways, 371, 372; Central Press Photos, 354; Dulwich College Picture Gallery, by permission of the Governors, 13; The London Museum, 29, 88; *Radio Times* Hulton Picture Library, 64, 104, 138, 221, 223, 231, 236, 238, 248, 294, 298, 299, 300, 301, 320; Ministry of Works, by permission of the Controller of H.M. Stationery Office, 349, 350; The National Buildings Record, 355; 321 is reproduced by permission of the executors of the late Sir William Nicholson; 11 is copyright reserved.

In addition, a number of illustrations are from our own collection.

HELMUT AND ALISON GERNSHEIM

# CONTENTS

attack on the Queen. End of her unpopularity. State visit of the Shah. Disraeli's return to power. Marriage of Prince Alfred. Suez Canal shares bought by Disraeli. Queen Victoria proclaimed Empress of India. Russo-Turkish War. The Congress of Berlin. Death of Princess Alice. Marriage of Prince Arthur. Gladstone returns to power. Queen Victoria's imperialism. Death of Disraeli. Another assassination attempt. Marriage and death of Prince Leopold. Death of John Brown. The Queen blames Gladstone for General Gordon's fate. Marriage of Princess Beatrice. Prince Henry of Battenberg enlivens the Royal Household. Queen Victoria's relations with her children. 'This mad, wicked folly of Women's Rights.' The Golden Jubilee.

Accession of the Emperor Frederick III. Queen Victoria's visit to Berlin. Death of Frederick III. The Kaiser quarrels with the Prince of Wales. His visits to England. Death of the Duke of Clarence. Marriage of the Duke of York. The Queen's relief at Gladstone's retirement. Visit to Coburg for inter-marriage of two of her grandchildren. Birth of an heir to the Duke of York. Princess Beatrice widowed. The Kaiser's provocative telegram to President Kruger. Visit of Czar Nicholas II to Balmoral. The Munshi's influence. The Diamond Jubilee. The Boer War. Visit to Ireland. Deaths of Prince Alfred and Prince Christian Victor. Failing health of the Queen. Death and funeral.

Drawn, painted and photographic portraits of Queen Victoria. Early daguerreotypes. Some notable early photographers. Queen Victoria and Prince Albert as patrons of photography. Prince Albert's Raphael catalogue. Photographs of the Crimean War. Prince Albert's suggestion of a photographic museum. The craze for cartes-de-visite. The Queen's and Prince's collections of photographs. Complete photographic catalogue of objects in the royal apartments. 100,000 surviving photographs. The royal photographers. First cinema film of Queen Victoria. The Queen's interest in new inventions: cinematography, the telephone, the phonograph, the bicycle.

Queen Victoria.
*Anaglyptograph by Henry Weigall. December 1837.*

# I

## FROM FIFTH IN SUCCESSION TO QUEEN

ON 6 November 1817 the twenty-one-year-old Princess Charlotte of Wales died with her still-born son after fifty hours of labour. Only child of the Prince Regent, later King George IV, Princess Charlotte had married in 1816 Prince Leopold of Saxe-Coburg-Saalfeld[1] (Plate 5)—an ancient but impoverished German dukedom. The Prince had done well for himself in obtaining the hand of the future Queen of England—as it seemed she would be—with Marlborough House as a London residence, Claremont near Esher for a country-seat, and an allowance of £50,000 a year, but on that tragic night he had no thought for such considerations, for he was very much in love with the unconventional tomboy Princess. In his grief he clung to his personal physician and friend, Christian Friedrich Stockmar, begging him never to leave him.

The unexpected death of Princess Charlotte left King George III, her grandfather, without a legitimate heir of the third generation, although Queen Charlotte had borne him no fewer than fifteen children, twelve of whom were still living. In the hope of securing the succession (Plate 8), three of

[1] In 1826 Saalfeld was exchanged for Gotha.

his middle-aged sons, the Dukes of Clarence, Kent and Cambridge, soon afterwards married German princesses, in accordance with the tradition of the House of Hanover.

Edward Augustus, Duke of Kent (1767–1820) (Plate 3), the fourth son of George III, had been living for the past twenty-seven years with Madame Julie de St. Laurent, a French lady of good family who is said to have borne him a son. She accompanied him wherever his military career took him: to Gibraltar, Canada, and the West Indies. Sober, punctual, and conscientious, in 1794 Prince Edward (as he then was) became Commander-in-Chief, Nova Scotia and New Brunswick, and five years later Commander-in-Chief, British North America (Canada). In 1802 he was appointed Governor-General of Gibraltar in the expectation of his being able to restore the discipline of the demoralized garrison: having been trained in the iron discipline of the Hanoverian army, the Duke was feared for his brutality, which had nearly led to his seizure by the troops in Canada. But parades, drill and exercises from dawn till dusk, the closing of half the wine-houses on the Rock, and merciless flogging for the smallest offences, resulted in a mutiny on Christmas Eve, 1802, and a conspiracy to assassinate the Duke. Order was restored by executing the ringleaders. The Duke was recalled to England, forbidden to return to Gibraltar, though retaining the Governorship. In 1805 he was gazetted a Field-Marshal.

Like his brothers, the Duke of Kent was extremely extravagant, and his debts were enormous, even without a run of bad luck which kept increasing them. Three times replacement outfits each costing £2,000 had been captured by the French during shipment to Canada. In addition, £11,000-worth of equipment was shipwrecked, in 1810 his bankers failed, and in 1814 his solicitor absconded. Even living quietly in Brussels with Madame de St. Laurent, the Duke could never hope to settle his debts, amounting to £200,000 by 1807, for almost three-quarters of his total income of £24,000 was mortgaged to his creditors.

Shortly after the death of Princess Charlotte the Duke of Kent decided, not without some misgivings, to abandon Madame de St. Laurent. The Duke had for some time been considering a union with the widowed Princess of Leiningen. The larger allowance which marriage would bring was strong grounds to 'fulfil his duty to the royal family'.

Princess Victoria Mary Louisa (1786–1861) (Plate 4), was the sister of Prince Leopold and widow of Prince Emich Karl of Leiningen. The Princess and her two children Charles (Plate 6) and Feodorowna, called Feodora (Plate 7) lived quietly at the family estate of the impoverished Leiningens—Amorbach, a small town not far from Aschaffenburg in Bavaria. The Principality of Leiningen had been mediatized in 1806. Though the Princess of Leiningen was aware of the Duke of Kent's long-standing attachment to Madame de St. Laurent, she was persuaded by her brother that marriage to him presented some small chance of becoming mother of an heir to the English throne. For both, the union was a matter of convenience; nevertheless they became very fond of each other. Neither was intellectual, both were cheerful, affectionate, and worldly.

The wedding took place at Coburg in the palace of the bride's father, the reigning Duke, on 29 May 1818, and was repeated a fortnight later according to Church of England ritual in the drawing-room at Kew Palace near London. At the same time and place the Duke of Clarence (Plate 2) married Princess Adelaide of Saxe-Meiningen (Plate 1). Soon afterwards the Duke and Duchess of Kent returned to Amorbach. Financially the marriage brought little improvement, for the Duke was granted only an additional £6,000 a year, instead of £25,000 as he had expected, and his debts remained as before unsettled. Yet despite this, he immediately spent £10,000 on stables and coach-houses, thirty-six horses and twenty carriages, without which Amorbach would not have been a princely court in the Kent style.

As the Duchess was wholly German and the Duke nearly so, they considered it important that their child should be born in England, to strengthen its position in the succession. Borrowing money for the journey, the Duke of Kent himself drove his wife and eleven-year-old stepdaughter through Germany to the coast, putting up at cheap inns. On arrival in London on 25 April 1819, they settled in the Duke's suite of rooms at Kensington Palace (Plate 9), where the Duchess gave birth to a daughter on 24 May 1819 (Plate 10). Exactly a month later the baby was christened in the Cupola Room at Kensington Palace. While the Archbishop of Canterbury held her over the font, a heated argument arose about her names, which had not yet been agreed upon. The first name, Alexandrina in honour of her chief sponsor Czar Alexander I, was accepted without opposition, but when the Prince Regent suggested as second name Georgiana, after himself, the Duke of Kent preferred Elizabeth. This savoured too much of sovereignty for the Regent's taste, and he put forward the mother's name, Victoria, which settled the matter. 'Alexandrina Victoria', the Archbishop repeated, glad to be able to christen the baby at last.[1]

To avoid his creditors and for economy's sake, the Duke of Kent rented Woolbrook Cottage, a small house at Sidmouth in South Devon. Here Victoria

[1] The name Victoria was later objected to by many people—among them Sir Walter Scott—and in 1831 two influential Members of Parliament urged that on accession the Princess should assume the title Queen Elizabeth II. 'Victoria', they urged, 'did not accord with the feelings of the English people.' It was considered a foreign name. Charlotte was put forward as an alternative to Elizabeth.

grew strong and healthy, 'too healthy, I fear, in the opinion of some members of my family, by whom she is regarded as an intruder', wrote her father. At Sidmouth the seven-months-old baby had her first narrow escape. A mischievous boy claiming to be sparrow-shooting carelessly fired into the nursery, missing the baby's head by a few inches. The pellets tore her sleeve, and her parents were at once suspicious of a plot.

So far, Victoria was only fifth in succession, and her chances seemed remote. George III, her grandfather, was still King. After him in line of succession were her uncles the Prince Regent, the Dukes of York and Clarence, and finally her father. Moreover, the Duke of Kent was only fifty-two years old, strong and healthy, and his wife but thirty-three, so the chances of a male heir were good. Apart from this, the Duchess of Clarence, whose infant daughter had died in March 1819, might reasonably be expected to have more children.[1] Yet within eight months of her birth the infant princess was two degrees nearer the throne. On 23 January 1820 her father died of inflammation of the lungs which had developed from a bad cold. Six days later his father the aged George III was also dead.

Prince Leopold hastened to fetch his bereaved sister and baby niece back to Kensington Palace. The Duke of Kent's finances were in such a bad state that his widow would have had no means even of leaving Sidmouth if her brother had not taken her under his care. On arrival in London they were very unkindly treated by the new King, George IV, whose great wish was to get Princess Victoria and her mother out of the country, and without Prince Leopold's assistance they could not have stayed. He constituted himself the Duchess's adviser, and unofficial guardian of her child, persuading her to resign the regency of Leiningen and live permanently in England for the sake of Victoria's prospects. This was a hard decision for the Duchess, who was aware of the dislike of all her brothers-in-law, could not speak English, and hated the climate. Nevertheless she felt it her duty to make the education of her younger daughter as possible Queen of England 'the whole object of her future life'. She was allowed to keep the apartments

[1] In fact the Duchess of Clarence bore one more daughter, at the end of 1820, who died twelve weeks later, and still-born twins in April 1822.

at Kensington Palace, but was left in very straitened circumstances, and until Parliament made adequate provision for her maintenance nearly six years later, she and her daughters were almost entirely dependent on the generosity of Prince Leopold.

Princess Feodora lived with her mother at Kensington Palace, and occasionally Prince Charles came over from Germany on visits. One of the very few children of about the same age who was sometimes allowed to play with Princess Victoria was Victoire Conroy, daughter of Sir John Conroy, the late Duke's equerry and friend, and now Comptroller of the Duchess's Household, and her friend.

The upbringing of Princess 'Drina', as she was called until her ninth year, was over-strict by modern standards. Treats were rare, few child friends were permitted, food was plain and dress simple.

Like most children, Princess Drina was often naughty and obstinate and 'set pretty well *all* at defiance', as she herself admitted. Before she was five she began reading and writing lessons. Her teacher, the Rev. George Davys (later Dean of Chester and Bishop of Peterborough), inquiring one day whether the little Princess had been good, learned from the Duchess that she had been good that morning, but on the day before there had been a little storm. Enjoying being the centre of attention, the little one triumphantly added, 'Yes, two storms —one at dressing, and one at washing.' On being reproved by the Duchess, 'When you are naughty like this, you make me and yourself very unhappy', the child corrected her: 'No, Mamma, not *me*, not myself, but *you*!' 'I hope your Highness will attend to her book and read a good lesson', admonished Dr. Davys as he departed. 'Yes', replied Drina, eager for the last word, 'and I will eat a good dinner.'

As she grew older, wilfulness remained the Princess's chief fault. When her music master told her, 'There is no royal road to music, Princess; you must practise like everybody else', she at once locked the piano, retorting, 'There, now! you see there is no *must* about it at all.'

From her fifth to her eighteenth year Princess Victoria was entrusted to the care of Princess Feodora's governess, Louise Lehzen, daughter of a Lutheran clergyman in Hanover. Princess Victoria stood in awe of her strictness, but wholeheartedly responded to her affection, in which Lehzen was more demonstrative than the Duchess. 'Lehzen often said that she had never seen such a passionate and naughty child as I was', yet despite this she loved Victoria devotedly.

As the death of the Duke of York in 1827 brought Princess Victoria a step nearer the throne, George IV appointed Dr. Davys resident director of her education, and created Lehzen a Hanoverian baroness.

Shortly before this, the Duchess of Kent and her daughters had been invited by George IV to stay with him at Windsor. This visit made a great impression on Victoria, for owing to George IV's strained relationship with her father and mother, it was the first time that she met her 'Uncle King'.

When we arrived at the Royal Lodge the King took me by the hand, saying: 'Give me your little paw.' He was large and gouty but with a wonderful dignity and charm of manner . . . Then he said he would give me something for me to wear, and that was his picture set in diamonds, which was worn by the Princesses as an order to a blue ribbon on the left shoulder. I was very proud of this, and Lady Conyngham pinned it on my shoulder. (Plate 15.)

George IV was very pleased with his niece, who replied with fine tact when asked to name her favourite tune for the band to play: 'Oh, Uncle King, I should like "God Save the King".' Upon his enquiry what she had most enjoyed at Windsor, the equally diplomatic answer was: 'The drive I took with you, Uncle King.'

The seclusion in which the Princess was brought up was a constant source of friction between George IV (and later William IV) and his sister-in-law, who rightly considered that the Court was not a suitable place for a child. But in sheltering her daughters the Duchess of Kent, with the best of intentions, went too far and ruined the most impressionable years of childhood, which Queen Victoria recalled as 'rather melancholy', 'sad and lonely'. 'I was extremely crushed and kept under and hardly dared say a word.' Visits to Uncle Leopold at Claremont remained the most enjoyable memories for Princess Victoria and her half-sister Princess Feodora, who married Prince Ernst von Hohenlohe-Langenburg in 1828.

I always left Claremont with tears for Kensington Palace. When I look back upon those years, which ought to have been the happiest in my life, I cannot help pitying myself. Not to have enjoyed the pleasures of youth is nothing, but to have been deprived of all intercourse, and not one cheerful thought in that dismal existence of ours, was very hard. My only happy time was going or driving out with you [Victoria] and Lehzen; then I could speak and look as I liked. I escaped some years of imprisonment, which you, my poor darling sister, had to endure after I was married.

Whilst hitherto great care had been taken to avoid premature disclosure to Princess Victoria of her closeness to the throne, after the death of George IV on 26 June 1830 Baroness Lehzen slipped a genealogical table into a history book. This was to supply the answer to Victoria's awkward question that had once put Lehzen in a fluster: 'Why do all the gentlemen raise their hats to me and not to Feodora?' 'I never saw that before', remarked the Princess. 'I see I am nearer the throne than I thought'—and tradition has it that she added: 'I will be good.'

Feodora, by eleven years her senior, was very beautiful. Victoria was not. Charles Greville, Clerk to the Privy Council, with his usual outspokenness called her 'a short, plain-looking child'. Lehzen, obviously partial, gave this flattering description of her charge. 'She is not tall, but very pretty; has dark blue eyes, and a mouth which, though not tiny, is good-tempered and pleasant; very fine teeth, a small but graceful figure, and a very small foot. Her whole bearing is so childish and engaging that one could not desire a more amiable child.' (Plate 17.)

Six months after the accession of the Duke of Clarence as William IV a Bill was passed appointing the Duchess of Kent Regent in case her daughter should succeed to the throne during her minority (Plate 16). An additional £10,000 p.a. was granted to the Duchess for the upkeep and education of the Princess.

Wishing to create confidence in her methods of up-bringing, the Duchess of Kent had, during the consideration of the Regency Bill, arranged for Princess Victoria to be examined by the Bishops of London and Lincoln and the Archbishop of Canterbury, who pronounced her system of education 'very judicious'. Princess Victoria received the ordinary education of a girl of good family, though extra stress was naturally laid on English history, which remained her main reading matter throughout her life, in preference to literature.

Up to the age of ten or eleven the Princess spoke English with a strong German accent, but endowed with a natural aptitude for languages, she later spoke English well, German perfectly, French fluently, and Italian moderately well. The Princess was, of course, instructed in all the social accomplishments befitting a young lady of the period: singing, playing the piano and harp, and sketching. In the latter she displayed considerable talent and sketching remained a lifelong recreation. Her singing was charming, whilst her piano playing was only considered sufficiently good 'to give much pleasure to herself and mild pleasure to others'. Finally, dancing lessons gave her that graceful deportment which is always referred to as one of Queen Victoria's greatest attractions.

Though very friendly with Queen Adelaide, the Duchess of Kent was on extremely bad terms with William IV, particularly since her refusal to allow Princess Victoria to attend his coronation in September 1831, on grounds of ill-health. Everyone knew that the Duchess's pride had been outraged when William IV correctly insisted on the heir-presumptive taking precedence over her mother. Princess Victoria never forgot this disappointment. 'Nothing could console me, not even my dolls' (of which she had no fewer than 132), she told her children many years later. King William was also annoyed at the airs and graces the fashionable Duchess gave herself as mother of the future Queen, and derided 'little Victoria's royal progresses', during which the Duchess of Kent had royal salutes fired in their honour until the King put a stop to it. The regally ceremonious arrangements for these journeys were made by Sir John Conroy, a conceited and ambitious Irishman, whose presence on them, and the status he assumed as a kind of prime minister, also gave rise to much criticism. Moreover, the Duchess of Kent's dependence on her husband's old friend after her brother Prince Leopold was no longer at hand, having accepted the crown of the new kingdom of Belgium in 1831, caused malicious gossip, fanned by Greville. The Clerk to the Privy

Letter written to her mother by Princess Victoria at the age of eight.

Council was, however, not always reliable in his information, judging from the biting couplet which made the round of London after his death:

> For forty years he listened at the door;
> He heard some secrets, and invented more.

Whilst these travels round the country were ostensibly to train Princess Victoria for public functions—in 1830 she opened the Royal Victoria Park at Bath, the first instance of the countless associations of her name with English topography—they afforded her mother an excellent opportunity for pushing herself forward in her favourite rôle of Regent-to-be. The trio and their suite visited many of the famous houses of the aristocracy, and stayed at watering places such as Tunbridge Wells and St. Leonards (Plate 20). For Princess Victoria, life certainly became more varied after 1830, and the journal in which from 1832 onward she recorded events of her daily life betrays her keen enjoyment. She now went frequently to concerts and the opera, and many entries close with the happy remark, emphatically underlined: 'I was *very much* amused.'

In 1836 the disagreements between William IV and his tactless sister-in-law came to a head. In August he invited her to come to Windsor with Victoria for eleven or twelve days prior to his birthday on the 21st. Wishing to shorten the visit, the Duchess excused herself from coming before the 20th, which annoyed the King greatly. His irritation increased when he found that the Duchess had taken over several additional rooms at Kensington Palace which he had previously refused her, and at the State banquet in honour of his birthday his rage got the better of his manners as host. Replying to a toast to his health, he burst into an extraordinary tirade against the Duchess of Kent.

> I trust in God that my life may be spared for nine months longer, after which period, in the event of my death, no regency would take place. I should then have the satisfaction of leaving the royal authority to the personal exercise of that young lady [pointing to Princess Victoria], the heiress presumptive of the crown, and not in the hands of a person now near me [the Duchess of Kent], who is surrounded by evil advisers, and who is herself incompetent to act with propriety in the station in which she would be placed. I have no hesitation in saying that I have been insulted —grossly and continually insulted—by that person; but I am determined to endure no longer a course of behaviour so disrespectful to me. Amongst many other things, I have particularly to complain of the manner in which that young lady has been kept away from my Court; she has been repeatedly kept from my Drawing-rooms, at which she ought always to have been present; but I am fully resolved that this shall not happen again. I would have her know that I am King, and I am determined to make my authority respected; and for the future I shall insist and command the Princess do upon all occasions appear at my Court, as it is her duty to do.

The hundred or so guests were aghast. Poor Queen Adelaide, who had always striven to keep the peace between her husband and sister-in-law, was deeply distressed, Princess Victoria burst into tears, while her mother, speechless, rose to order her carriage. With difficulty she was persuaded to remain at Windsor overnight.

King William was spared the annoyance of dying before his niece's coming-of-age, but he was too ill to attend the State ball in celebration of her eigh-teenth birthday. Soon afterwards, rumours reached him of the Duchess of Kent's plot to force on her daughter an extension of the Regency on the grounds of her youth, inexperience, and lack of intellectual ability, and to accept Sir John Conroy as her private secretary. In trying to gain Lord Melbourne's approval, the Duchess represented her own and Conroy's ambitions as the Princess's own wish. On learning, however, that Princess Victoria was not only unaware of but also hostile to the plan, the Prime Minister revealed the plot to the King.

To remove his niece from the scheming influence of her mother, the King proposed an independent Household for the Princess—a suggestion which the Duchess peremptorily refused to consider. Thereupon the King sent Princess Victoria direct an offer of £10,000 a year, which she gladly accepted, much to the resentment of her mother. The journal which Princess Victoria kept from the age of thirteen until within ten days of her death had at that time to be submitted to her mother's inspection, and so naturally gives no indication of their disagreements, beyond such phrases as 'Felt very miserable and agitated. Did not go down to dinner.' The seriousness of the quarrel is revealed, however, in King Leopold's letter of 25 May 1837, the day following Princess Victoria's coming-of-age.

> My dearest child,
>     You have had some battles and difficulties of which I am completely in the dark . . . Two things seem necessary; not to be fettered by any establishment other than what will be *comfortable to you*, and then to avoid any breach with your mother . . . Be steady, my good child, and *not* put out by *anything*; as long as I live *you will not want a faithful friend and supporter*.

For several years King Leopold had been moulding his niece for her future position. His letters were always full of sound advice on current affairs of State, and he endeavoured to instil in her a broad philosophical view of things in general. Part of a sermon he had once sent her concerned—as many foreigners think—a peculiarly English failing.

> *Hypocrisy* is a besetting sin of all times, but *particularly of the present*, and many are the wolves in sheep's clothes. I am sorry to say, with all my affection for old England, the very *state of its Society and politics*

renders many in that country *essentially humbugs and deceivers*; the *appearance* of the thing is generally *more* considered than the *reality*; provided matters go off well, and opinion may be gained, the *real good is matter of the most perfect indifference*.

When Princess Victoria came of age, King Leopold, at the request of William IV, sent Baron Stockmar (Plate 147) to London to act as her adviser. Stockmar had great influence behind the scenes, but no personal ambition. His statecraft was admired by sovereigns and their ministers all over Europe. Lord Melbourne called him 'one of the cleverest fellows I ever saw, the most discreet man', and Lord Palmerston, though not liking Stockmar personally, nor his political views, nevertheless considered him the only absolutely disinterested man he had come across in his life. So Princess Victoria had been entrusted to the best possible man. Nevertheless, in the certainty of King William's approaching death, Uncle Leopold took the reins into his own hands. Letters from Brussels arrived now almost daily.

17 June 1837. The moment you get official communication of the King's death, you will entrust Lord Melbourne with the office of retaining the present Administration as your Ministers ... I have already— if you would read it over, and perhaps let Stockmar see it—written to you some months ago on the subject of the necessity of maintaining the influence of conservative principles, and of protecting the Church... Concerning foreign policy I shall write on some future occasion ... I have taken into consideration the advantage or disadvantage of my coming over to you *immediately*. The result of my *examen* is that I think it better to visit you later ... People might fancy I came to enslave you ... as if I thought of ruling the realm for *purposes of my own*.

A few days later he advised:

say as often as possible that you are *born* in England ... You never can say too much of your country and its inhabitants. Two nations in Europe are really almost ridiculous in their own exaggerated praises of themselves; these are the English and the French. Your being very national is highly important, and as you happen to be born in England and never to have left it for a moment, it would be odd indeed if people tried to make out to the contrary.

Before William IV's offer to Princess Victoria of an annuity sufficient for a separate establishment could be put into effect, he died at the age of seventy-two. This is how she learned the news.

20 June 1837. I was awoke at 6 o'clock by Mamma, who told me that the Archbishop of Canterbury and Lord Conyngham were here, and wished to see me. I got out of bed and went into my sitting-room (only in my dressing-gown), and *alone*, and saw them. Lord Conyngham [the Lord Chamberlain] then acquainted me that my poor Uncle, the King, was no more, and had expired at 12 minutes past 2 this morning, and consequently that I am *Queen*. Lord Conyngham knelt down and kissed my hand, at the same time delivering to me the official announcement of the poor King's demise. (Plate 26.) The Archbishop then told me that the Queen was desirous that he should come and tell me the details of the last moments of my poor, good Uncle ...

Since it has pleased Providence to place me in this station, I shall do my utmost to fulfil my duty towards my country; I am very young and perhaps in many, though not in all things, inexperienced, but I am sure, that very few have more real good will and more real desire to do what is fit and right than I have ...

At 9 came Lord Melbourne, [the Prime Minister] whom I saw in my room, and of *course quite alone*, as I shall *always* do all my Ministers. He kissed my hand and I then acquainted him that it had long been my intention to retain him and the rest of the present Ministry at the head of affairs, and that it could not be in better hands than his ...

At half past eleven Queen Victoria held her first Council in the Red Saloon—now the entrance hall of the London Museum. Her paternal uncles, the Dukes of Cumberland and Sussex, and Lord Melbourne led her in. She bowed to the assembly, took her seat, and read her Declaration in a clear voice without any sign of nervousness. (Plate 27.)[1]

Never was anything like the first impression she produced, [wrote Greville] or the chorus of praise and admiration which is raised about her manner and

[1] Sir David Wilkie's well-known painting of this Council depicts the Queen in a *white* dress for the sake of artistic effect. With her characteristic love of truth, the Queen raised objections to this artistic licence, and the painter had some difficulty in overcoming her scruples. In fact she was wearing neither white, nor mourning for her uncle, but a brown silk dress, which is preserved at the London Museum.

behaviour, and certainly not without justice. It was very extraordinary, and something far beyond what was looked for. Her extreme youth and inexperience, and the ignorance of the world concerning her, naturally excited intense curiosity to see how she would act on this trying occasion . . .

After she had read her speech, and taken and signed the oath for the security of the Church of Scotland, the Privy Counsellors were sworn, the two Royal Dukes first, by themselves; and as these two old men, her uncles, knelt before her, swearing allegiance and kissing her hand, I saw her blush up to the eyes, as if she felt the contrast between their civil and their natural relations, and this was the only sign of emotion which she evinced . . . She went through the whole ceremony . . . with perfect calmness and self-possession, but at the same time with a graceful modesty and propriety particularly interesting and ingratiating.

Not only the critical Greville, but everyone else present was immensely impressed by the new sovereign's first official appearance. 'If she had been my own daughter', said the Duke of Wellington, 'I could not have wished that she should do better. Why, she not only filled the chair, she filled the room!'

In the official documents prepared on the first day of her reign the Queen's name figured as Alexandrina Victoria, and in this style the Proclamation of her accession was made the following day at St. James's Palace (Plate 28), where the cheering crowds moved her to tears. But henceforth it was her wish to be known as Victoria only.

In the young Queen's mind, crowded with new impressions, the strongest impression of all was unmistakably the feeling of independence from her mother. This feeling of freedom comes out again and again in her journal, in the reiteration of that significant word alone . . . alone . . . alone. Until her accession Victoria had never even been allowed to walk downstairs without someone holding her hand. But now that she could see her Ministers alone, she also insisted on sleeping alone. It was unthinkable for a Queen to continue sharing the room with her mother (Plate 11).

Knowing that it would be easier to manage her mother in her own house, the Queen decided to move as soon as possible into Buckingham Palace, the building and furnishing of which had only been completed during William IV's last illness. Her father had been born in Buckingham House on the same site, which from 1825 onward John Nash rebuilt for George IV. Nash's slowness and extravagance were so great, however, that William IV entrusted the work to another architect, Edward Blore. Well over a million pounds had been spent on Buckingham Palace by the time Queen Victoria was at last able to make it the London residence of the sovereign. The Marble Arch at that time formed an imposing entrance to the Palace, which was built round three sides of a courtyard (Plate 331). In the late 'forties, in view of 'the total want of accommodation for our little family', the east side of the courtyard was enclosed by a fourth wing built by Blore (Plate 332).[1] This made the Marble Arch look insignificant, and since it was, in addition, too narrow for the State coach to pass through, it was removed to the north-east corner of Hyde Park in 1851, where its once intended effect is completely lost owing to the proximity of much taller buildings.

It was not without feelings of regret that Queen Victoria left her birthplace. 'I have gone through painful and disagreeable scenes here, 'tis true, but still I am fond of the poor old Palace.' After inspecting her new residence she took her dog for a walk in the pretty forty-acre grounds. 'Dear *Dashy* was quite happy in it.' The opinion of Dash, the King Charles spaniel (Plate 23), set the seal of approval on it. A present from Sir John Conroy to the Duchess of Kent, Dash had been adopted by Victoria, and no odium attached to him from his origin with Conroy, whom she detested.

The day after moving in, Queen Victoria was dismayed to find that the Palace lacked a throne. The cost of £1,000 was, of course, borne by the Treasury, but there were other heavy moving-in expenses, and until financial provision had been made for the Queen by Parliament, she was obliged to borrow from Coutts's Bank. Eventually she was voted an annual allowance of £385,000,[2] in addition to the considerable revenues from the Duchies of Cornwall and Lancaster.

[1] The façade of this wing was greatly altered in 1913 by Sir Aston Webb.
[2] George IV's income had been £1,057,000. The spending power of the pound was then about five times as much as it is today, and there was no income tax!

The Queen at once settled her father's debts, making in addition a gift of plate to the patient creditors. She also paid her mother's outstanding bills, and continued the personal allowances of her illegitimate FitzClarence cousins, the children of William IV and the actress Mrs. Jordan.

At Buckingham Palace the Queen was at last mistress of her own household. Her mother, whose domineering interference had been a constant source of annoyance to her up to the day of her accession, was now excluded from all share in her public and private life. Both had their own suite of rooms. Their relationship, which since the Regency plot had considerably cooled, deteriorated further when the Queen pensioned off Conroy with £3,000 a year and a baronetcy, his request for an Irish peerage being refused. Princess Lieven, wife of the Russian Ambassador, expressed her doubts whether mother and daughter would remain long under the same roof: 'The Duchess of Kent is overwhelmed with vexation and disappointment. Her daughter behaves to her with kindness and attention, but has rendered herself quite independent of the Duchess, who painfully feels her own insignificance. The almost contemptuous way in which Sir John Conroy has been dismissed must be a bitter mortification to her.'

The young Queen was most fortunate in her Prime Minister, Viscount Melbourne (1779–1848). A charming elderly man of the world, he knew how to pilot the inexperienced Queen through the welter of political matters and personal problems. He was a Whig, the party to which the Duke of Kent had belonged, and in the ideals of which the Queen had been brought up. Lord Melbourne proved, above all, a real friend. Up to the time of the Queen's marriage he practically gave up his private life to devote himself to her entirely, as Prime Minister, political tutor, and *de facto* private secretary. His tact and integrity as her adviser won universal approval. Melbourne knew, of course, that his pupil was also receiving instruction from Baron Stockmar and King Leopold, who had reminded his niece directly after her accession, 'Before you decide on anything important I should be glad if you would consult me.'

Lord Melbourne's companionship greatly contributed to the Queen's happiness in the first few years of her reign; it broadened her knowledge of the world, and gave her confidence. Sitting beside him on the sofa after dinner, the Queen bombarded him with questions on every subject that came into her head, hanging upon his explanations with parted lips. Sometimes he amused her with scandals about her predecessors, which had been carefully kept from her by her mother. He regaled her with social and political gossip of the present and of former times, such as Lady Holland's admiration for Napoleon and the parcels of chocolate she sent to St. Helena, and King George III's delusion that he was married to Lady Pembroke. Sometimes he ventured a personal remark, teasing the Queen about the quantity of dresses and bonnets to be packed for Windsor, and if he offered no comment on her dress or hairstyle, the Queen would ask his opinion.

The young Queen threw herself into her new life with zest for both work and pleasure. In these early years work was, as a rule, restricted to the morning hours, and the days were similarly organized whether the Court was at Buckingham Palace or at Windsor Castle.

The Queen got up between eight and half past and read or wrote letters while her hair was being dressed. The morning was spent transacting State business with the Prime Minister. At two, she went riding with him and a large suite (Plates 31 & 33), which always included some members of the Paget family, nine of whom held positions at Court. Afterwards the Queen practised music, or enjoyed a game of battledore and shuttlecock.

Formality reigned from dinner onward, which was served at eight, Lord Melbourne always sitting on the Queen's left. After dinner the gentlemen were expected to join the ladies within a quarter of an hour, thus avoiding the drunkenness which had disgraced the previous Courts. The Queen passed round the drawing-room exchanging a few words with each of her guests—arid dialogues consisting of question and answer on such topics as the weather and riding. Then the Duchess of Kent was settled with partners for her favourite game of whist. Sometimes the Queen played cards, draughts, or chess, but more often the party gathered round the table on which lay the latest publications illustrated with engravings, and listened to Lord Melbourne's informative and witty comments which 'kept us in fits of laughter'.

During and after dinner the band played music by Rossini, Bellini, and Donizetti. Some of the Queen's ladies would play the piano or sing. Occasionally the party would insist on hearing the Queen, for everyone admired her voice, and she would consent, 'literally shaking with fear and fright'.

On one occasion Thalberg, the rival of Liszt, played his fantasias for piano on operatic themes, and the Queen was 'quite in ecstasies and raptures with him'. Her taste was for modern Italian operas, Bellini's *I Puritani* being her favourite at that time, and Giulietta Grisi always remained her ideal singer. She also admired Auber and Meyerbeer; Mozart, however, she considered 'old-fashioned' and Handel 'heavy and tiresome'. There is no mention of the newer German composers such as Beethoven, Weber, and Schubert, though later the Queen sang Mendelssohn's songs with pleasure and feeling.

Usually the Queen retired between eleven and half past, but if there were a ball she loved to dance until dawn. Dancing was at that period her greatest delight, and it was her constant regret to be restricted to quadrilles; for the sovereign to waltz in the arms of a subject was then considered undignified.

A three weeks' visit to Windsor of 'dearest and most beloved' King Leopold and Queen Louise (a daughter of King Louis-Philippe) in September made the first summer of her reign the pleasantest the Queen had ever experienced. Fortunately both her advisers got on well together, and perfectly agreed on politics. 'The sound observations they make, and the impartial advice they give me would make a most interesting book.'

Towards the end of his visit King Leopold and the Duke of Wellington accompanied the Queen to a review of the Guards. Queen Victoria, proud of being a soldier's daughter and head of the army, wore the navy-blue and scarlet Windsor uniform (Plate 30).

All too quickly the time came for King Leopold and his wife to depart and for the Court to leave Windsor. The Queen felt sad, for she had spent such a wonderful time there. Life was good and full of promise. Much of her enjoyment, she reflected,

was due to the companionship of Lord Melbourne, for whom she felt ever-increasing affection and admiration.

The more I see of him and the more I know of him, the more I like and appreciate his fine and honest character. I have seen a great deal of him, every day, these last 5 weeks, and I have always found him in good humour, kind, good, and most agreeable; I have seen him in my Closet for Political Affairs, I have ridden out with him (every day), I have sat near him constantly at and after dinner, and talked about all sorts of things, and have always found him a kind and most excellent and very agreeable man. I am very fond of him.

After a month at Brighton (Plate 32) in George IV's fantastic Pavilion, the Court settled down again at Buckingham Palace. On 9 November Queen Victoria visited the City for the first time as sovereign to attend the Lord Mayor's banquet at the Guildhall. Wearing a pink satin dress embroidered with silver, and a splendid diamond tiara, she set out from Buckingham Palace in the State coach drawn by eight horses (Plate 34). The procession and banquet lasted nearly eight hours. The Queen was deeply moved by her brilliant and enthusiastic reception. 'It is much more than I deserve, and I shall do my utmost to render myself worthy of all this love and affection.' On this occasion one of the Sheriffs, Moses Montefiore, became the first Jew to receive the honour of knighthood, and the country warmly approved of this distinction.

On 28 June 1838, just over a year after her accession, Queen Victoria was crowned.

It was a fine day, and the crowds of people exceeded what I have ever seen; many as there were the day I went to the City, it was nothing, nothing to the multitudes, the millions of my loyal subjects, who were assembled *in every spot* to witness the Procession. Their good humour and excessive loyalty was beyond everything, and I really cannot say *how* proud I feel to be the Queen of *such* a Nation. I was alarmed at times for fear that the people would be crushed and squeezed on account of the tremendous rush and pressure.

At Westminster Abbey 10,000 guests had assembled several hours before the Queen and her eight train-bearers and procession walked slowly up the nave to the throne amidst thunders of applause and handkerchiefs and scarves waving. Despite her lack of height, she looked majestic in the crimson velvet ermine-lined Parliament Robes (Plate 41), and wearing a diamond circlet on her head.

Everyone who has watched the coronation of Queen Elizabeth II in the Abbey, on television or in the cinema, will remember it as the most wonderful and colourful spectacle that pageantry can offer. The moment of crowning in particular, when all the peers and peeresses put on their coronets as the Archbishop places the crown on the Monarch's head, is an impressive and unforgettable sight. Queen Victoria's coronation (Plates 37–40) was marred by a few awkward incidents, due in the main to lack of rehearsal. 'Pray tell me what I am to do, for they [the clergy] don't know' whispered the Queen at one point to the Sub-Dean. The bishops started the litany before the delivery of the regalia, and as they could not be stopped, both proceeded simultaneously. By mistake the coronation ring had been made to fit the Queen's little finger, but the Archbishop insisted on forcing it on the correct, fourth, finger, which caused her great pain and difficulty in getting it off again. During the Homage, the eighty-eight-year-old Lord Rolle had the misfortune to slip and roll down the steps of the throne. A gullible foreign visitor was assured by a wag that Lord Rolle's *roll* was intentional, his family holding their title on condition of performing this feat at every coronation! Considering the many archaic details in the coronation ritual, that explanation seemed plausible enough. Towards the end of the ceremonies the Bishop of Bath and Wells, having turned over two pages at once, informed the Queen that the service was over and she retired to Edward the Confessor's Chapel. The Sub-Dean enquired of the Lord Chamberlain whether Her Majesty were ill. Lord Melbourne thought the omission did not matter, but the clergy insisted on completing the service, and after much consultation the Queen was fetched back. Even then the confusion was not at an end. Before the final procession of the crowned sovereign, 'the Archbishop *ought* to have delivered the Orb to me, but I had already got it, and he (as usual) was *so* confused and puzzled and knew nothing, and went away'.

Five hours after her arrival at the Abbey the Queen re-entered the State coach. In the immense sea of people watching the return procession to Buckingham Palace stood Carlyle, who was overheard saying as the Queen drove past, now in her purple velvet Robes of State, wearing the crown and holding the orb and sceptre, 'Poor little Queen, she is at an age at which a girl can hardly be trusted to choose a bonnet for herself; yet a task is laid upon her from which an archangel might shrink.'

Rather incongruously, the first thing the crowned and anointed Queen did after returning to Buckingham Palace was to give Dash a bath. Afterwards there was a small private dinner party, and it was well after midnight when she wrote in her journal a detailed account of that eventful day which 'I shall ever remember as the proudest of my life.'

To judge Queen Victoria's appearance at that time by the innumerable published portraits would certainly be misleading. Most of them are derivative illustrations, and even those artists who were favoured with a sitting served their contemporaries —and posterity—ill by their excessive flattery. Louisa Costello's water-colour (Plate 25) painted on the day of the Queen's Proclamation probably comes closest to a truthful likeness. Contrary to the impression given by some contemporary illustrations, the young Queen was not in any way remarkable for her looks, and far too short (about 4 feet 9 inches) to impress with her figure. 'We are rather small for a Queen', she regretted. But all who saw her found these failings of nature amply compensated for by her charm of manner and dignity. 'She possesses a composure', wrote Princess Lieven, 'an air of command, and of dignity, which with her childlike face, her tiny figure, and her pretty smile, create one of the most extraordinary impressions that it is possible to imagine.'

The Queen never, at any time, could have been called pretty, [wrote her lifelong friend the Duchess of Cleveland] but when she came to the throne, she was distinctly attractive: her small fair head well set on extremely pretty shoulders, singularly graceful in all her movements, with a great charm of manner, the brightest and gayest of smiles, and a remarkably clear and musical voice.

There was something pathetic, too, in her extreme

youthfulness: her face had still the flush and flower-like look of childhood, from which, small and slim[1] as she was, she might easily be supposed to have not yet emerged. Yet this little figure was not one to be over-looked. She had so much natural dignity, and such an air of distinction, that . . . in whatever dress, or even disguise, she might appear, she would always be recognized as a great personage when she came into the room.

On unofficial occasions the Queen was as natural as any girl of her age could have been.

A more homely little being you never beheld, when she is at her ease, and she is evidently dying to be always more so. [wrote Thomas Creevey] She laughs in real earnest, opening her mouth as wide as it can go, showing not very pretty gums . . . She eats quite as heartily as she laughs, I think I may say she gobbles . . . She blushes and laughs every instant in so natural a way as to disarm anybody.

1839 opened with a Court scandal which excited more interest than any matter of a public or political character, 'played the devil with the Queen's popularity, and cast dreadful odium and discredit on the Court'.

In January it was noticed that Lady Flora Hastings, Lady of the Bedchamber to the Duchess of Kent, appeared to be pregnant. As the change in her figure became more and more pronounced, the rumour spread that Lady Flora was either privately married, or ought to be. Lady Flora, who had already consulted the Court physician Sir James Clark because she had been feeling ill for some time, was indignant when Clark urged her to confess. He told her that nothing short of a thorough medical examination would satisfy the ladies of the Court—with which demand the Queen identified herself. The Queen, in fact, sent a message to her mother that Lady Flora was not to appear at her dinner table until a medical examination had decided matters. The Duchess of Kent demonstrated her complete trust in her lady by dismissing Clark from her service and refusing to appear at the Queen's table for several weeks. The rupture between the Queen and her mother was complete. Having submitted to the indignity of an examination by Clark

[1] The Queen was rather plump by the time of her marriage.

and another doctor in the presence of Lady Portman, one of her accusers, Lady Flora was given a certificate stating that no pregnancy had ever existed. Queen Victoria expressed with tears her deepest regret to Lady Flora in private, but, badly advised, did not acknowledge her error publicly by dismissing Clark for fanning the suspicions before an examination had taken place. Lady Flora's mother and brother were not satisfied with private apologies. Having tried in vain to obtain some sort of official action which would have gone some way to repair Lady Flora's injured reputation, they decided to publish their correspondence with the Prime Minister and the Queen. As a result, the whole country was furious with the Queen and sympathetic to 'the victim of a depraved court'. To make matters worse, the two doctors had been so concerned with the alleged pregnancy that they had omitted to seek the real cause of Lady Flora's condition, and early in July the unfortunate woman died of enlargement of the liver at the age of thirty-four. Although her funeral procession left Buckingham Palace at four in the morning, to avoid attracting attention, the carriage which the Queen sent to take part was stoned. At the Ascot races the Queen was hissed by the Duchess of Montrose and Lady Sarah Ingestre, and some gentlemen called out 'Mrs. Melbourne' as her carriage passed.

Almost concurrently with the Hastings affair there was a political crisis. The emancipation of the slaves in Jamaica caused the planters who owned them to rebel. A Government proposal to suspend the constitution of the island was passed on 7 May by so small a majority that Lord Melbourne and his colleagues felt obliged to resign. Queen Victoria's grief at the prospect of 'this dreadful change' was profound. On the advice of Lord Melbourne she sent for the Duke of Wellington, and he in turn, feeling too old and deaf for the task, advised her to ask Sir Robert Peel to form a new Ministry. Peel was a stiff, shy man with embarrassed nervous manners and an unfortunate habit of pointing his toes like a dancing master. 'Oh! how different, how dreadfully so, to that frank, open, natural and most kind, warm manner of Lord Melbourne', sighed the Queen. As a Tory, Peel was not happy about the fact that all the Queen's Ladies of the Bedchamber were Whigs, and several of them closely related to Whig Ministers. He asked the Queen as a mark of confidence in his Government to change some of the ladies—a request which she flatly refused. Despite several harassing interviews, the Queen remained obstinate, explaining that she felt unable to adopt 'a course which she conceives to be contrary to usage and repugnant to her feelings'. In these circumstances Sir Robert Peel declined to form a Government, and the so-called 'Bedchamber Plot' ended in the *status quo ante*. Many years later the Queen admitted that she had acted unreasonably in insisting on keeping *all* her ladies, but at the time she felt so elated and triumphant at getting her own way that she danced till the early morning hours with the Grand Duke Alexander of Russia (later Czar Alexander II). Afterwards she confided to her journal: 'I felt so sad to take leave of this dear, amiable young man, whom I really think (talking jokingly) I was a little in love with.' More than ever the Queen realized what happiness she was missing by having so few young people of her own rank for company, and she began to feel lonely in her exalted position. Her only real friends were all elderly—Baroness Lehzen, Lord Melbourne, Baron Stockmar. Marriage would, of course, have offered a solution but having only so recently gained independence from her mother's control Queen Victoria did not welcome the idea of a new tie through marriage as wholeheartedly as did other girls of her age. As the months went by, everyone seemed to expect a decision, however, especially as various family factions, as well as the nation's interest, got involved in the question. On her accession, the kingdom of Hanover, which had been ruled by English sovereigns since George I became King of England in 1714, had passed to her uncle the Duke of Cumberland, a woman being debarred from succession in Hanover under the Salic law. Until Queen Victoria had a child, her un-popular Uncle Ernest was heir to the English throne.

Particular admirers of the Queen were Lord Elphinstone, and Lord Alfred Paget, who wore the Queen's portrait round his neck, as did his dog. But the Queen agreed with Lord Melbourne that it was not advisable to marry one of her subjects. Apart from the jealousy it might cause, 'marrying a subject was making yourself so much their equal, and brought you so in contact with the whole family'. Some relations suggested her cousin Prince George of Cambridge as a suitable husband; another branch of the family even had hopes she might marry the blind son of her Uncle Ernest so as again to secure the kingdom of Hanover to the English crown. But Queen Victoria put all these matchmaking schemes aside, for dear Uncle Leopold had his own wise plans.

Ever since the birth of her grandson Albert, three months after Victoria, the Dowager Duchess of Saxe-Coburg, mother of Albert's father and Victoria's mother, schemed for the union of her grandchildren, and in this she had the active support of her other son, King Leopold. The idea of this marriage was instilled in both children. To Victoria, their close relationship seemed a strong point in favour of it, for from early childhood onward she was imbued with an extraordinarily strong, one might even say exaggerated, family feeling—a German trait. She well remembered how handsome Prince Albert had seemed to her at their first meeting in 1836. It was shortly before her seventeenth birthday when Prince Albert and his elder brother Prince Ernest arrived on a visit to Kensington Palace, together with their father the Duke of Saxe-Coburg-Gotha. The cousins quickly found common interests in sketching and playing the piano, and Victoria remembered her delight when Albert and Ernest, too, were 'in perfect ecstasies' over her favourite opera, *I Puritani*. In honour of her birthday King William had given a ball to which he had invited a suitor of his own choice—a son of the Prince of Orange who had once been a claimant for the hand of Princess Charlotte. Victoria betrayed no favouritism, though Albert was the choice of her heart. He showed no emotion for his cousin, if he had any. Writing to his stepmother, his only comment about Victoria was rather cool—'very amiable'. Accustomed to a simple, studious way of life, he was outspoken about his sufferings: the late entertainments caused him 'many hard battles against sleepiness'; the English climate, the way of life, and the food also upset him. In fact, he looked forward to getting back to his studies and a quiet and regular mode of life. Victoria, in contrast, 'cried bitterly, very bitterly' when 'those *dearest*, beloved Cousins, whom I *do* love so *very very* dearly' departed.

Uncle Leopold was very satisfied with the result of the visit. Everything had gone as he had hoped.

I must thank you, my beloved Uncle, for the prospect of *great* happiness you have contributed to give me, in the person of dear Albert . . . He possesses every quality that could be desired to render me perfectly happy. He is so sensible, so kind, and so good, and so amiable too. He has, besides, the most pleasing and delightful exterior and appearance you can possibly see.

I have only now to beg you, my dearest Uncle, to take care of the health of one, now *so dear* to me, and to take him under *your special* protection . . . I hope and trust that all will go on prosperously and well on this subject of so much importance to me.

The two princes continued their studies in Brussels under the wing of King Leopold. Then followed a year and a half at Bonn University, after which Baron Stockmar accompanied them on a tour of Switzerland and Italy. Prince Albert was 'intoxicated with delight' at the Italian art galleries, and felt more at home in discussions with scholars than in the company of young ladies. Indeed he viewed with dismay King Leopold's directive that 'I am to go into society, learn the ways of the world, and vitiate my culture with fashionable accomplishments, the last of which would appear to be an extraordinarily good testimonial in V.'s eyes.' His uncle's matchmaking filled Prince Albert with apprehension. 'V. is said to be incredibly stubborn, and her extreme obstinacy to be constantly at war with her good nature; she delights in court ceremonies, etiquette and trivial formalities. These are gloomy prospects.'

The young Queen, too, sometimes had misgivings. 'I have always had my own way . . . Suppose he should endeavour to thwart me, and oppose me in what I like, what a dreadful thing it would be!' In April 1839 she confided to Lord Melbourne that she 'dreaded the thought of marrying; I was so accustomed to have my own way, that I thought it was 10 to 1 that I shouldn't agree with any body. Lord M. said, "Oh! but you would have it still" (my own way).' Reverting to the 'odious subject' again in July, the two agreed that since Prince Albert knew there was a possibility of such a union, it would be unfair to keep him in suspense. Frankly speaking, Lord Melbourne did not consider a foreign prince a popular choice; the Coburgs in particular, he warned,

were not liked abroad, and in addition, he advised against marriage between first cousins.

Such arguments naturally strengthened Queen Victoria's own doubts, and in her emotional instability she emphatically informed her uncle that the feelings she had expressed three years earlier with regard to Albert should not be construed as a promise.

I am anxious that you should acquaint Uncle Ernest [the Duke of Saxe-Coburg] that if I should like Albert, I can make *no final promise this year*, for, at the *very earliest*, any such event could not take place till *two or three years hence* . . .

Though all the reports of Albert are most favourable, and though I have little doubt I shall like him, still one can never answer beforehand for *feelings*, and I may not have the *feeling* for him which is requisite to ensure happiness. I *may* like him as a friend, and as a *cousin*, and as a *brother*, but not *more*; and should this be the case (which is not likely), I am *very* anxious that it should be understood that I am *not* guilty of any breach of promise, for *I never gave any*.

Fearing that any delay now might conspire against the union of his niece and nephew towards which he had striven for so long, King Leopold proposed that Prince Albert and his brother should come to England—an idea which filled Queen Victoria with alarm. She postponed the visit on a threadbare pretext, but when Prince Albert in turn put off his departure from Brussels she was offended. At last, on 10 October the Princes arrived at Windsor, and from the moment the Queen set her eyes on Prince Albert again, all doubt vanished, as her uncle had foreseen.

It was with some emotion that I beheld Albert—who is *beautiful* . . . so excessively handsome, such beautiful blue eyes, an exquisite nose, and such a pretty mouth with delicate moustachios and slight but very slight whiskers; a beautiful figure, broad in the shoulders and a fine waist. (Plate 42.)

Within four days Prince Albert had conquered. When Lord Melbourne learned the Queen's decision to marry, he assured her 'You'll be much more comfortable; for a woman cannot stand alone for long, in whatever situation she is.' Discussing Prince Albert's future title and position, they took his assent for granted: it never entered their minds that he had come to Windsor 'with the quiet but firm resolution to declare, on my part, that I also, tired of the delay, withdrew entirely from the affair'.

On the fifth morning the Queen plucked up her courage to propose, Prince Albert's lower rank making it impossible for him to speak first (Plate 43). At about half past twelve she received him alone in her sitting-room, talking nervously at first about different matters to gain time. Daguerreotypes had only lately been introduced, and she showed Albert the first specimens that had been left with her that morning. Next she spoke of the great tournament which had recently been held at Eglinton Castle— and then suddenly, after a pause, came to the point. 'I think you must be aware why I asked you to come', adding, with tears in her eyes, 'Could you forsake your country for me? It would make me *too happy* if you would consent to what I wish.'

We embraced each other, and he was *so* kind, *so* affectionate. I told him I was quite unworthy of him,— he said he would be very happy 'das Leben mit dir zu zubringen'. I really felt it was the happiest brightest moment in my life.

The Queen was in ecstasies.

Oh! dear Uncle, I *do* feel so happy! I do so adore Albert! He is quite an angel, and so very very kind to me, and seems so fond of me, which touches me much. I trust and hope I shall be able to make him as happy as he *ought* to be! . . . I shall do everything in my power to render the sacrifice he has made (for a *sacrifice* in my opinion it is) as small as I can . . . My feelings are a *little* changed, I must say, since last Spring, when I said I couldn't *think* of marrying for *three or four years*; but seeing Albert has changed all this.

Prince Albert informed his step-grandmother, Caroline, Duchess of Saxe-Coburg-Altenburg, of his engagement in less glowing terms:

Victoria is really most good and amiable, and I am quite sure heaven has not given me into evil hands, and that we shall be happy together . . . Oh, the future, does it not bring with it the moment when I shall have to take leave of my dear, dear home and of you! I cannot think of that without deep melancholy taking possession of me. . . .

The period of our marriage is already close at hand. The Queen and the Ministers wish exceedingly that it should take place in the first days of February, in which I acquiesced.

The official announcement of the engagement caused some disappointment, for this small German dukedom, which Bismarck was later to dub 'the stud farm of Europe', was unimportant in every other respect, and the royal families of Europe resented the way these Coburgs climbed on to thrones by marriage or election. Satirical broadsheets like the following expressed John Bull's disapproval of Prince Albert.

He comes the bridegroom of Victoria's choice,
The nominee of Lehzen's vulgar voice;
He comes to take 'for better or for worse'
England's fat Queen and England's fatter purse.

At least twice a week Queen Victoria wrote to her fiancé who had returned to Coburg on 14 November, and she was 'quite miserable' when once no letter came from him for ten days.

His Royal Mistress, mournful and depressed,
Pined in his absence, whom she valued best—
Missed the hoarse whispers of his German tongue,
And the moustache above his lip that hung:
That dear moustache which caused her first to *feel*,
And filled her bosom with pre-nuptial zeal.

Meanwhile the Queen studied the question of titles for her future husband. Taking the precedent of Mary I's husband Philip II of Spain who was given the title of King, she suggested the same for Prince Albert, but Lord Melbourne pointed out that if Parliament had the power to make a King they could also unmake one. King Leopold thought that his nephew should have an English name and title analogous to the precedent of Queen Anne's husband Prince George of Denmark, who was created Earl of Kendal and Duke of Cumberland. To avoid the impression, however, that Prince Albert 'meant to play a political part'—a thought far from the Queen's intention at that time—the idea of a peerage was dropped.[1] Parliament refused to pass a Bill granting

---

[1] This was the reason given by Queen Victoria. Prince Albert told his brother in 1857 (when he was given the title Prince Consort) 'I refused the title of a Peer as being below my dignity.'

Prince Albert precedence immediately after the Queen, but on the advice of Baron Stockmar the Queen got over this difficulty by issuing a Royal Warrant, which, however, only applied in Britain. A Tory amendment was passed by Parliament reducing the proposed annuity for Prince Albert from £50,000 to £30,000,[1] although previous Prince Consorts and Queen Consorts had been granted the larger amount. The Queen was furious, and complained that the Tories, who had voted solidly for the reduction, were 'doing everything they can to be personally rude to me'. Prince Albert was equally annoyed by the slight, particularly as the reduction limited his philanthropic plans and his desire to be a patron of the arts. He also objected to having his gentlemen-in-waiting chosen for him, and above all, his private secretary, but the Queen insisted that *he* was not in a position to judge who would be suitable, and appointed Lord Melbourne's private secretary George Anson.[2] Prince Albert was quite surprised at the lack of consideration shown by his bride for his own wishes and feelings in these matters concerning his future happiness. In particular he must have objected to the patronizing tone in which some of her decisions were phrased. He was told, for example, that he had 'no right to quarter the English Arms, but the Sovereign has the power to *allow* it by Royal Command: this was done for Uncle Leopold by the Prince Regent, and I will do it again for

you. But it can only be done by Royal Command.' When he expressed disappointment at Victoria's decision to restrict the honeymoon to a couple of days, she replied: 'You forget, my dearest Love, that I am the Sovereign, and that business can stop and wait for nothing.' It really seemed as though England's Queen were determined to wear the trousers, as a lampoonist had warned:

> She's all my Lehzen painted her,
> She's lovely, she is rich,
> But they tell me when I marry her
> That she will wear the *britch*.

These and other annoyances cast a gloom over Prince Albert's last months at home—and Coburg always remained *home* to him. Although the Queen sent two gentlemen of her Household to Gotha with the insignia of the Garter, with which Prince Albert was invested by his father (a Knight of the Order), King Leopold found him 'rather exasperated and pretty full of grievances' when the party broke their journey in Brussels. Indeed, a number of remarks convey the impression of a somewhat faint-hearted bridegroom conscious that his 'future lot is high and brilliant but also plentifully strewn with thorns', yet consoling himself with the thought that his high position would enable him to do good, 'using his powers and endeavours for a great object—that of promoting the welfare of multitudes of his [new] countrymen'. With these objects in mind he sailed for England, on 6 February 1840, in accordance with his previous assurance to Stockmar, 'I will not let my courage fail me.'

[1] Actually £30,000 equalled the total income of the Duchy of Saxe-Coburg.

[2] It says much for Prince Albert's amiable disposition that he did not take an instant dislike to Anson, but on the contrary soon gave him his entire confidence and friendship.

Queen Victoria in Robes of State.
*Painting by F. Winterhalter, 1859.*

1 The Duchess of Clarence (later Queen Adelaide),
Queen Victoria's aunt by marriage.
*Miniature by Mary Green, c. 1818.*

2 The Duke of Clarence (later King William IV),
Queen Victoria's uncle.
*Miniature by J. P. Fisher, 1818.*

3 The Duke of Kent, Queen Victoria's father.
*Miniature after a painting by Sir William Beechey,
c. 1818.*

4 The Duchess of Kent, Queen Victoria's mother.
*Miniature by Alfred Chalon, 1829.*

5   Leopold I, King of the Belgians, Queen Victoria's uncle.
*Photograph, c. 1855.*

6  Prince Charles of Leiningen, Queen
Victoria's half-brother.
*Miniature by Acland, 1821.*

7  Princess Feodora of Leiningen (later von
Hohenlohe-Langenburg), Queen Victoria's
half-sister.
*Miniature by Henry Collen, 1828.*

8  Cartoon showing members of the royal family in the race for an heir. *L. to R.:* The Duke and
Duchess of Clarence, the Duke and Duchess of Cambridge with baby Prince George, the Duke
and Duchess of Kent two months before the birth of Princess Victoria, the Duke and Duchess of
Cumberland and the Duchess of York.
*Coloured lithograph published March 1819.*

9 Kensington Palace, where Queen Victoria was born on 24 May 1819.
*Engraving by J. Storer after a drawing by T. Taylor, 1802.*

10 The room in which Queen Victoria was born, as it looked when she visited Kensington Palace on 15 May 1899. The room is on the ground floor in the south-east corner. Unlike her bedroom and sitting-room (mistakenly called nursery), this room is no longer furnished but is used for exhibiting part of the London Museum's collection of costumes.

11 Queen Victoria's bedroom at Kensington Palace on the first floor facing south, as it is today.

12  The Duchess of Kent and Princess Victoria, aged three.
*Engraving by William Skelton published April 1823, after a painting by*
*Sir William Beechey, 1822.*

13  Princess Victoria, aged four.
*Painting by S. P. Denning, 1823.*

14  Princess Victoria, aged five.
*Engraving by William Ward after a painting by
William Fowler, 1824.*

15  Princess Victoria, aged seven. The 'order'
on the Princess's left shoulder is a miniature of
King George IV set in diamonds and pinned to
a blue ribbon. He gave it to her at Windsor in
1826.
*Engraving by T. Woolnoth, 1832, from a painting
by Anthony Stewart, 1826.*

16 'Design for a Regency.' Prince Leopold with Princess Victoria on his knee, the Duchess of Kent enthroned as Regent, right background Sir John Conroy presiding at an imaginary meeting of the Privy Council.
*Cartoon by William Heath, July 1830.*

17 Princess Victoria, aged eleven, with sketch-book.
*Painting by Richard Westall, who was appointed her drawing master in 1830.*

18 Princess Victoria, aged ten.
*Lithograph by Hullmandel from a drawing by Richard J. Lane, 1829.*

19 The Duchess of Kent and Princess Victoria, aged fifteen.
*Lithograph by R. J. Lane from a drawing by Sir George Hayter, 1834.*

20 Arrival of the Duchess of Kent and Princess Victoria at St. Leonards, 4 November 1834.
*Coloured lithograph by J. J. Dodd.*

21  Princess Victoria, aged seventeen.
*Engraving by T. Woolnoth after a miniature by Henry Collen, 1836.*

22  Princess Victoria, aged seventeen.
*Silhouette by F. Frith, 1836.*

23   Princess Victoria, aged sixteen, and her spaniel Dash.
*Engraving by James Bromley after a painting by Sir George Hayter, 1835.*

24 Queen Victoria, aged nineteen.
*Copy by Charles Heath of a miniature by
Sir William Ross, 1838.*

25 Queen Victoria on the day of her
Proclamation, 21 June 1837.
*Pen and wash drawing by Louisa S. Costello.*

26 Queen Victoria receiving the news of her accession from the Lord Chamberlain, Lord
Conyngham, and the Archbishop of Canterbury at Kensington Palace on 20 June 1837.
*Painting by H. T. Wells.*

27 Queen Victoria's first Privy Council, held at Kensington Palace on the morning of her accession. The Prime Minister, Lord Melbourne, holds the pen for the Queen to sign her Declaration. Behind and to his left is Lord Palmerston, and to his right Lord John Russell. On Lord Melbourne's left sits the Archbishop of Canterbury (with wig), next to him the Duke of Cumberland, the Queen's eldest uncle. The Duke of Wellington stands in front of the column, Sir Robert Peel next to him, and seated nearest to the spectator is the Duke of Sussex, another uncle of the Queen.

*Painting by Sir David Wilkie.*

28 Queen Victoria hears the Proclamation of her accession, at the window of the Audience Chamber, St. James's Palace, 21 June 1837.

*Engraving after a drawing by H. Melville.*

29

29   Queen Victoria.
*Lithograph by I. W. Gear, 1837.*

30  Queen Victoria (wearing the Windsor uniform) leaving Windsor Castle with King Leopold of the Belgians (*left*), the Duke of Wellington (*right*), and Lord Hill, Commander of the Forces (*behind*), to review the Guards on 28 September 1837.
*Lithograph by W. Clark from a sketch by T. C. Wilson.*

31  'Susannah and the Elders.' Queen Victoria between Lord Melbourne (Prime Minister) and Lord John Russell (Home Secretary and Leader of the House).
*Sketch by John Doyle, October 1837.*

32 Queen Victoria's first visit to Brighton, 4 October 1837. *Lithograph by W. Walton from a sketch by I. Cordwell.*

33 Queen Victoria riding. In the background, Buckingham Palace and the Marble Arch. *Coloured lithograph, 1837.*

34 Queen Victoria driving through Trafalgar Square on her way to the Lord Mayor's banquet at the Guildhall on 9 November 1837.

35 Queen Victoria's first visit to Covent Garden Theatre since her accession, 17 November 1837. *L. to R.:* The Marquess of Conyngham (Lord Chamberlain), the Duchess of Sutherland (Mistress of the Robes), the Marchioness of Tavistock (Lady of the Bedchamber), the Queen, the Duchess of Kent, the Earl of Albemarle (Master of the Horse).

*Coloured lithograph by W. Drummond.*

36 Queen Victoria wearing the Garter.
*Engraving by Finden after a drawing by R. J. Lane, May 1838.*

THE CORONATION

of Her Most Sacred Majesty

Admit *Comte Philippe de Rohan-Chabot* Secretary to the French Embassy.

INTO WESTMINSTER ABBEY.

West Door

N° 35.

*Norfolk Earl Marshal*

37 Admission ticket of Comte Philippe de Rohan-Chabot to Queen Victoria's Coronation, 28 June 1838.

38 Queen Victoria's Coronation, 28 June 1838.
*Coloured engraving by C. Hunt after a drawing by T. Kearnan.*

39 Queen Victoria's Coronation. Lord Melbourne is beside the Queen, bearing the Sword of State. The Duke of Wellington is a prominent figure in the group of peers at the left centre. On the left is the Archbishop of Canterbury, who has just crowned the Queen.

*Painting by Sir George Hayter.*

40 Queen Victoria receiving the Sacrament from the Archbishop of Canterbury after being crowned. Near the Queen stand Lord Melbourne and the Duke of Wellington. Next to him is the Duchess of Kent. Behind the Queen stand the Duchess of Sutherland (Mistress of the Robes) and some of the train-bearers.

*Painting by C. R. Leslie.*

35

41  Queen Victoria in Coronation robes. The robes are now in the London Museum.
*Painting by Alfred Chalon.*

42   Prince Albert of Saxe-Coburg-Gotha.
*Mezzotint from a drawing by V. Gortz, .Gotha, c. 1838.*

# II

## VICTORIA
## AND ALBERT

THE morning of the royal wedding day, 10 February 1840, was dark and dreary, with rain and fog. 'God help me, or rather, God be my stay!' was all Prince Albert could say as he set out from Buckingham Palace with his father and brother for the Chapel Royal, St. James's Palace, where the marriage ceremony was to take place at one o'clock. He wore Field-Marshal's uniform and the insignia of the Garter, with the enormous white rosettes which are worn on 'Collar Days' (Plate 44). Half an hour later the bride followed with her mother and the Duchess of Sutherland, Mistress of the Robes. Queen Victoria's *décolleté* white satin dress had an overskirt of Honiton lace, and a veil of similar lace hung from her wreath of orange-blossom (Plate 44). The collar of the Garter and diamond and sapphire jewellery added a touch of brilliance. Her long train, trimmed with orange-blossom, was borne by twelve peers' daughters dressed in white, with white roses, the crimson and gold drapery of the Chapel Royal forming a splendid setting for the bridal procession.

Before the wedding, the Archbishop of Canterbury had enquired whether the Queen wanted to make any alteration in the part of the service containing the promise to obey. He received the reply that 'though not as a *queen*, as a *woman* she was ready to promise all things contained in that portion of the Liturgy'.

The Queen was given away by her uncle the Duke of Sussex, and at the moment when the ring was placed on her finger by Prince Albert a royal salute was fired and all the bells in London began to peal, so that every citizen should know that his sovereign was a wife (Plate 45).

After the short ceremony the register was signed (Plate 46) in the Throne Room at St. James's Palace, and the bride and bridegroom returned to Buckingham Palace, being heartily cheered on the way by the crowds, though it was noticed that the Duke of Wellington received a still greater ovation.

A brilliant assembly gathered for the wedding breakfast at Buckingham Palace. The huge cake measured nine feet in circumference and weighed over 300 lbs. On top of it stood a foot-high figure of Britannia blessing the bride and bridegroom. They left for Windsor at four: 'I and Albert alone.'

As the royal carriage drove off the sun came out for the first time. In every village Victoria and Albert drove through, people were waiting to cheer them, and Eton and Windsor were brilliantly illuminated. The pleasure of being alone was soon interrupted, however, for even on this their first evening the bridal couple dined with half a dozen ladies- and gentlemen-in-waiting, though the Queen felt unwell. Complaining of a sick headache, she lay on the sofa for the rest of the evening.

Early next morning Victoria and Albert went for a walk in the grounds. 'Strange that a bridal night should be so short,' mocked Greville. Surely this was 'not the way to provide us with a Prince of Wales'. At breakfast Prince Albert appeared in a black velvet jacket without a cravat, and to his wife it seemed that 'anything more beautiful—and more youthfully manly and perfect—never was seen'. Snatching a little time from adoring her bridegroom, she poured out her happiness to King Leopold.

Windsor Castle,
11th February 1840

My dearest Uncle,

I write to you from here, the happiest, happiest Being that ever existed. Really, I do not think it *possible* for anyone in the world to be *happier*, or *as* happy as I am. He is an Angel, and his kindness and affection for me is really touching. To look in those dear eyes, and that dear sunny face, is enough to make me adore him. What I can do to make him happy will be my greatest delight.

The honeymoon was ended on the third day by the arrival of the Duchess of Kent, the Duke of Saxe-Coburg, Prince Ernest, Lord Melbourne, and the entire Court. The two following evenings were spent dancing, and on the 14th they all returned to London.

The Duchess of Kent, whose suite of rooms was now needed for Prince Albert, moved to Ingestre House in Belgrave Square, until the death of Princess Augusta (a daughter of George III) some months later left vacant Clarence House and Frogmore House in Windsor Home Park. Prince Albert, who was very fond of his aunt-mother-in-law, eventually succeeded in effecting a reconciliation between her and the Queen, which gradually warmed into a tender companionship far more loving than had ever existed before.

He himself was soon sorely in need of friends, for he found far more thorns strewn in his path than he had anticipated. Difficulties from a quite unexpected quarter threatened his peace and caused him to complain that he was 'only the husband and not the master in the house'. Baroness Lehzen, who on the Queen's accession had refused any official appointment in the Household, had made herself *de facto* superintendent of the royal establishment and of the privy purse, besides acting as the Queen's personal private secretary. She was consulted about everything, and even without emphasizing it on her letter paper bearing the picture of a railway engine with the motto 'I am coming', her power was felt everywhere. Prince Albert naturally considered her activities as his prerogative now, and expected that Lehzen would respect his authority. But far from it. Lehzen felt responsible only to the Queen, and the Queen refused to take sides between her two 'angels'. During the difficult period prior to her accession Lehzen had supported Princess Victoria against her mother most loyally, and she felt then 'I shall never be able to repay her sufficiently for all she has *borne* and done for me but by my love and gratitude. She is the *most affectionate*, *devoted*, *attached* and *disinterested* friend I have, and I love her most *dearly*.' Leaving Prince Albert and Lehzen to work out a solution brought none, and gave him no alternative but to ask the baroness to leave. Yet again she defied him, saying that he had not the power to turn her out of the Queen's house.

Another irritation of which the Prince complained to the Queen was her 'want of confidence [in him] in trivial matters, and in all matters connected with the policy of the country'. It was humiliating for the father-to-be of the next sovereign to find himself excluded from his wife's interviews with her Ministers. His hopes of sharing her life in everything, and taking King Leopold's place as her political adviser, were sadly dashed. Having been subservient to her mother's wishes for so long, the Queen's attitude should be seen as a natural reaction against any interference, rather than lack of confidence in her husband. Her pride in her exalted position could not endure any advice or difference of opinion even from him. It tended to make her assume a haughty and even imperious manner, which naturally aggravated the difficulty immeasurably. Prince Albert once said to Anson, his private secretary and friend: 'The Queen always sees what is right at a glance, but if her feelings run contrary, she avoids the Prince's arguments, which she feels sure agree with her own, and seeks arguments to support her wishes against her convictions from other people.' Underlying this difficulty was a clash on principle: Prince Albert resolutely refused to take orders from his wife, who had promised to obey him on marriage, yet who stubbornly insisted that he should obey the Queen. Three months after their marriage, King Leopold—probably at the request of his nephew—wrote to Queen Victoria rather pointedly about his marriage with Princess Charlotte, in which a similar difference in rank might have caused difficulties:

> I know that you have been told that she ordered everything in the house, and liked to show that she was mistress. It was not so. On the contrary, her pride was to make me appear to my best advantage, and even to display respect and obedience ... to show very clearly that she considered me as her lord and master. ... I must say that I was much more the master of the house than is generally the case in private life.

Prince Ernest, who stayed on with the young couple for the first two months, could not help noticing that they 'could not yield to each other'. Indeed, it took them several years to find a *modus vivendi*, and in this gradual adaptation the intensity of her love made the Queen give way more readily to her husband than his intellectual superiority permitted him to submit to her sometimes unreasonable will. Several amusing anecdotes show his tactics in endeavouring to tame her.

After a quarrel Prince Albert retired to his study. The Queen hurrying after him and finding the door locked, imperiously demanded entry. 'Who is there?' enquired the Prince in a calm voice. 'The Queen', came the haughty reply. 'The Queen must wait', answered the voice from within. For a moment she was dumbfounded. Such an unbelievable situation had never occurred before. Again and again she beat upon the door, and again and again came the same question and answer, until at last, bursting

into tears, the Queen sobbed, 'Your wife, Albert. Your poor unhappy *Weibchen*.' The door opened, and Prince Albert tenderly took his wife into his arms.

On another occasion Prince Albert attended the Royal Academy banquet. At ten-thirty the Queen, it is said, sent him a note asking him to come home. Finding the conversation more animated than he had expected, Prince Albert stayed a little longer. Half an hour later another note arrived from Buckingham Palace. This time he was ordered to return at once. Resenting this treatment, Prince Albert decided to teach his wife a lesson. He told the astonished coachman to drive to Windsor Castle, and kept the Queen in suspense until the next morning.

In the first years of their marriage, the Queen and Prince breakfasted at nine and took a short walk with the dogs soon afterwards in the grounds of Buckingham Palace, or in Windsor Park as the case might be. Then came a few hours' work—which in later years assumed vast proportions—and, time permitting, they made drawings or etchings (Plate 375). After luncheon at two o'clock, the Prime Minister usually saw the Queen on State business. Between five and six the Queen and Prince went driving in a phaeton, or she drove with two of her ladies, the Prince accompanying them on horseback. After dinner at eight came the inevitable albums of engravings, a little amateur music-making, and small-talk which caused the Prince agonies of boredom from which he escaped at the earliest opportunity in a game of chess. He would have liked to enliven the interminable tedious evenings by inviting leading writers and scientists, but was unable to have his way because the Queen, aware of her inability to meet them as an intellectual equal, did not fancy remaining silent, and was equally unwilling to risk revealing her ignorance. Prince Albert did not care for society and above all the unintellectual English Court. He had in fact little in common with most of the aristocrats surrounding the Queen, and strongly disapproved of the lax moral standards of many of them. They in turn found him stiff, reserved in manner, lacking in humour and social graces, and prim. The Duke of Wellington thought him 'extremely strait-laced and a great stickler for morality'. Those who came into close contact with the Prince invariably became very attached to him, but few were given the opportunity, for few matched his intellect and idealism. Highly cultivated in many fields and a patron of art and science, Prince Albert was also a talented musician. He played the organ well—in his opinion the greatest and most expressive of all instruments—and wrote several compositions for it, including a *Te Deum* which was performed at Westminster Abbey. Singing and playing the piano with the Queen in private was one of his greatest pleasures. Sometimes they would sing a duet at a concert at Court. No less a musician than Mendelssohn thought highly of their attainments. Musical entertainments which did not tax his intellect, however, sent the Prince quickly to sleep, much as he struggled against it. Guizot, French Ambassador to the Court of St. James's in 1840, wrote of a concert at Buckingham Palace: 'The Queen took a more lively interest in it than the greater part of her guests. Prince Albert slept. She looked at him, half smiling, half vexed. She pushed him with her elbow. He woke up, and nodded approval of the piece of the moment. Then he went to sleep again, still nodding approval, and the Queen began again.'

Exactly four months after marriage, an attempt was made on the Queen's life (Plate 49) while she and Prince Albert drove up Constitution Hill. Her calmness aroused such admiration that Edward Oxford's attack had the effect of restoring some of the popularity the Queen had lost through the Hastings and Bedchamber affairs a year earlier. Addresses of congratulation were presented by both Houses of Parliament, and for several days when the royal couple went for their afternoon drive many ladies and gentlemen on horseback spontaneously formed a bodyguard.

At the time of the attack—the first of seven during her reign—the Queen was already expecting a child, and early in August Prince Albert was appointed Regent in the event of the Queen's death during the minority of the heir to the throne. The Bill passed both Houses of Parliament without opposition—except from the Duke of Sussex—a fact which was the more gratifying, Lord Melbourne told the Queen, because it was 'entirely owing to the golden opinions the Prince had won on all sides

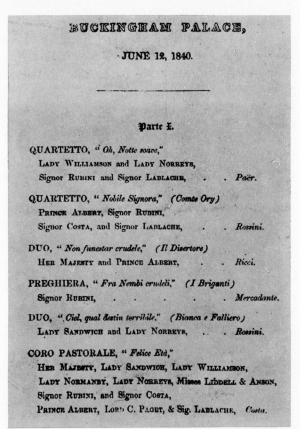

Programme of concert in which Queen Victoria and Prince Albert took part.

since his arrival in the country'. Baron Stockmar's diplomatic discussions with leaders of the Tory party had also done much to mollify the Opposition. When the Queen prorogued Parliament on 11 August Prince Albert drove with her to the House of Lords and sat on a chair of State beside the throne (Plate 51). On this occasion the Duke of Sussex had Lord Albemarle, the Master of the Horse, and Baroness Lehzen as allies in protesting against the elevated position the Queen accorded to her husband, but the precedent of Prince George of Denmark's accompanying Queen Anne settled the matter.

The following month Prince Albert was made a Privy Councillor. Giving the news to his brother he noted with satisfaction this further evidence of the Queen's changing attitude. 'Now Victoria is also ready to give up something for my sake, I, everything for her sake.' Baron Stockmar was also informed: 'I have come to be extremely pleased with

Victoria during the past few months. She has only twice had the sulks ... altogether she puts more confidence in me daily. I am constantly provided with interesting [Foreign Office] papers.'

On 21 November 1840 Queen Victoria gave birth to a daughter in the presence of Prince Albert, the Duchess of Kent, and some Ladies of the Bedchamber, in addition to three doctors and a nurse. The crying baby was immediately taken into the ante-room—the door of which had remained open—where a distinguished company, whose constitutional duty it was to be present at the birth of royal children, was anxiously waiting. It included Lord Melbourne, Lord John Russell (Home Secretary), Lord Palmerston (Foreign Secretary), the Archbishop of Canterbury, the Bishop of London, the Duke of Sussex, and a number of other peers and Privy Councillors. Rejoicing throughout the country was great, for the danger that the unpopular King of Hanover would inherit the crown of England was averted. 'Victoria is as well as if nothing had happened', reported Prince Albert to his father two days later. 'The little one is very well and very merry ... I should certainly have liked it better if she had been a son, as would Victoria also; but, at the same time, we must be equally satisfied and thankful as it is.'

Prince Albert watched over the Queen with the devoted care of a mother. No one but he ever lifted her from bed to sofa, and he always helped to wheel her into the next room. For this purpose he would come instantly when sent for from any part of the Palace. 'A kinder, wiser, or more judicious nurse there could not be', felt the Queen as her husband waited on her. In the circumstances it seemed natural that he should read and discuss the secret Government dispatches that arrived daily, and deal with her private correspondence. The latter had hitherto been the privilege of Baroness Lehzen, but with the Queen's growing dependence on her husband, Lehzen's influence was on the wane. From the beginning of 1841 Prince Albert was virtually the Queen's Private Secretary.

The Queen and Prince Albert spent their first Christmas together at Windsor Castle. Three Christmas trees adorned the hall, and smaller ones stood on the tables where the presents were laid out.

This German custom was popularized by Queen Victoria and Prince Albert, but the introduction of the Christmas tree into England is not due to them, as is generally assumed, but to Queen Adelaide, who was a princess of Saxe-Meiningen.

Every day Prince Albert went skating on the pond at Frogmore, the country house of the Duchess of Kent near by, and sometimes the Queen joined in the fun (Plate 54).

Though for the time being Prince Albert was still thwarted in his ambition to share fully in the Queen's political duties, he had plenty of outlets for his diverse talents. He was responsible for many of the programmes of 'The Antient Concerts' organized by the Philharmonic Society. In 1841 Sir Robert Peel placed him at the head of the Fine Arts Commission on the decoration of the new Houses of Parliament. Two years later the Prince accepted the presidency of the Society of Arts, a position which he held until his death. Under his aegis technological and scientific developments were encouraged as never before because, being of a progressive turn of mind, Prince Albert foresaw their importance in the rapidly expanding industrialization of England and the corresponding growth of national prosperity which was bound to come. As a philanthropist he was much concerned with the abolition of the slave trade in other countries and in social improvements at home. He himself designed and had erected on sites belonging to the Duchy of Cornwall some blocks of working-class dwellings with bathrooms—an unheard-of luxury for the poor.

The same foresight, thoroughness and hard work which Prince Albert bestowed on public and philanthropic projects is also shown in his investigation of the management of the royal household. Having been brought up in a small and economical Court, Prince Albert was amazed at the waste and extravagance that was going on at Windsor Castle and Buckingham Palace. At Windsor Castle, for instance, dinner was served to 113,000 people in the course of one year, not including ball suppers, etc. Even when the Court was not in residence, at least fifteen or twenty large joints of meat were roasted every day for a total of eighty-five resident members of the household. Wherever the royal family was in residence Prince Albert noticed that each day hundreds of wax candles were put in the candelabras and chandeliers, and removed again at bed-time even if they were only partly burned or had not been lighted at all. Ever since the reign of Queen Anne these 'Palace ends' had been sold by the servants for extra pocket money. His study of the account books revealed many ancient sinecures, such as that of a half-pay officer at Windsor Castle who continued to receive thirty-five shillings a week for 'Red Room Wine' for the officer of the guard in that room, though it had only been temporarily used as a guardroom in the days of George III.

Bad organization in the household arrangements was another cause of wastage, inefficiency, and much discomfort. Many of the responsibilities were shared between the Lord Steward's and the Lord Chamberlain's departments in an inexplicable way. The Lord Steward's department, for instance, laid the fires and the Lord Chamberlain's lit them: on the other hand, the Lord Chamberlain provided the lamps and the Lord Steward was responsible for cleaning, trimming and lighting them. The Office of Works, being responsible for the exteriors of palaces, cleaned the outside of the windows, but not the inside of the panes which came in the province of the Lord Chamberlain. Such a division of labour was bound to result in inefficiency.

The Queen was surprised when she learned of these matters, but thought it wiser not to stir up dust. Prince Albert, however, was determined to put the arrangements on a more efficient footing. He enlisted the aid of Baron Stockmar, who drew up in January 1841 a memorandum with typical German thoroughness and a typical long-winded title: 'Observations on the present state of the Royal Household; written with a view to amend the present scheme and to unite the greater security and comfort of the Sovereign with the greater regularity and better discipline of the Royal Household.'

The reforms made Prince Albert extremely unpopular with the staff, for apart from measures designed to avoid waste (candles, for example, were ordered to be burned down to a small end), he actually reduced wages and the number of servants, and saw to it that everyone did fair work for fair money. His economy drive saved the Queen no less

than £70,000 up to 1844, when he introduced the most fundamental change—the delegation of the administrative powers of the Lord Steward, the Lord Chamberlain, the Master of the Horse and the Office of Works, to one man, the Master of the Household.

In May 1841 Lord Melbourne's Ministry was defeated and the change so much dreaded by the Queen became inevitable. When the new Parliament, which had a large Tory majority, assembled in August, the Queen, still annoyed at their treatment of Prince Albert a year and a half before, abstained from opening it. She tried, nevertheless, to avoid another clash with Sir Robert Peel over the Bedchamber question, which—to save embarrassment on either side—was negotiated beforehand between George Anson and Peel. The Duchess of Sutherland and two other ladies closely connected with the retiring Whig Ministers 'voluntarily' resigned and were replaced by three Tory ladies.

At the instigation of Prince Albert, the retiring Prime Minister on whose advice the Queen had hitherto relied, impressed upon her the inestimable advantage of the Prince's assistance: 'Your Majesty cannot do better than have recourse to it, whenever it is needed, and rely upon it with confidence. . . . You will find a great support in the Prince; he is so able. You said when you were going to be married that he was perfection, which I thought a little exaggerated then, but really I think now that it is in some degree realized.' The Queen assured Lord Melbourne that she was prepared to follow his advice.

Strange as it may seem, up to the age of twenty Prince Albert had been totally indifferent to politics, and it was with difficulty that Baron Stockmar persuaded him to read even one daily newspaper. All this was now changed. Prince Albert studied politics assiduously, took lessons in English Law, read Hallam's *Constitutional History of England*—and there was always the faithful Stockmar at hand, who was respected as an *Éminence grise*, though it is difficult to assess the actual extent of his political influence. Until 1857 the Baron spent every autumn, winter and spring at the royal residences, living with his family in Coburg only during the summer months. But even from Coburg he bombarded

Prince Albert with long memoranda and platitudes such as 'never fail in princely worth and nobleness'.

The new Prime Minister, Sir Robert Peel (1788–1850), came from a rich cotton-spinning family. With his awkward manners he formed a strange contrast to the courtly Melbourne, but Prince Albert found him congenial. Being highly educated, serious and high-minded, Peel had much in common with the Prince and they soon became firm friends. This naturally made the Queen change her attitude to Peel also.

On 9 November 1841 a male heir to the throne was born—the first for seventy-nine years. Delighted at having a boy, the Queen prayed fervently 'to see him resemble his angelic dearest Father in *every, every* respect, both in body and mind'—pious hopes which were doomed to disappointment.

On 25 January the Prince of Wales was baptized Albert Edward at St. George's Chapel, Windsor Castle (Plate 57). The chief sponsor was King Frederick William IV of Prussia, who came over on a State visit. The extravagance of the christening ceremony, banquet and subsequent festivities formed an astonishing contrast to Prince Albert's household economies, to which allusion is made in a contemporary cartoon (Plate 58).

In May the Queen gave a splendid fancy-dress ball at Buckingham Palace in an attempt to stimulate the Spitalfields silk weaving industry, which was in a depressed state, as was trade in general. All the guests wore fourteenth-century costume, the Queen and Prince appearing as Edward III and Queen Philippa (Plate 63) in dresses copied from their effigies in Westminster Abbey. Shortly before the ball Richard Monckton-Milnes (later Lord Houghton) sent to the *Morning Chronicle* a fictitious report of an alleged debate in the Chamber of Deputies, during which a deputy, taking offence at Prince Albert's representation of France's ancient enemy, was supposed to have asked 'whether the French Ambassador in England had been invited to the *bal masqué* to be given by the haughty descendants of the Plantagenets for the purpose of awakening the long-buried griefs of France in the disasters of Crécy and Poitiers and the loss of Calais, and whether he were going with his *attachés* with bare feet and halters round their necks,

representing the unfortunate burghers of Calais?' No one could have been more surprised at the success of this hoax than its author. The Home Secretary rushed into Sir Robert Peel's room with the *Morning Chronicle* saying 'There's the devil to pay in France about this foolish ball!' and a French newspaper, without first checking the debate, suggested by way of retaliation holding a similar ball in Paris at which the Duke of Orleans should impersonate William the Conqueror. Still more surprising is the fact that even so conscientious a biographer of Queen Victoria as Sir Sidney Lee was taken in by Monckton-Milnes' joke sixty years after the event.

A fortnight after the Plantagenet Ball, Prince Albert thought he saw a man in the crowd aiming a pistol at the Queen during their drive back to Buckingham Palace from a service at St. James's Chapel. Neither the Queen nor the Prince could bear the idea of staying at home until the man had been traced—an almost impossible task. The Queen declared 'she would much rather run the immediate risk at any time, than have the presentiment of danger constantly hovering over her'. It was therefore decided to tempt the would-be assassin to reveal himself. The next afternoon the Queen and Prince Albert courageously acted as bait by driving out as usual, the Queen's ladies being left at the Palace without explanation. The two equerries, however, rode close to the carriage, which drove faster than usual. The plan succeeded. In Constitution Hill, at the same spot at which Oxford had made his attempt two years previously, a destitute cabinet-maker named John Francis fired without effect, and was immediately arrested by plain-clothes policemen who were out in force (Plate 64). The whole country was relieved at the Queen's renewed escape, and very proud of the extremely courageous behaviour of the royal couple, who were greeted with prolonged cheers on arrival at the Italian Opera that evening.

Only a month later the Queen had yet another frightening experience. This time a crippled youth named Bean aimed a pistol at her. He was seized but escaped for a time, leaving his weapon in the hands of the man who struggled with him, and who then had the greatest difficulty in convincing the police that *he* was not the assailant. When the pistol was examined it was found to be loaded with paper, pieces of clay pipe and powder, but no bullet. Under the existing law even such harmless demonstrations as Bean's were treated as high treason, but a new Act was passed reducing the death sentence for such criminal offences to transportation for seven years or imprisonment for up to three years.

On 14 June the Queen and Prince Albert made their first railway journey—on the new Great Western line from Slough, near Windsor, to London. The Master of the Horse carefully inspected the locomotive, and the royal coachman insisted that it was his duty to ride on the pilot engine which, to test the line, steamed in advance of every royal train at least up to 1901. But finding his scarlet livery and white wig covered with smuts on arrival at Paddington station, he did not press his rights on later journeys. The Queen expressed herself 'quite charmed' with the experience, but the Prince protested, 'Not quite so fast next time, Mr. Conductor, if you please.' The distance of 21½ miles was covered in twenty-five minutes—less than most trains take today.

The royal train in those days consisted of four carriages: the first after the engine and tender was for luggage, then came the royal saloon, topped by a crown (Plate 72), for the royal family and the ladies-in-waiting. The last two carriages were for the equerries, other attendants, and officials of the railway company. Railway travel was still sufficiently novel for large crowds to gather and wave as their Queen sped past. When the royal train passed through Coventry in November 1843 the line was thronged with 10,000 spectators for two miles; at one local station troops presented arms, and a band played 'God Save the Queen' as the train passed through—about as appropriate an occasion for the national anthem as when George III took a dip in the sea at Weymouth. But one never knew. These new-fangled inventions were dangerous.

In September 1842 Victoria and Albert paid their first visit to Scotland. On account of Chartist riots in the Midlands and north of England, the journey was made by sea. Leaving their babies in the care of their governess Lady Lyttelton, the Queen and Prince embarked at Woolwich on the *Royal George* under the command of the Queen's cousin Lord Adolphus Fitzclarence, a son of William IV and the actress Mrs. Jordan.

At Tilbury the royal squadron, consisting of nine ships, was saluted by the guns of the fortress, and all the way up the East Coast was received with the greatest enthusiasm. Civic authorities in their robes came out in steamers to pay homage to the Queen, and crowds of people in gaily decorated boats cheered and waved, while bands played 'God Save the Queen', church bells rang, and cannons boomed.

The second evening out the sea became choppy. The straining of the *Royal George* (a sailing vessel) on the tow-ropes attaching her to two steamers with members of the Household on board aggravated the motion. Everybody on the royal yacht was seasick (Plate 65).

At a quarter to one on the morning of 1 September, the third day out, the *Royal George* anchored for the night off Inchkeith near Edinburgh (Plate 66). Arthur's Seat presented a beautiful sight in the night: an enormous bonfire on top, 40 feet in diameter and containing 25 tons of coal, 40 cartloads of wood and 180 barrels of tar, made it into an artificial Vesuvius.

The Scottish capital had planned a great welcome for the previous day, but learning that the royal party would arrive too late, the reception was called off. Victoria and Albert landing at Granton pier at the unexpectedly early hour of ten minutes past eight upset all plans. The ceremony of delivering to the Queen the keys of Edinburgh could not be performed because the royal visitors had driven past the city boundary long before the Lord Provost knew they were there, though the Royal Company of Archers, in their green uniforms and plumed caps and carrying bows and arrows, had hastily assembled to escort the Queen's carriage. The escort of dragoons, ignorant of the Archers' ancient privilege, opposed them and the noblemen were badly pushed about. The Lord Provost and Councillors racing in their carriages by various short cuts at last managed to get in front of the procession, now on its way to Dalkeith where the royal party were to be the guests of the Duke of Buccleuch.

The Queen and Prince were both much impressed with Edinburgh and Arthur's Seat towering above it. 'Albert said he felt sure the Acropolis could not be finer.' At Dalkeith and at the estates of other Scottish noblemen, Prince Albert had his first experience of deerstalking, which became his favourite sport. A good shot, he found it 'one of the most fatiguing, but also one of the most interesting of pursuits'. One day he bagged nineteen roe deer and three brace of grouse, but this feat was not so imposing as it sounds, for 150 men were engaged as beaters and he was the only person to shoot.

Victoria and Albert were both enchanted with Scotland and vowed to come again soon. The picturesque scenery, the natural friendliness of the people, and the climate, appealed to the Queen and to Prince Albert, who was strongly reminded of his native Thuringia, and took an immediate liking to the simple folk—the gillies and *jaeger*—with whom he spent much time deerstalking.

Unable to face another voyage in the old sailing yacht (in which the Duke and Duchess of Kent had crossed the Channel in 1819), the Queen and Prince made the homeward journey on the fast steamship *Trident*, which they liked so much that immediately after her return the Queen commissioned the building of a royal steam yacht.

In the autumn, Baroness Lehzen, seeing her power gradually eclipsed by Prince Albert, decided to return to Germany for good. Her departure came as an immense relief to the Prince, in whose eyes she had always been 'a house dragon spitting fire', and even the Queen realized its necessity now, for Lehzen had 'got to be rather trying . . . never from any evil intention, only from a mistaken idea of duty and affection for me'. To console her old governess and faithful friend in her loneliness the Queen wrote to her regularly once a week and later monthly until Lehzen's death.

As Queen Victoria came more and more under the influence of her husband she began to appreciate and share his high principles and lofty attitude towards life. This caused her to see the years between her accession and marriage as 'a life of constant amusement, flattery and excitement'.

What an artificial sort of happiness *mine* was then, and what a blessing it is I have now in my beloved Husband *real* and solid happiness, which no Politics, no worldly reverses *can* change; it could not have

lasted long, as it was then, for after all . . . it was but in Society that I had amusement, and I was only living on that superficial resource, which I *then fancied* was happiness! Thank God! for *me* and others, this is changed, and I *know what real* happiness is.

Court life, too, changed through the influence of Prince Albert, who insisted on spotless character. Originally the Queen's attitude had been more broadminded: 'one ought always to be indulgent towards other people', she argued, 'if we had not been well brought up and well taken care of, we might also have gone astray'. But Prince Albert's admonition to be more strict in her appointments to the Household prevailed. In his opinion, great harm had resulted to the Court from some of Lord Melbourne's 'very careless' appointments, 'and though Lord Melbourne had declared "that that damned morality would undo us all", we had found great advantage in it, and were determined to adhere to it'.

Prince Albert's attitude may seem narrow, but at any rate he did not expect more from other people than from himself. He told Anson that he never feared temptation with regard to women because he had no inclinations in that respect, and vice disgusted him. He could not have been more different from his brother Ernest, who led a dissipated life. Even so close an observer as Lord Melbourne could hardly believe that this state of affairs could last for ever. When the Queen boasted to him one day of the Prince's utter indifference to the attractions of other women, he cynically remarked that 'these were early days to boast', which made her very indignant. But then, Lord Melbourne was a relic of the Regency.

In the spring of 1843, when the birth of a third child drew near, Prince Albert held *levées* in place of the Queen's Drawing-rooms. After three years of married life the Queen had come to realize the desirability of that unity of purpose towards which Prince Albert had been striving all the time. 'He and I must be one, and God knows, he, dear Angel, *deserves* to be *highest* in everything.' Yet this sign of Prince Albert's growing authority was by no means well received by the Press and public.

Strong family feeling even for relations she did not care for, led Queen Victoria to invite the King of Hanover to be one of the sponsors at the christening of Princess Alice, who was born on 25 April (Plate 67). The King, however, arrived too late to attend the ceremony, and was annoyed that they had not waited for him. Soon afterwards he made himself thoroughly disagreeable at the wedding of his niece, Princess Augusta of Cambridge. Having always resented the fact that 'a paper Royal Highness'—as he disparagingly called Prince Albert—took precedence over him in England, the King took up a position in front of him, but the Prince gave him a sharp push down the steps of the chapel, and he left. At the signing of the register, however, King Ernest turned up again and manœuvred to sign immediately after Queen Victoria. Realizing his design, the Queen seized the register and dodging round to the other side of the table, quickly handed the pen to her husband. Royal visitors to London included the Queen's favourite uncle Leopold as well as the 'Ogre', and being anxious to give Uncle Leopold precedence over Uncle Ernest, she consulted the Duke of Wellington. He advised using the same system as at the Congress of Vienna. 'How was that?' asked the Queen, 'by the first arrival?' 'No, Ma'am', replied the Iron Duke, 'alphabetically: and then, you know, B [Belgium] comes before H [Hanover].'

Queen Victoria's affection for King Leopold's wife Louise, and her peculiar enthusiasm for all family connections, had long made her eager to meet Queen Louise's father, King Louis-Philippe. A visit was arranged for the early autumn, preceded by a cruise in the Channel to try out the new royal steam yacht *Victoria and Albert*. On their arrival off Tréport, near Cherbourg, on 2 September 1843, Queen Victoria put on a purple satin dress and a bonnet trimmed with yellow feathers, and watched with emotion the royal barge come out to the *Victoria and Albert*, where she and Prince Albert received a warm welcome from the King of the French, his sons, the Prime Minister Guizot, and other officials.

The landing was a fine sight, which the beauty of the evening and the setting sun enhanced. Crowds of people (all so different from ours), numbers of troops (also so different from our troops), the whole Court, and all the authorities, were assembled on the shore.

The King led me up a somewhat steepish staircase, where the Queen received me with the kindest welcome (Plate 78). . . . The cheering of the people and of the troops crying '*Vive la Reine! Vive le Roi!*' wellnigh overcame me.

It was Queen Victoria's first trip abroad, and the first time that an English reigning sovereign had set foot on the soil of France since the Field of the Cloth of Gold, 323 years earlier. The entertainment was perhaps not quite so sumptuous as at the meeting of Francis I and Henry VIII. The Citizen King had ordered from England large quantities of Cheddar cheese and bottled beer (Plate 80) in the hope of making his English guests feel at home. In this he succeeded entirely. Queen Victoria was 'delighted at being in the midst of this admirable and truly amiable family . . . we are quite at home as if we were one of them'. Staying at the historic Château d'Eu (Plate 79), the Queen 'felt as though it were a dream that my favourite air castle[1] for so many years was at length realized. But it is no dream, it is a pleasant reality.'

Queen Victoria got on very well with Louis-Philippe, Queen Marie-Amélie, and the whole large Orleans family, who were simple and domestic in their tastes like herself. 'They are all so kind and delightful, so united, that it does one's heart good to see this family. . . . I feel so gay and happy with these dear people.' She thoroughly enjoyed a banquet, a military review, a concert conducted by Auber, and, most of all, two *fêtes champêtres*. The effect of so much French conversation is very evident in her diary.

6 September 1843. At two we set off with the whole company in *char-à-bancs* . . . We arrived at St. Catherine, a *garde-chasse*. The day was beautiful, and the *endroit* of the *forêt* charming. After walking about for some little time in the garden, we all sat down to a *déjeuner* under the trees, I sitting between the King and Queen. It was so pretty, so merry, so *champêtre*; and it is quite wonderful the rapidity with which everything had been arranged (Plate 81).

Both monarchs took sincere pleasure in their meeting. Louis-Philippe, who had been slighted by the Courts of Europe all the thirteen years of his

[1] Queen Victoria's English was sometimes rather Germanic.

reign, felt flattered. Queen Victoria, overcome by the King's friendliness and hospitality, was in the seventh heaven. All too soon the five days were over.

> I got up, heavy-hearted at the thought that we must leave this dear family . . . At last the *mauvais moment* arrived, and with great regret we were obliged to take leave (Plate 82).

At Eu, the sovereigns and their Ministers, Guizot and Lord Aberdeen (Foreign Secretary) had taken the opportunity to discuss a question of some importance to both countries: the choice of a husband for Queen Isabella of Spain. It was known that Louis-Philippe had secret ambitions for his own family, but aware of British objections to an extension of French influence in Spain, was not pressing the point. The suitor most favoured by the young Queen's mother, the Regent of Spain, was Prince Leopold of Saxe-Coburg, a brother of the Prince Consort of Portugal and first cousin of Victoria and Albert. But Louis-Philippe did not want to see the power of the Coburgs increased, despite the fact that several of his children had married Coburgs, so the first round in this marriage game ended in a draw. Feeling his way very carefully, Louis-Philippe enquired whether the British had any objection to the marriage of one of his younger sons, the Duke of Montpensier, to the Queen of Spain's younger sister. The British, still fearing possible extension of French influence in Spain should Queen Isabella die childless, were equally cautious in their counter-move. They did not object, provided the Duke of Montpensier did not marry the Infanta until Queen Isabella had married a non-Coburg Prince and had children. As the Queen was only thirteen at the time, this compromise solution to which both sides agreed, allowed time for the fruition of a plot which Louis-Philippe and Guizot were hatching.

On their return from Eu the Queen and Prince Albert spent a few days at the Royal Pavilion, Brighton, and then sailed for Ostend, where they were met on 13 September by the King and Queen of the Belgians (Plate 83). The same evening they attended a gala banquet at the Hôtel de Ville, and during the next few days visited Bruges, Ghent, Brussels and Antwerp, which no English sovereign had entered since Edward III in 1338.

No wonder that after these first exciting trips to the Continent the Queen feared 'these *two* never-to-be-forgotten *voyages* and *visits* have made me think Windsor and its daily occurrences very dull'.

The relationship between Victoria and Albert continued to improve with the arrival of each child, and in particular since Baroness Lehzen's departure. In November Albert was able to report to his brother with teutonic matter-of-factness: 'Victoria has greatly improved, and has become very reasonable and good-natured.' Victoria, writing to Uncle Leopold, was as usual more effusive in her praise: 'I *am* grateful for possessing (*really without* vanity or flattery or *blindness*) the *most perfect* being as a husband in existence, or who ever did exist; and I doubt whether anybody *ever* did love or respect another as I do my dear Angel!'

The following January the Duke of Saxe-Coburg died suddenly. Two months later Prince Albert went to Coburg for a fortnight to help his brother put the affairs of the Duchy in order. To let him go alone was, the Queen felt, a terrible sacrifice. 'I have *never* been separated from him even for *one night*, and the *thought* of *such* a separation is quite dreadful.' Even thirteen years later, when the Prince attended the wedding of Princess Charlotte of Belgium to the Archduke Maximilian of Austria, the Queen told her uncle

> You cannot think how much this costs me, nor how completely forlorn I am and feel when he is away, or how I count the hours till he returns. All the numerous children are as nothing to me when he is away. It seems as if the whole life of the house and home were gone.

On one of the rare occasions when Prince Albert's public duties took him away from home the Queen, in what she acknowledged as 'a very discreditable fit of pettishness', reproached him for having gone away without taking her miniature with him. The Prince rebuked her gently, saying 'I carry your dear picture within me, and no miniature can come up to this image. I do not need to put a picture on my table to be reminded of you.'

During 1844 Victoria and Albert entertained

three foreign sovereigns. In June the King of Saxony and Czar Nicholas I came to England, and in October, two months after the birth of Prince Alfred, Louis-Philippe paid a visit to Windsor. Incredible as it may seem, the Citizen King was the first French reigning monarch ever to set foot in the British Isles voluntarily. Queen Marie-Amélie, who did not accompany her husband, feared that he might over-eat, and strict instructions about his diet were sent to Queen Victoria. Another unusual request concerned his bed—it must be a hard mattress laid on planks. Considering that the Czar had slept on a leather sack stuffed with straw from the stables, this habit of the Citizen King seemed less eccentric, though one would like to know what the royal servants had to say about the habits of these 'uncivilized foreigners'.

Louis-Philippe was greatly impressed by Windsor Castle, the most ancient and stately of the English royal residences, founded by William the Conqueror (though no building of his date survives) (Plates 341–343). He stayed in the sumptuous suite of rooms now known as the State Apartments, built for Charles II by Hugh May, decorated with paintings by Verrio and wood-carvings by Grinling Gibbons. The royal family's apartments had been built for George IV by Sir Jeffrey Wyatville with the comfort expected in the nineteenth century (Plates 344–348). Wyatville also restored the somewhat neglected exterior of the Castle and added other, more doubtful, 'improvements'. The total cost of the work carried out in the reign of George IV amounted to over one million pounds—a quarter of which was for furnishings.

Louis-Philippe admired everything: the grand view from the North Terrace overlooking the Thames and Eton, no less than the wealth and magnificence of the art treasures in the State Apartments. 'I never saw anybody more pleased, or more amused in looking at every picture and every bust', wrote the Queen. 'He is enchanted with the Castle, and repeated to me again and again (as did also all his people) how delighted he was to be here' (Plates 90, 92).

His investiture with the Order of the Garter (Plate 91), which was placed on his leg by Prince Albert, pleased Louis-Philippe more than anything else, for until he received this honour he said he did not feel he belonged to the 'club' of European sovereigns.

The King endeared himself to the Queen particularly by his respect for her husband, saying 'Le Prince Albert, c'est pour moi le roi', and astonished her with reminiscences of his life in exile, when he taught under an assumed name in a Swiss school for twenty pence a day and had to clean his boots himself.

Whilst Windsor Castle and Buckingham Palace were well adapted for Court ceremonial, Victoria and Albert felt the need for a country estate of their own to which they could retire for rest and privacy. The Royal Pavilion at Brighton, though intended as a holiday residence, no longer afforded these amenities since the town had grown up so closely around the building; moreover, for them the Prince Regent's exotic taste excluded all serious consideration of the Pavilion as a home on aesthetic grounds. Indeed, a Bill to provide for its demolition was prepared, but execution averted by the town's decision to purchase the building in 1850 for £50,000.

Remembering some enjoyable childhood visits to the Isle of Wight, the Queen had enquiries made for a suitable house there. On learning that Lady Isabella Blachford was considering the sale of her 800-acre estate of Osborne (originally called Auster-bourne) near East Cowes, she rented it in 1844 for a trial period of one year. Both Queen and Prince were charmed with its situation.

> It is impossible to imagine a prettier place, with woods and valleys, and *points de vue* which would be beautiful anywhere; but when these are combined with the sea (to which the woods grow down), and a beach which is quite private, it is really everything one could wish.

Early in 1845 the Queen bought the estate for £26,000. The eighteenth-century house, however, proved too small for the royal Household, and it was decided to replace it by a larger mansion in Italian Renaissance style designed by Prince Albert in collaboration with the London builder Thomas Cubitt, who was entrusted with its construction. The foundation-stone was laid in June of that year, and the royal apartments (Plate 349) were ready for occupation by September 1846, but the remaining wings for the Household were not completed until 1851 (Plate 350).

Usually the royal family paid three or four visits a year to their 'sweet, peaceful, little abode'. Prince Albert found much enjoyment in laying out the grounds, which were increased by subsequent purchases to about 2,300 acres. The total cost of the estate, house, and furnishing amounted to about £200,000, which came from the Queen's private purse. In 1854 Prince Albert had a full-size Swiss châlet erected about half a mile from the house (Plate 357). It was brought from Switzerland in sections, and served the ideal Victorian dual function of providing instruction and amusement for the royal children. There was a carpenter's shop for the princes, and a kitchen where the princesses learned housekeeping and cookery. Besides a dining-room and a dressing-room, the châlet had a sitting-room in which they often entertained their parents and other visitors to tea and home-made cakes. Every day a dish prepared by one of her daughters was served at Queen Victoria's dining-table.

Prince Albert also arranged for the children a little natural history museum of objects which they collected. In the garden they grew flowers and vegetables, each having his own tools marked with the owners' initials. Unlike Marie Antoinette's, they were not golden toys, and the young princes were put to work alongside labourers at farming and building under the supervision of a foreman, who had to criticize their work and enter it on a time-sheet. They received the rate for the job from their employer, Prince Albert, who in this way endeavoured to instil in them understanding and sympathy for the working classes. But since their earnings were merely pocket-money for the princes, they could have had no inkling of how far such wages had to go in a poor family.

In August 1845 Queen Victoria paid her first visit to Coburg and Schloss Rosenau, the country-seat of her brother-in-law, and her husband's birthplace. It was the place the Prince loved most, and she had heard so much about it that she felt almost as though her own childhood had been spent there. She experienced an indescribable feeling, something 'which touches me so, and which goes to my heart, and makes me inclined to cry. I never felt at any other time that sort of pensive pleasure and peace which I felt there. I fear I almost like it too much.'

The return journey was broken by a brief visit to the Château d'Eu. At Tréport the tide was too low to disembark from the royal barge, and Louis-Philippe suggested landing from a bathing machine (Plate 95). His ingenious but unconventional plan worked perfectly, but was much ridiculed in the English Press.

A few months later the honeymoon of France and England nearly ended in an abrupt divorce. The cause was the Spanish marriage on which both countries had reached a compromise solution in September 1843. Despite Queen Isabella's youth, settlement of the question had become urgent, for, as a Spanish diplomat bluntly put it, the Queen was so hot-blooded that there was danger the heir might arrive before the husband. Without referring the matter to Queen Victoria, Lord Palmerston, the Foreign Secretary, instructed the English Ambassador in Madrid to communicate to the Queen Mother the names of three possible suitors for Queen Isabella. One of these was Prince Leopold of Saxe-Coburg. When Guizot and Louis-Philippe heard of this, they considered that perfidious Albion had played them a trick, and consequently their promise was no longer binding. Assuming that the English were still intriguing for the Coburg suitor, Louis-Philippe now pressed the Queen Mother to marry Isabella to her cousin the Duke of Cadiz, and the fourteen-year-old Infanta Fernanda to his son, the Duke of Montpensier. His advice was taken. The whole point of this arrangement, so far as the French were concerned, was that the Duke of Cadiz had the reputation of being effeminate. Louis-Philippe had, therefore, strong hopes that his own son might father the future sovereign of Spain. Victoria and Albert were completely taken by surprise at this turn of events, and naturally furious. Prince Albert told his brother, 'We have been shamefully betrayed and now the other party triumphs.' The *entente* between England and France was ruined. Moreover, France did not reap any benefit, for Queen Isabella bore twelve children, of whom only five survived infancy.

By the time Queen Victoria saw Louis-Philippe again, the Citizen King was no longer King but an exile. After the revolution of 1848 the Orleans family lived at Claremont, made available by King Leopold. They were kindly received by the Queen, whose resentment had vanished partly out of sympathy for Louis-Philippe's plight, partly because Lord Palmerston was as much to blame for his rash action.

England, like most continental countries, was going through a difficult period, with a great rise in the price of wheat, economic depression, Chartist disturbances, and civil war and starvation in Ireland following the complete failure of the potato crop for two years running. Seeing several kings toppling from their thrones on the Continent, Queen Victoria felt insecure too. 'When one thinks of one's children, their education, their future—and prays for them', she wrote to King Leopold in July 1848, 'I always think and say to myself: "Let them grow up fit for *whatever station* they may be placed in— *high or low*"—this I never thought of before, but I *do* always now.' In the circumstances it was not deemed advisable to carry out a planned State visit to Ireland, but in August 1849 Victoria and Albert paid a private visit in the royal yacht, taking with them their four eldest children, the Princess Royal, the Prince of Wales, Princess Alice and Prince Alfred. Princesses Helena and Louise, born in May 1846 and March 1848 respectively, were left at home. After visiting Cork, the royal family were the guests of the Lord-Lieutenant of Ireland, the Earl of Clarendon, at his official residence in Phoenix Park, Dublin. The Queen's reception in the capital left nothing to be desired. 'It was a wonderful and striking scene, such masses of human beings, so enthusiastic, so excited, and yet such perfect order maintained—a never-to-be-forgotten scene when one reflected how lately the country had been in open revolt and under martial law.'

From Dublin the royal party sailed to Belfast, where again thousands had assembled at the landing-place to give them a very hearty reception. The town was beautifully decorated with flowers, hangings, and triumphal arches bearing the motto '*Ceade mille failte*' which means a hundred thousand welcomes. Lord Londonderry and numerous deputa-tions with addresses came on board, including the Mayor, whom the Queen knighted (Plate 100).

For the Christmas festivities of 1848 Prince Albert and his private secretary arranged the first Royal Command performance at Windsor Castle. It was *The Merchant of Venice*, produced and acted by Charles Kean and his company in the Rubens Room (Plates 97, 98). The Queen had never seen the play before and much admired Shakespeare's wit and his knowledge of human nature. The first experiment went off smoothly, and in the course of the next thirteen years, thirteen other plays by Shakespeare and nineteen lighter comedies were put on, including Sheridan's *School for Scandal*, *The Rivals* and *The Critic*, and even farces such as *Box and Cox* and *The Loan of a Lover*.

During 1849 preparations began for the Great Exhibition of the Works of Industry of All Nations. It was a grand conception to bring the nations of the world in contact with one another for their mutual benefit, but Protectionists and ultra-conservative elements like the notorious Colonel Sibthorp, M.P., vilified Prince Albert's plan in every conceivable way in attempts to wreck it. They roused the suspicion and prejudice of the naturally insular British against foreign products and foreign visitors alike, making the most ludicrous prophecies of social and moral upheaval that would follow in the wake of the exhibition. (Sir) Joseph Paxton's novel design for a building of iron and glass (the 247th plan submitted to the Building Committee) was the work of an amateur architect, and the Astronomer Royal published calculations proving that the building was bound to collapse like a house of cards. But however loudly Colonel Sibthorp thundered in Parliament against this 'sieve, oven, and lightning conductor', none of the 293,655 panes of glass got broken by hailstones as he forecast. The Press, and especially *The Times*, was openly hostile, and *Punch* conducted a campaign of ridicule against Prince Albert. But the Prince and (Sir) Henry Cole, a civil servant assisting him, battled their way through the most ferocious opposition. When ten months before the exhibition was due to open Sir Robert Peel was killed by a fall from his horse, it was believed that the project would fail without his support. But this was not so, and eventually the proposed site in Hyde Park was agreed to and the foundations were laid in August 1850. Paxton's 1,848-foot-long palace of glass—a kind of giant conservatory—arose with miraculous speed, made possible by novel mass-production and pre-fabrication methods. By the end of January 1851 the main structure was complete, a fortnight later exhibition items began to arrive, and on 1 May 1851 the Great Exhibition was opened in the Crystal Palace.

The 26,000 people who had the privilege of being present surged round the galleries and nave when, amidst a flourish of trumpets, the Queen and Prince Albert with the Princess Royal and the Prince of Wales entered the building. Outside the sun gleamed on the gigantic glass and iron edifice, upon which the flags of all nations were flying. Inside, the scene was breathtaking. The vastness of the building, the myriads of exhibits, the colourful flags and banners, the elms and palm trees, the huge crystal fountain at the intersection of the nave and transepts, the tremendous cheering of thousands of people everywhere, as far as the eye could see, and 'Albert the creator of this peace festival uniting the industry and art of all nations'—this was indeed a moving moment, never to be forgotten, a festival 'a thousand times superior to the Coronation' and 'a day to live for ever'. The opening ceremony (Plate 104) was short. After the national anthem and the reading of the report of the Commissioners by Prince Albert, to which the Queen replied briefly, the Archbishop of Canterbury offered a prayer. Then followed Handel's 'Hallelujah Chorus', without which no Victorian festival was a festival. This performance was on a massive scale commensurate with the immensity of the building: a choir of 600 plus an orchestra of 200 plus the organ at full blast. Afterwards the Queen and Prince Albert, the Government, the Diplomatic Corps and the exhibition officials walked in a long procession through the cheering crowds in the building, and amidst another fanfare the royal party left. Hyde Park and the Green Park presented a scene just like Coronation day; one mass of densely crowded human beings in the highest good humour and most enthusiastic—not a sign of Colonel Sibthorp's assassins and pickpockets.

During the afternoon the eighty-two-year-old Duke of Wellington came to the Palace bringing birthday greetings to his little godson Prince Arthur, who was born on his birthday the year before and named after him (Plate 103).

Describing the many events of that momentous day to King Leopold, the Queen called it

the *greatest* day in our history, the *most beautiful* and *imposing* and *touching* spectacle ever seen, and the triumph of my beloved Albert. . . . It was the *happiest, proudest* day in my life, and I can think of nothing else. Albert's dearest name is immortalised with this *great* conception, *his* own, and my *own* dear country *showed* she was *worthy* of it. The triumph is *immense*, for up to the *last hour* the difficulties, the opposition, and the ill-natured attempts to annoy and frighten, of a certain set of fashionables and Protectionists, were immense; but Albert's [good] temper, patience, firmness, and energy surmounted all.

The feeling was universal in the country that the exhibition was a great achievement. Over 100,000 exhibits worth about two million pounds—excluding the Koh-i-noor diamond which alone was worth that sum—were shown by nearly 14,000 exhibitors, of whom about half were foreign. Among the numerous novelties which aroused the Queen's curiosity during her thirty-four visits to the Crystal Palace was an ingenious bed for heavy sleepers which tipped up when the attached alarm-clock rang, pitching the occupant into a tub of cold water 'without the slightest personal danger'. Two winged 'thoughts' moulded on an elaborate papier-mâché chair called 'The Day Dreamer' whispered suggestions in the occupant's ear. A garden seat carved out of one huge block of coal was acquired for Osborne House. There were hats made from the leaves of the Australian cabbage-tree, mittens knitted from the wool of French poodles, a combined dressing-table and fire-escape, a fountain with a group of three statues, which could be converted into a fireplace in winter, and a stove in the form of a knight in armour. Most tasteless of all was a collection of stuffed animals dressed up and posed in human action, which the Queen found 'really marvellous'.

In the fine art division was a profusion of sculptured female nudes 'the seducing loveliness' of which stirred the usually restrained British to extravagant praise. New techniques and new materials were tried out in bewildering quantity on suitable and unsuitable objects alike. The Queen had the satisfaction of seeing statues of herself, Prince Albert, and his greyhound Eos cast in zinc. Duke Ernest of Saxe-Coburg exhibited some fruit stones which, with a penknife, he had carved into rabbits.

Admittedly many of the objects shown were over-elaborate, unsuitable in design, or downright tasteless, but it would be a grave error to put all the blame for so-called 'Victorian junk' on the Great Exhibition. It is the industrial revolution which is chiefly to blame for mid-nineteenth-century taste, as is shown by the objects in other international exhibitions held subsequently. On the credit side, the international display of goods stimulated new manufacturing processes and boosted Britain's trade with foreign countries and its prestige as the leading manufacturing country in the world as no event had before, while its educational influence on the population is incalculable.

Contrary to the Cassandra-like prophecies of failure, the Great Exhibition proved a triumphant success. When it closed on 11 October it had been visited by over six million people and had made a net profit of £186,000, which by judicious management is still producing an annual income of about £29,000. From all over Britain people had come on cheap excursions, and a woman of eighty had walked all the way from Cornwall. 'Foreigners also came, their bearded visages conjuring up all the horrors of Free Trade', wrote *The Times*, but there was no revolution.

The Exhibition seemed to mark the zenith of Queen Victoria's reign, and now that the Hungry 'Forties were over, it was expected to herald increasing technical progress, prosperity, and an era of international goodwill and peace. Yet within two and a half years of its closing, England was drawn into the first European war for thirty-nine years.

In December 1851 Queen Victoria had the satisfaction of seeing Lord Palmerston dismissed from the Foreign Office. She was jubilant, for ever since Palmerston's second term of office in 1846 his behaviour had been a constant source of irritation to her and Prince Albert. Their dislike of 'Pilgerstein' (Prince Albert's translation of Palmerston) was in fact so great that one is tempted to impute to their authorship a lampoon which made the round of the German courts.

*Hat der Teufel einen Sohn,*
*So ist er sicher Palmerston.*

If the Devil has a son,
You may be sure he's Palmerston.

Palmerston was not only in the habit of taking action without consulting the Queen (as, for instance, in the Spanish marriage question) but he also altered dispatches after they had been approved by her. In the autumn of 1851 he was reproved for his independent action in receiving the Hungarian revolutionary leader Kossuth, and for accepting from his supporters in London an address in which the Emperors of Austria and Russia were stigmatized 'odious and detestable assassins' and 'merciless tyrants and despots'. Soon afterwards he got himself into hot water again for expressing approval of Louis Napoleon's *coup d'état*, which Count Walewski, the French ambassador in London and first cousin of the new dictator, was only too glad to interpret as official approval by the British Government. For this last piece of reckless diplomacy, Lord John Russell removed Lord Palmerston from office, but the Queen's respite was of short duration. Two years later he was back at the Foreign Office and in 1855 he even became Prime Minister.

Added to Palmerston's political offences was a *faux pas* he had been guilty of early in the Queen's reign. Once while staying at Windsor Castle he wandered into the bedroom of a lady he was accustomed to sleep with. To his dismay, the room was now occupied by one of the Ladies of the Bedchamber, who raised the alarm. The Queen considered Palmerston's behaviour a gross insult to herself.

As the years went by, Queen Victoria took less and less active interest in politics. She now had seven children and the flow of arrivals showed no sign of ceasing. Finding it difficult to divide herself between domestic and public duties she decided to leave politics more to Prince Albert, who, she informed her uncle in February 1852, 'grows daily fonder and fonder of politics and business, and is so wonderfully *fit* for both—such perspicacity and *courage*—and I grow daily to dislike them more and more'. She regretted that Prince Albert's preoccupation with these public duties should 'take a little off from the gentleness of his character', adding 'I *cannot* enjoy these things, *much* as I interest myself in *general* European politics; but I am every day more convinced that *we women*, if we *are* to be *good* women, *feminine* and *amiable* and *domestic*, are *not fitted to reign*.' Nothing could reveal more clearly the complete reversal of outlook the Queen had undergone since the time of her engagement, when she feared that Prince Albert might meddle in politics. Now, he took the greater burden. Lord Clarendon, who became Foreign Secretary in 1853, considered that the way in which the Queen in her own name, but with the assistance of Prince Albert, exercised her functions, was exceedingly good. She constantly asked for detailed memoranda about all important matters, and frequently referred to her records of all the reports she had received. None of her predecessors had ever done this.

It is in fact the act of Prince Albert, [said Lord Clarendon] who is to all intents and purposes King, only acting in her name. All his views and notions are those of a Constitutional Sovereign, and he fulfils the duties of one, and at the same time makes the Crown an entity, and discharges the functions which properly belong to the Sovereign.

In April 1853 the Queen gave birth to her eighth child, who was named Leopold after the King of the Belgians—'a name which is the dearest to me after Albert, one which recalls the almost only happy days of my sad childhood'.

Meanwhile Prince Albert had bought for £31,500 Balmoral House near Braemar, Aberdeenshire, an unpretentious house erected about 1830 by Sir Robert Gordon in late medieval style. The estate had been on lease to Prince Albert since 1848, and as the attractive first impression was borne out by further enjoyable autumn holidays in 1849, 1850 and 1852, the purchase was decided upon and the estate eventually extended to cover some 30,000 acres of deer forest. Surrounded by woods and mountains, with the River Dee near by, the situation of Balmoral House was most attractive, and the view from it immediately reminded Prince Albert and the Queen of the Thüringerwald. 'It was so calm, and so solitary, it did one good as one gazed around; and the pure mountain air was most refreshing. All seemed to breathe freedom and peace, and to make one forget the world and its sad turmoils.'

The house, a pretty little castle with a picturesque tower (Plate 359), proved too small and it was decided to replace it with a larger and more stately residence (Plates 360, 364). This Prince Albert designed himself, and in September 1853 the foundation-stone was laid by the Queen with the solemnity for which she and the Prince had such a strong feeling. The constructional work was entrusted to an Aberdeen architect, William Smith.

The Court returned to Windsor earlier than usual in consequence of the critical state of affairs in eastern Europe. Russia, under the pretext of protecting Christian Turkish subjects in the Balkans, had sent troops across the Danube. As a result Turkey declared war on Russia on 23 October 1853. Public opinion in England was strongly in favour of her ally Turkey. Lord Aberdeen, the Prime Minister, tried to avert war, but the firebrand Palmerston, then Home Secretary, wanted England to intervene and resigned in protest. The public, believing that Prince Albert was acting as a hostile influence against the popular Palmerston, considered him guilty of treasonable intrigue. 'You will scarcely credit', wrote the Prince to Baron Stockmar, 'that my being committed to the Tower was believed all over the country,—nay, even "that the Queen had been arrested". People surrounded the Tower in thousands to see us brought to it.' In January 1854, when Parliament met, the calumnies against the Prince were of course completely refuted, but the warmongers won the day and on 28 March Britain declared war on Russia. France, and later Sardinia, affirmed their readiness to fight with Britain and Turkey. With the landing of the Allied forces in the Crimea in September, the Russo-Turkish War, which for many months had been waged in the Danube basin, entered a new phase. Failing to take the fortified naval base of Sebastopol, the Allies settled down to a long siege for which they were unprepared. During the winter they suffered heavy casualties from the loss of supplies and consequent exposure to cold, and malnutrition. Incompetence and mismanagement led to the greatest disaster—insanitary conditions—which brought an outbreak of cholera and other diseases accounting for seven-eighths of all casualties. The Queen expressed her deep concern about the troops to the British Commander in the Field. 'The Queen trusts that Lord Raglan will be very strict in seeing that no unnecessary privations are incurred by any negligence of those whose duty it is to watch over their wants.'

(Sir) William Howard Russell's frank revelations in *The Times* of the appalling conditions could not be denied or explained away, and on 30 January 1855 Lord Aberdeen's Government resigned. After every other possibility had been tried, the Queen was obliged to accept Lord Palmerston as Prime Minister.

Meanwhile Florence Nightingale's and other nursing parties had gone to the East, new supplies of winter clothing, tents and huts were arriving, cooking and sanitary conditions improved, and with the coming of spring, the health and morale of the army began to recover. Queen Victoria and Prince Albert frequently visited the military hospitals at Chatham (Plate 138). In order to express her gratitude for the bravery of her soldiers the Queen made it her duty to present each decoration personally, a function that had never before been performed by an English sovereign. In May she distributed the Crimean medal on Horse Guards Parade, and from the highest officer to the lowest rank all received the same distinction for brave conduct.

Noble fellows! I own I feel as if they were my own children—my heart beats for them as for my nearest and dearest! They were so touched, so pleased—many, I hear, cried; and they won't hear of giving up their medals to have their names engraved upon them, for fear they should *not* receive the identical one put into *their hands by me*! Several came by in a sadly mutilated state. None created more interest or is more gallant than young Sir Thomas Troubridge (Plate 128), who had at Inkermann one leg and the other foot carried away by a round shot, and continued commanding

his battery till the battle was over. . . . He was dragged by in a bath chair, and when I gave him his medal I told him I should make him one of my aides-de-camp for his very gallant conduct; to which he replied, 'I am amply repaid for everything.'

The Victoria Cross, designed by Prince Albert and instituted by Queen Victoria as the highest reward for valour, was first distributed by her at a military review in Hyde Park in June of the following year.

To cement the alliance of France and Britain and to further the prosecution of the war, the Emperor Napoleon III and the Empress Eugénie paid a State visit to England in April 1855. Against her expectation, Queen Victoria was quite captivated by the charm of the Imperial pair, whom she had hitherto regarded as upstarts. 'The impression is very favourable. There is great fascination in the quiet, frank manner of the Emperor, and *she* is very pleasing, very graceful, and very unaffected.' During the five days' visit two Councils of War were held, Queen Victoria invested the Emperor with the Order of the Garter, they attended a military review, a banquet at Windsor Castle, paid a State visit to the Opera (Plate 126) and enjoyed a brilliant ball which moved the Queen to muse on the relativity of human and political values. 'How strange to think that I, the granddaughter of George III, should dance with the Emperor Napoleon, nephew of England's great enemy, now my nearest and most intimate ally, in the Waterloo Room, and this ally only six years ago living in this country, an exile, poor and unthought of!' The alliance was progressing more swiftly than anyone could have foreseen.

For the last day of their stay, 20 April, a visit was arranged to the Crystal Palace, which had been re-erected the previous year in an enlarged form at Sydenham (Plate 121). As on all other public engagements, the Imperial couple were enthusiastically received by a huge crowd[1] (Plate 127). Somewhat anxious for her guest's safety, the little Queen, forgetting her own narrow escapes, leaned on the Emperor's arm feeling 'that I was possibly a

[1] The instantaneous photograph of this historic occasion showing Napoleon III seated on the right of Queen Victoria and the Empress Eugénie on her left with Prince Albert next to her, is one of the earliest news photographs ever taken.

protection for him. All thoughts of nervousness for myself were passed. I thought only of him; and so it is, Albert says, when one forgets oneself, one loses this great and foolish nervousness.'

Four months later Queen Victoria and Prince Albert paid a return visit to the Emperor and Empress. Accompanied by their two eldest children they sailed from Cowes early on 18 August in the newly completed *Victoria and Albert* (the second yacht of this name) for Boulogne, where they were met by Napoleon III. Paris was reached by train at 8.30 in the evening. No English sovereign had visited the French capital since Henry VI was crowned there as an infant 433 years earlier, and the city spared no effort to give Victoria and Albert a rousing welcome as they drove to the Palace of St. Cloud. It was a triumphal entry accompanied by endless shouts of '*Vive la Reine d'Angleterre! Vive l'Empereur! Vive le Prince Albert!*' (Plate 129).

With her immense capacity for enjoyment, Queen Victoria was enchanted by the most magnificent reception she had ever experienced, at home or abroad, and was ready to believe Marshal Magnan when he told her with a touch of Gallic flattery that such enthusiasm had not been seen in Paris even in the time of Napoleon I's triumphs.

In Queen Victoria's eyes the most significant moment of the State visit was her homage at the tomb of Napoleon I in the chapel of the Hôtel des Invalides.

There I stood, on the arm of Napoleon III, his nephew, before the coffin of England's bitterest foe; I, the granddaughter of that King who hated him most, and who most vigorously opposed him, and this very nephew, who bears his name, being my nearest and dearest ally! The organ of the Church was playing 'God save the Queen' at the time, and this solemn scene took place by torchlight, and during a thunderstorm. Strange and wonderful indeed!

The effectiveness of this rather theatrical scene was enhanced when the Queen bade the Prince of Wales kneel at the coffin of England's arch-enemy—a gesture which caused some French generals present to burst into tears.

It seems, as if in this tribute of respect to a departed and dead foe, old enmities and rivalries were wiped out, and the seal of Heaven placed upon that bond of unity, which is now happily established between two great and powerful nations. May Heaven bless and prosper it!

The many official engagements included visits to the International Exhibition, Versailles, the Opera, a review of 40,000 troops on the Champs de Mars (Plate 130) and a ball at the Hôtel de Ville (Plate 131). But above all, Victoria and Albert enjoyed the novel experience of driving *incogniti* through Paris on a sightseeing tour, the Queen disguising herself in 'a common bonnet with a black veil down and a black mantilla'. Now she could really feel something of the magic of the French capital which was not put on for her sake, and she thought she 'never saw anything more *beautiful* and gay'.

The splendour of a fête and ball at Versailles, arranged by the Empress after a print of a fête given by Louis XV was 'one of the finest and most magnificent sights we had ever witnessed; there had not been a ball at Versailles since the time of Louis XVI'. The Queen was entranced by a firework display ending in a fairy-like representation of Windsor Castle. Then came dancing in the Galerie des Glaces, which was one blaze of light from countless chandeliers and candelabras. Supper for 400 was served on the stage of the theatre, enviously watched by hungry spectators in the boxes.

That evening the priceless Koh-i-noor sparkled in Queen Victoria's diadem. In other respects her lavish but dowdy outfit for the Paris visit could not rival the superb elegance of her hostess. Although Queen Victoria had a dress allowance of £5,000 a year and was far from economical, she never managed to look *chic*. Her skirts were not wide enough and her bonnets not small enough for Parisian taste. It seems that Prince Albert, who was always present when she tried on new dresses and bonnets, acted as a brake on any desire to wear the latest fashions. 'I remember so well, when my French coiffeur came from Paris every year, and brought over things which were tried on, the Prince has come in and said, *Das trägst Du nicht!* (That you shan't wear!)'

Victoria and Albert formed a great affection for the beautiful and fascinating Empress. Napoleon too endeared himself to the royal family. The thirteen-year-old Prince of Wales begged to be allowed to stay on, and told the Emperor that he would like to be his son, and the Queen wrote to Baron Stockmar:

I know *no* one who puts me more at my ease, or to whom I felt more inclined to talk unreservedly, or in whom involuntarily I should be more inclined to confide, than the Emperor! . . . Wonderful it is that this *man*—whom certainly we were *not* over well-disposed to—should by *force* of *circumstances* be drawn into such close connection with us, and become *personally* our friend, and *this* entirely by his *own personal* qualities . . . he *has* the power of *attaching* those to him who come near him and know him, which is *quite incredible.*

In short, the brilliant but exhausting State visit to the French capital had given Queen Victoria 'the *pleasantest* and most *interesting* and triumphant ten days that I think I ever passed. . . . The *complete* Union of the two countries is stamped and sealed in the most satisfactory and solid manner.'

Two years later Napoleon and Eugénie paid a private visit to Osborne (Plate 154) and affection deepened into real friendship. 'We are all in love with her . . . Albert, who is seldom much pleased with ladies or princesses, is very fond of her, and her great ally.'

After the very hot August days spent in Paris, Queen Victoria longed for the reviving effect of the bracing Scottish air, and early in September the Court moved to the new, partially-completed granite castle at Balmoral (Plate 360).

An old shoe was thrown after us into the house, for good luck, when we entered the hall. The house is charming, the rooms delightful, the furniture, papers, everything perfection. . . . The view from the windows of our rooms, and from the library, drawing-room, &c. below them, of the valley of the Dee, with the mountains in the background, which one could never see from the old house, is quite beautiful.

Their happiness was complete when on 10 September a telegram arrived from General Simpson, the Commander-in-Chief in the Crimea, announcing 'Sebastopol is in the hands of the Allies.'

Our delight was great; but we could hardly believe the good news, having so long, so anxiously expected it . . . Albert said they should go at once and light the bonfire which had been prepared when the false report of the fall of the town arrived last year, and had remained ever since, waiting to be lit.

All the scattered population of Deeside climbed to this beacon on top of Craig Gowan, and for once Prince Albert threw dignity to the winds. 'We performed towards midnight a veritable Witches' dance, supported by whisky.'

Four days after this celebration, Prince Frederick William of Prussia came on a visit in order to ask for the hand of the Princess Royal (Plate 135). 'He is a dear, excellent, charming young man whom we shall give our dear child to with perfect confidence,' wrote the Queen, who had long hoped for this alliance between England and Prussia (as had also Prince Albert and Baron Stockmar). The Princess was only fourteen (her suitor was ten years older) and the proposal seemed somewhat premature, but in the end the Queen consented, feeling that in spite of her extreme youth the Princess Royal was mature enough for a decision.

The following summer Victoria and Albert found Balmoral Castle quite complete. The cost of about £100,000 was borne by Prince Albert. The Queen was delighted with her royal Highland residence, 'this dear Paradise' on which her heart became more fixed every year, and 'so much more so now, that *all* has become my dearest Albert's *own* creation, own work, own building, own laying out, as at *Osborne*; and his great taste, and the impress of his dear hand, have been stamped everywhere'.

Compared with the grandeur of Windsor Castle, Buckingham Palace, and Osborne House, the furniture was simple. It was chiefly of light-coloured wood such as maple and birch—the latter rather a novelty at this date—and supported a heavy load of curiously devised and elaborately executed articles which grew in quantity as birthdays were celebrated, while trophies of the chase multiplied each autumn. Plates 365 and 366 show the rooms in their original state. The drawing-room carpet was specially woven in the red Royal Stuart tartan, with curtains and furniture covers of Dress Stuart tartan. The blue wallpaper was powdered with golden thistles, and the candelabra were in the form of Highlanders. 'All highly characteristic and appropriate, but not all equally *flatteux* to the eye', commented Lady Augusta Bruce (later Lady Augusta Stanley)—a remark which equally applies to the letter paper designed by Sir Edwin Landseer, the Queen's favourite artist (Plates 361, 362).

Always looking after the welfare of his tenants, Prince Albert built cottages for them—as he had at Osborne—and a school, and he and the Queen provided a library for the local people.

Henceforth part of each spring and autumn was spent in Scotland, 'that beloved and blessed land', 'the birthplace of valour, the country of worth'. Queen Victoria had a real longing for Scotland. 'It is not alone the pure air, the quiet and beautiful scenery, which makes it so delightful—it is the atmosphere of loving affection and the hearty attachment of the people around Balmoral which warms the heart, and does one good.'

Here in this private residence the Queen had the feeling that she was living a simple life, as indeed it was compared with Windsor Castle and Buckingham Palace. On occasion she even walked about unattended, visiting the cottagers for a chat, or leaving gifts of warm petticoats. Frequently she sketched the scenery or people while Prince Albert was out shooting (Plates 385, 386).

The climate suited the Queen extremely well. She probably suffered from high blood pressure for she could not stand heat. Her journal is full of remarks that it was too hot to go out (in May and early June), and dislike of mild weather in winter. Even on the coldest days she would drive in an open carriage, or go riding all day in the Highlands despite snow or icy winds. Indoors, too, she liked it cool. Fires were lit only in the coldest weather, and even then the room temperature was usually kept at 56°F. and *never* allowed to exceed 60°F. Once, in later years, when the Queen unexpectedly called on the family of her Private Secretary, General Sir Henry Ponsonby, they hastily put out the drawing-room fire with a bucket of water.

Much as the Queen was delighted at the engagment of her daughter to Fritz Wilhelm, constant chaperoning of the loving couple during Fritz's longish visits got rather on her nerves. It took away so much of her precious time from other duties,

Sketch by Queen Victoria in a letter to a friend.

for she was always hard-worked and the only way to get through it all was to organize the day with rigid precision. Quite apart from this, she found intimacy with her children in general difficult, as she revealed in a very frank disclosure of her feelings to Princess Augusta of Prussia, mother of Fritz Wilhelm.

Even here, [Balmoral] where Albert is very often away all day long [deerstalking] I find no especial pleasure or compensation in the company of the elder children. . . . Only very occasionally do I find intimate intercourse with them either agreeable or easy. You will not understand this, but it derives from various causes. Firstly, I am really only *à mon aise* and quite happy when Albert is with me; secondly, I am used to carrying on my many affairs quietly and alone; then, I grew up quite alone, always accustomed to the society of adult (and never with younger) people—lastly, I cannot yet quite get used to the fact that Vicky is nearly grown up. To me she still seems the child who has to be kept in order and therefore must not become too intimate.

The official announcement of the engagement was deferred until May 1857. Politically the union was not liked in either country. Nevertheless, Parliament granted the Princess Royal a liberal dowry of £40,000 and an annuity of £8,000 on marriage. The engagement was celebrated with prolonged festivities, into which fell also the christening of the Queen's ninth and last child, Princess Beatrice, born on 14 April (Plate 152). There were State visits to the theatre, and balls, and the whole Court attended the first Handel Festival at the Crystal Palace on 17 June (Plate 153) at which *Judas Maccabeus* was performed by a massed choir of 2,500.

On 25 June the Queen conferred on her husband by Royal Letters Patent the title of Prince Consort. For seventeen years the question of an English title for Prince Albert had remained unsettled, for the Queen had always hoped to obtain approval for her original intention that the crown should be jointly borne by her and Albert as it had been by William III and Mary. Yet however much she insisted that he ought to be King Consort, 'and is above me in everything really, and therefore I wish that he should be equal in rank to me', everyone, including Stockmar, strongly advised against this step, and

Prince Albert disdained the idea of being King of England only in title like Philip of Spain. It was annoying that at foreign Courts Prince Albert's official position was only that of a younger brother of the Duke of Saxe-Coburg. Though sometimes he was given precedence as the Queen of England's husband out of courtesy, at other times a foreign sovereign was placed in the dilemma of either offending Prince Albert, and the Queen, or one of his other guests. Any duke could claim precedence over him. This the Queen rightly felt was 'derogatory to the dignity of the crown of England'. Even the title Prince Consort was not a rank conferred upon him by Parliament, and it was humiliating to the Queen to think that he took precedence only by the forbearance of their children.

The marriage of the Princess Royal took place on 25 January 1858 in the Chapel Royal, St. James's Palace, the Queen having in no uncertain manner instructed the Foreign Secretary to dispose of the Prussian desire for the ceremony to be performed in Berlin.

The assumption of its being *too much* for a Prince Royal of Prussia to *come* over to marry *the Princess Royal of Great Britain in* England is too *absurd*, to say the least. . . . Whatever may be the usual practice of Prussian Princes, it is not *every* day that one marries the eldest daughter of the Queen of England. The question therefore must be considered as settled and closed.

The well-known punctuality of the royal family was not in evidence on the wedding morning. The sitting with the daguerreotypist W. E. Kilburn at Buckingham Palace before the ceremony took longer than anticipated. In picture after picture the Queen moved through nervousness. Regretfully she observed of the final photograph (Plate 155), 'I trembled so, my likeness has come out indistinct.' She was wearing a dress of lilac and silver moiré antique with a flounce of Honiton lace, and a train of lilac velvet. Among her magnificent diamonds sparkled the Koh-i-noor, now set as a brooch. The seventeen-year-old bride wore white moiré and Honiton lace, and her eight sylphide-like bridesmaids (Plate 158) in tulle with large wreaths looked like a bevy of Taglionis. The wedding in that very place where she and Albert had joined hands eighteen years earlier vividly recalled to the Queen many memories of that day. 'I felt as if I were being married over again myself, only much more nervous, for I had not that blessed feeling which I had then, which raises and supports one, of giving myself up for life to him whom I loved and worshipped—then and ever.'

After a short honeymoon at Windsor Castle (Plate 160) the 'dreadful moment' of parting arrived. 'Such sickness came over me, real heartache, when I thought of our dearest child being gone, and for so long—all, all being over! . . . Such desolation!' Queen Victoria was inclined to be either in the seventh heaven or in the depths of woe. She felt every emotion to an exaggerated degree and made no effort to control it. It seems that a hundred years ago the proverbial English self-control was not an admired characteristic. On the contrary, not to make a show of emotion was considered to be lacking in proper feeling. The Hall at Buckingham Palace witnessed a heartrending scene. All the princesses sobbed loudly, and the Queen 'howled as much as I possibly could'. 'I think it will kill me to take leave of dear papa', cried the bride, who had in recent years become the close intellectual companion of her father. The Prince Consort only wished that the Prince of Wales had Vicky's intelligence. The fact that Bertie, as he was called in the family, was a poor scholar greatly distressed him and the Queen, who bemoaned his 'defective mental powers'. Neither attached sufficient importance to the Prince of Wales's attractive personality, friendliness and tact, which later made him so popular a king.

This first parting from the Princess Royal was not of long duration. The Prince Consort paid a short visit to the young couple in June, and in August both he and the Queen went to spend a fortnight with them at their castle of Babelsberg near Potsdam, where they also met again their old friend Baron Stockmar, who promised to watch over the affairs of the Princess Royal. Baroness Lehzen, on the other hand, whom Queen Victoria had once called her greatest friend, had to be content with waving her handkerchief when the royal train steamed through Bückeberg station.

The Prince Consort's birthday was celebrated at Babelsberg with the customary presentation of gifts, both useful and decorative, all neatly arranged by the Queen on a drawing-room table: a life-size oil-painting of the baby Princess Beatrice; a collection of photographs of Gotha, Rosenau, Coburg and the surrounding countryside, specially taken for the Queen by Francis Bedford; a paper-weight of Balmoral granite and deer's-teeth, designed by the Princess Royal; an iron chair for the garden at Balmoral; a drawing by the Princess Royal, a small oil portrait of her, and two bronze statues. A similar mixture of paintings, sculpture, sketches and photographs graced every birthday and Christmas table, plus stuffed animals and albums for the Prince and shawls or sunshades for the Queen and Princesses. A variety of knick-knacks can be discerned in the photographs (Plates 164, 166, 177, 178), which are eloquent proof of that extraordinary conglomeration of useful and useless, always decorative but rarely aesthetically satisfying presents (according to our taste, at least) which gradually filled the private rooms of royal residences to overflowing.[1] Anniversaries in general played an important part in the life of the Queen, who had an almost superstitious reverence for them. Whenever possible, family events such as weddings or christenings were arranged to take place on the anniversary of another event such as her own wedding day. Occasionally she was carried away by her passion for remembering anniversaries, and achieved four in one sentence of a letter sent to King Leopold on 1 May 1855. 'On this day, the fifth birthday of our darling little Arthur—the anniversary of the opening of the Great Exhibition—the *once* great day at Paris, viz. the poor King's [Louis-Philippe's] name-day—and also the birthday of the dear old Duke, [of Wellington] I write to thank you for your kind and affectionate letter.'

While at Babelsberg, a brusquely worded draft proclamation to the people of India was submitted to the Queen. Despite the ghastly massacres of English women and children during the recent Mutiny, the Queen showed toleration and common sense in the resettlement of India. She was determined that the Indian people 'should know that

[1] By 1883 the Queen's four private rooms at Windsor Castle contained nearly 250 pictures.

there is no hatred of a brown skin, none; but the greatest wish on their Queen's part to see them happy, contented, and flourishing'. The proclamation setting forth the principles on which the government of India was in future to be carried on was rewritten, giving prominence to the principles of toleration and conciliation, and to the protection of native religions and customs. The absorption by the Crown of the territories and power of the East India Company added over 800,000 square miles and 200 million people to the British dominions, and the Governor-General was elevated to the position of Viceroy.

Just a year after the wedding of the Princess Royal, Queen Victoria became a grandmother at the age of thirty-nine. Prince Wilhelm (later the Kaiser) had for his christening no fewer than forty-two godparents, probably a record number even for a royal baby, and the Queen was bitterly disappointed at not being able to attend the ceremony. 'It almost breaks my heart not to witness our first grandchild christened! I don't think I ever felt so bitterly disappointed about anything as about this!'

The 'gentle, sensible, and amiable' Princess Alice took the Princess Royal's place as her mother's constant companion, but afraid of losing her too, the Queen resolved at the time of Alice's confirmation in April 1859 (when the Princess was sixteen) 'Not to let her marry as long as I can reasonably delay her doing so'—a resolve which she renewed with each daughter in turn. The Princesses Alice and Helena were allowed to accompany their parents for the first time to the opening of Parliament in January 1860. In July the Prince of Wales left on a three-months' tour of Canada and America, where, to the surprise of his parents, he made an excellent impression. Prince Alfred, who was in the Navy, at the same time visited the Cape of Good Hope.

In the autumn Queen Victoria, the Prince Consort and Princess Alice left for Coburg, where they were to meet the Princess Royal with her husband (Plate 176) and—most important of all—Willi, 'Our darling grandchild, such a little love! He has Fritz's eyes and Vicky's mouth, and very fair curly hair. We felt so happy to see him at last!'

On account of the death of Prince Albert's step-mother the visit was a quiet one. The royal family were relieved that they could go for walks in the town without being followed about. The greater part of their stay was, however, spent at the Duke of Saxe-Coburg's country-seat, Rosenau, about four miles from Coburg. It was in this neighbourhood that the Prince Consort had a narrow escape on 1 October, driving alone into Coburg. Frightened by an approaching train, the horses suddenly ran away and crashed into the bar of a level-crossing. One of the horses was killed and the coachman badly injured, but the Prince had leapt from the open carriage at the last moment, and escaped with slight cuts on the nose. In gratitude for her husband's wonderful escape, the Queen established the 'Victoria Stift', a trust fund of £1,000, the interest on which was to be distributed each year on this anniversary to deserving young men and women of Coburg towards setting them up in a useful occupation.

Every year on her wedding anniversary Queen Victoria was wont to write to her uncle, who had been instrumental in bringing her and Albert together. These letters are largely taken up with praise of Albert, and provide interesting variations on the Queen's favourite theme. Two examples may suffice. The eighteenth anniversary: 'This blessed marriage which has brought such universal blessings on this country and Europe. For *what* has not my beloved and perfect Albert done? Raised monarchy to the *highest* pinnacle of *respect*, and rendered it *popular* beyond what it *ever* was in this country!' Twenty-first anniversary (the last before the Prince Consort's death): 'a day which has brought to us, and I may say to the world at large, such incalculable blessings! Very few can say with me, that this husband at the end of twenty-one years is not only full of the friendship, kindness, and affection which a truly happy marriage brings with it, but of the same tender love as in the very first days of our marriage.'

The following month a deep shadow passed over the Queen's life—the death of her mother, the Duchess of Kent (Plate 182). Though her severe and ambitious nature had embittered the Queen's childhood and girlhood, a great change had come over the Duchess after the pernicious influence of

Sir John Conroy had been removed. Moreover, the Queen's own domineering spirit had been modified since Baroness Lehzen's departure by Prince Albert, who brought mother and daughter together in reconciliation. Neither the Duchess nor the Queen could have believed then that the years would so completely heal the rift and bring about such sympathy and warmth of affection which in the end united them in true love.

> Oh! I am wretched to think *how, for a time, two people* [Conroy and Lehzen] *most* wickedly estranged us! . . . To miss a mother's friendship—not to be able to have her to confide in—when a girl *most* needs it, was fearful! I *dare not* think of it—it drives me *wild* now! But thank God! that is all passed *long, long* ago, and she had forgotten it, and only thought of the last very happy years. And all that was brought about by my good angel, dearest Albert, whom *she* adored.

The Queen was overwhelmed with grief and morbid misery. She pitied herself as an orphan, which though true, seems hardly the right expression to use at the age of forty-one. Nor should a happily married woman with nine children consider the death of a mother at the ripe age of seventy-four 'a life sorrow'. Yet such was her grief on this 'the most dreadful day of my life'. It was deep and sincere, yet in her constant dwelling upon it—one might even say wallowing in it—one cannot avoid the suspicion that, like a child, she almost enjoyed it and began playing to the gallery. 'The *weeping*, which day after day is my welcome friend' demonstrated her sensibility, and she was quite proud of the effect. 'The general sympathy for *me*, and approval of the manner in which I have shown my grief, is *quite wonderful and most touching*.' The Prince Consort carefully kept from her unpleasant rumours that her mind was unbalanced by her grief, but he exerted all his influence to make her use more self-control.

The usual autumn holiday at Balmoral brought some solace to the Queen. After describing a long ride in the mountains, she ended, 'Have enjoyed nothing as much, or indeed felt so much cheered by anything, since my great sorrow.'

Some extremely strenuous outings were undertaken, partly by carriage, partly on ponies and on foot. On one of these expeditions the Queen and Prince Consort, with Princess Alice and Prince Louis of Hesse, covered 129 miles in two days. They spent the night *incogniti* at an inn at Dalwhinnie where unfortunately there was hardly anything to eat.

The Duke of Atholl met the royal family with twelve of his men, and after a short visit to his castle, Blair Atholl, the party set off again. In a few minutes they were at the celebrated ford of the Poll Tarff, which was almost impassable after heavy rain. The Duke offered to lead the Queen's pony on one side, and her favourite attendant John Brown took the reins on the other. The guide, and two pipers playing all the time, formed the spearhead and other attendants the rearguard at the crossing, wading waist deep through the stream (Plate 185), which had a strong current from the high waterfall. 'This was the pleasantest and most enjoyable expedition I *ever* made, and the recollection of it will always be most agreeable to me, and increase my wish to make more!' Within a week, another excursion was undertaken, in which Princess Helena participated for the first time. Lunch was eaten on a high plateau, 'a very precipitous place, which made one dread anyone moving backwards (Plate 186). I made some hasty sketches; and then Albert wrote on a bit of paper that we had lunched here, put it into the Selters-water bottle, and buried it there. . . . We came down by the Month Eigie, a steep hill covered with grass—down part of which I rode, walking where it was steepest; but it was so wet and slippery that I had two falls . . . we returned much pleased and interested with this delightful expedition. Alas! I fear our *last* great one!' (meaning that year). To this diary entry the Queen added after the Prince Consort's death, '*It Was Our Last One!*'

In preparation for the dreaded return to Windsor, full of memories of the Duchess of Kent, the Prince Consort begged the Queen to be less preoccupied with her feelings and to take more interest in things unconnected with them. He gave the Princess Royal this very clear analysis of her mother's state of mind: 'For your Mama, who lives much in the past and future, perhaps more than in the present, it is a spiritual necessity to cling to moments that are flown and to recollections, and to form plans for the future.' These words seem almost prophetic, considering that this mental attitude—only a thousandfold exaggerated—became the Queen's normal state of mind after her husband's death. Feeling everything so intensely and knowing her great difficulty in holding back her tears when speaking of anything that distressed or annoyed her, the Queen used to send notes to the Prince about such matters, to which he also replied in writing.

During the last two years the Prince Consort had frequently complained of feeling unwell, due to minor causes such as indigestion, neuralgia, and catarrh. The strain of years of overwork had left its mark. At forty-two, the Prince looked at least ten years older, and when disease came, he had neither the physical resistance nor the will-power to struggle against it.

During November, the Prince fulfilled a number of engagements in cold, wet weather, feeling miserable, full of rheumatic pains, and great weariness from insomnia. 'Have scarcely closed my eyes at night for the last fortnight', he complained on 24 November, two days after inspecting the Royal Military Academy at Sandhurst, which exposed him to more fatigue and cold. The recent deaths from typhoid fever of his first cousins King Pedro of Portugal and his brother had already acutely depressed him, when other worries burdened his mind. The eight-year-old Prince Leopold, who was very delicate, suffering from haemophilia, had been sent to Cannes for the winter; now it was learned that the serious illness of the old general who accompanied him necessitated the immediate appointment of a successor. Worse still was the news that the Prince of Wales, who was studying at Cambridge, had got involved with a girl. This nearly broke his father's heart, and though very ill, he felt it required his presence in Cambridge to straighten matters out. On his return to Windsor on 26 November, the Prince Consort felt much worse, yet three days later he forced himself to watch a review of Eton College volunteers from the South Terrace. The weather was mild, but despite his fur-lined overcoat the Prince felt as though cold water were being poured down his back. Instead of resting in bed, the Prince Consort gave all his attention to another urgent matter.

The American Civil War had been going on for eight months when the British ship *Trent*, carrying among her passengers two envoys from the Confederate States to the British and French Courts, was stopped by a Federal warship, and the envoys and their secretaries were forcibly removed. News of this violation of a neutral power was received only when the *Trent* reached Southampton on 27 November. Understandably it aroused great indignation in Britain, and 8,000 troops were at once dispatched to Canada. The draft of a brusquely worded Foreign Office note to the British Ambassador in Washington was submitted to the Queen on the evening of 30 November. Realizing that its delivery would almost certainly lead to war, the Prince Consort considered it throughout a sleepless night. At his usual hour of seven he rose, and before eight brought the Queen his draft of the amended dispatch, remarking that he could hardly hold his pen to write it (Plates 188, 189). His tactful suggestion that the Federal captain must have misunderstood his instructions was accepted by Washington, and the four Confederates were released in January. Thus the Prince Consort's moderation is generally considered as having avoided war.

All these worries and the accumulative effect of the Prince's neglect of his condition, lowered his resistance to the disease which was already attacking his system. Suffering from great restlessness, he changed from room to room two or three times during one night. On 3 December Sir James Clark gave his opinion that the illness would *not* turn to 'low or gastric fever'—as typhoid fever was then called—and felt confident enough not to call in another doctor, reassuring the Queen that there was no cause for alarm. Three days later, however, his colleague (Sir) William Jenner had to inform the Queen that her husband *was* suffering from this dreaded fever, which was attributed to 'great worry, and far too hard work for long'. The nature of the illness was kept from the patient, who had a particular horror of it, and had only recently remarked, in speaking of his cousins' deaths, that it would certainly be fatal to him too. Not long before his illness, he had told the Queen that he did not cling to life as she did, and would give up at once if attacked by a severe illness. The Queen had absolute faith in the comforting phrases with which her Court physician deceived himself and her. 'My heart was ready to burst, but I cheered up, remembering how many people have fever' (without dying).

The Queen's Ministers, however, had not forgotten what a fool Sir James Clark had made of himself with his mis-diagnosis of Lady Flora Hastings's condition over twenty-two years earlier, and urged on the Prince's private secretary, Sir Charles Phipps, the necessity of calling in more doctors. 'If it is unavoidable that the highest interests of the nation must be sacrificed to personal and professional jealousy', wrote Lord Palmerston, 'there is no help for it and so it must be. I could say much about the past, but my thoughts are wholly engrossed with the future.' Lord Clarendon wrote in similar vein. The advice, though much resented was followed, and (Sir) Thomas Watson and Sir Henry Holland were called in. But by then it was too late.

On 7 December the Prince moved into the Blue Room, a bright room, in which George IV and William IV had died, clearly in preparedness for his own death. As it was a Sunday he asked for a chorale, and Princess Alice played in the next room Luther's hymn 'Eine feste Burg ist unser Gott'.

It is typical of Queen Victoria's temperament that in the depths of her misery any faintly comforting expressions at once brought about a reaction which almost banished anxiety. Two days before the Prince's death she told King Leopold 'There is nothing to cause alarm.' Up to the very last hours she was tormented by alternating fear and hope. Even on the morning of the fatal 14 December, Dr. Henry Brown, physician to the late Duchess of Kent, who was supposed to be thoroughly acquainted with the Prince's constitution, had no hesitation in telling the Queen that he thought the patient much better and 'there was ground to hope the crisis was over'. Whereupon the Queen telegraphed to Berlin: 'Dear Vicky. Papa has had a good night's rest and I hope the danger is over.' The eighteen-year-old Princess Alice was not so blind. Her father told her he was dying, but that he could not speak of it to her mother, and it was she who telegraphed to the Prince of Wales, who arrived from Cambridge before dawn on the day of his father's death. Throughout

that eventful 14 December the Queen anxiously watched her husband, sitting by his side. For long periods he lay dozing or gazing at unseen objects, taking no notice of anyone. Regaining consciousness he would try to comfort her, tenderly stroking her hand, or kissing his 'gutes Frauchen', and then his mind would wander once more. In the afternoon five of the children[1] came in, one after the other, to say farewell to their father, and then the Prince's private secretary, the Keeper of the Privy Purse and the Master of the Household were sent for. Everyone was dreadfully overcome. It was a terrible moment but the Queen was able to control herself, and remained outwardly calm.

At about ten in the evening the Queen, who had retired into an adjoining room to weep alone, was fetched back by Princess Alice. Having enjoyed little privacy on her honeymoon and none at all at the birth of her children, the Queen now had to endure her greatest agony before a gathering of twenty spectators. Doctors, relations, friends, and the members of the Household who were closest to the Prince Consort filled the death chamber. Kneeling by the bed the Queen held the Prince's hand, which was already cold, though he was still breathing gently, until shortly before eleven the breathing almost imperceptibly ceased. Crying 'Oh, this is death! I know it. I have seen this before', the Queen threw herself upon her husband's body, calling him by every loving name. In a state of collapse she was helped on to the sofa in the next room, and with an immense effort at self-control she embraced the children, saying she would try to live for them, and do her duty, and begging them to follow in their father's footsteps. She thanked the doctors, and then the Prince's equerries and other members of the Household, who had been waiting apprehensively for hours in the corridor, were called in one by one. Seizing their hands, the Queen gasped with a great effort, 'You will not desert me now? You will all help me?'

The Queen was persuaded by King Leopold that it was best to go to Osborne at once, but before leaving Windsor on the 19th she drove to Frogmore

[1] Prince Alfred was at sea, Prince Leopold at Cannes, the Princess Royal was informed too late of the seriousness of her father's condition, and Princess Beatrice was considered too young at four for a deathbed scene.

with Princess Alice to choose the site for a mausoleum where her husband and she herself might be buried together. She did not attend the funeral at St. George's Chapel, Windsor, on the 23rd, at which she was represented by the Prince of Wales.

At Osborne the Queen broke down completely. It seemed as though it was only now that she awoke to the full consciousness of her loss. In dumb despair she sat all day staring vacantly around her. Now and then her feelings would burst out in a letter to a close relation like King Leopold, but her journal entries ceased until New Year's Day.

My *own* dearest, kindest *Father*—for as such have I *ever* loved you! The poor fatherless baby of eight months is now the utterly broken-hearted and crushed widow of forty-two! My *life* as a *happy* one is *ended*! the world is gone for *me*! If I *must live* on (and I will do nothing to make me worse than I am), it is henceforth for our poor fatherless children—for my unhappy country, which has lost *all* in losing him —and in *only* doing what I know and *feel* he would wish, for he *is* near me—his spirit will guide and inspire me! But oh! to be cut off in the prime of life—to see our pure, happy, quiet, domestic life, which *alone* enabled me to bear my *much* disliked position, *cut off* at forty-two—when I *had* hoped with such instinctive certainty that God never *would* part us, and would let us grow old together (though *he* always talked of the shortness of life)—is *too awful*, too cruel! And yet it *must* be for *his* good, his happiness! His purity was too great, his aspiration *too high* for this poor, *miserable* world! His great soul is *now only* enjoying *that* for which it *was* worthy!

Albert will you
marry me?

43  Queen Victoria's proposal to Prince Albert,
15 October 1839.
*Lithograph.*

44  Study for the painting of Queen Victoria's wedding by
Sir George Hayter. The Queen's wedding dress (minus the
train and the lace flounce) is now at the London Museum.

45    The marriage of Queen Victoria and Prince Albert at the Chapel Royal, St. James's Palace, on 10 February 1840. Next to the Queen stands Lord Melbourne with the Sword of State, on his left the Duke of Sussex (with skull-cap), the Duchess of Kent wearing ostrich plumes. The group on the left includes the Dowager Queen Adelaide, Duke Ernest of Saxe-Coburg-Gotha (father of Prince Albert) and his son Prince Ernest. On the extreme left is the Duchess of Cambridge and her young daughter Mary (mother of Queen Mary). The ceremony was performed by the Archbishop of Canterbury.

*Painting by Sir George Hayter.*

46    Marriage register entry of Queen Victoria and Prince Albert.

*Be it remembered that the Queen's most Excellent Majesty was married to His Royal Highness Francis Albert Augustus Charles Emanuel, Duke of Saxe, Prince of Saxe Cobourg and Gotha, Knight of the Most Noble Order of the Garter, in the Chapel Royal at St. James's, on Monday the tenth day of February in the year of our Lord one thousand eight hundred and forty, and in the third year of Her Majesty's Reign, by me*

*W. Cantuar*

*This Marriage was solemnized between us this tenth day of February one thousand eight hundred and forty.*

*Victoria R*

*Albert.*

47 and 48   'The Royal Pear (Pair).'
*Coloured lithograph with moveable flap, 1840.*

49   Edward Oxford's attempt to assassinate Queen Victoria, 10 June 1840. An imaginary news picture
by an artist who did not know that Oxford was not a gentleman but a potboy.
*Engraving.*

50 Presentation of an Address from the University of Oxford, in the Throne Room, Buckingham Palace.
*Engraving after a drawing by H. Melville, 1840–41.*

51 Queen Victoria proroguing Parliament in the old House of Lords on 11 August 1840, when she was
for the first time accompanied by Prince Albert.
*Engraving by H. Melville after a drawing by T. H. Shepherd.*

52   Queen Victoria and Prince Albert at a service in the Chapel Royal, St. James's Palace.
*Engraving by W. Radclyffe after a drawing by T. H. Shepherd, 1840–41.*

53   The christening of the Princess Royal by the Archbishop of Canterbury in the Throne Room at
Buckingham Palace on 10 February 1841 (the first wedding anniversary). The Dowager Queen Adelaide
on the left of the font named the child Victoria Adelaide Mary Louisa. Others present include the Duchesses
of Gloucester and Kent, King Leopold of the Belgians, and the Duke of Sussex (all in the group on the left).
*Painting by C. R. Leslie.*

54   Queen Victoria and Prince Albert on the frozen pond at Frogmore.
*Coloured lithograph, c. 1840.*

55 'The Annuals.' Arrival of the Prince of Wales, November 1841. John Bull wonders what the child will cost him annually.
*Lithograph.*

56 'Royal *Dry* Nursing Extraordinary.' The Queen and Prince Albert are shocked to find that the nurse gives the Prince of Wales a stronger drink than was expected.
*Lithograph, 1842.*

57 The christening of the Prince of Wales at St. George's Chapel, Windsor Castle, on 25 January 1842. The two Archbishops and four Bishops officiated. Chief sponsor was King Frederick William IV of Prussia (fifth from the left, in group with the Duke and Duchess of Cambridge, and the Duchess of Kent). Behind the Queen and Prince Albert is the Duke of Wellington with the Sword of State, and on Prince Albert's left, the Duke of Sussex.
*Painting by Sir George Hayter.*

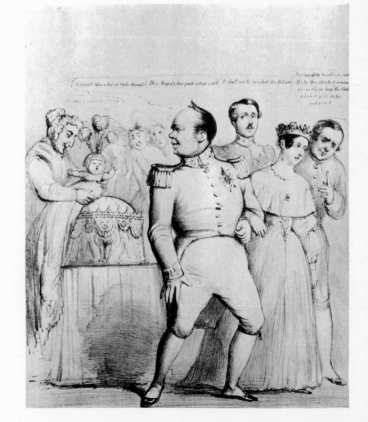

58 'The Royal Christening Cake.' 1842. This cartoon makes fun of Prince Albert's Household economies. *L. to R.:* The Prince of Wales, the King of Prussia, Prince Albert, Queen Victoria, Sir Robert Peel who advises the Queen to keep the cake whole for next year (i.e. the next christening).

59 Investiture of a Knight of the Garter in the Throne Room,
St. James's Palace.
*Engraving by H. Melville after a drawing by Gilbert, c. 1841.*

60 Queen Victoria.
*Miniature by Robert Thorburn, 1842.*

61 'Light Sovereigns, or the Balance of Power.' In the balance
against Queen Victoria are King Louis-Philippe of France, King Ernest
of Hanover, King Frederick William IV of Prussia, King Leopold I of
the Belgians, and the Emperor Ferdinand of Austria, all of whom are
outweighed by the Queen of England. 'Light sovereigns' is also an
allusion to the fact that in 1842 recently minted issues of sovereigns were
found to be under weight.
*Lithograph, 1842.*

62 Daguerreotype of Prince Albert taken at Brighton on 6 March 1842. The earliest photograph of the Prince, and in general a very early photograph, taken within a year of the first studio in Europe being opened.

63 Queen Victoria and Prince Albert in the costumes they wore at the Plantagenet Ball given at Buckingham Palace on 12 May 1842. The dresses were copied from the effigies of King Edward III and Queen Philippa in Westminster Abbey. *Watercolour*

64 Attack on Queen Victoria by John Francis, 30 May 1842. *Woodcut.*

75

65  Queen Victoria's first visit to Scotland, August–September 1842.  On board the *Royal George*—
the sudden separation of the Royal couple on the announcement of dinner.
*Lithograph.*

66  The *Royal George* off Inchkeith, in sight of Edinburgh, 1 September 1842.
*Watercolour by J. W. Carmichael.*

67 'Tender Annuals.' Arrival of Princess Alice, 25 April 1843. John Bull wonders how long it will continue at this rate.
*Lithograph.*

68 'The Royal Alphabet.' *L. to R.:* Prince Albert holding the Prince of Wales, the Princess Royal on the floor, Queen Victoria, Princess Alice in cradle.
*Sketch by John Doyle, July 1843.*

69 'A first lesson on the Welsh Harp.' In the royal nursery are seen *L. to R.*: Prince Albert, Queen Victoria holding Princess Alice, the Princess Royal, the Prince of Wales playing the Welsh harp, and his nurse. The pets are a lory on the perch, Prince Albert's greyhound Eos, the Queen's dogs, and two monkeys.                *Sketch by John Doyle, August 1843.*

70    The Yellow Drawing-room at Buckingham Palace.
*Engraving by H. Melville after a drawing by MacManus, c. 1843.*

TO THE
QUEEN'S PRIVATE APARTMENTS

THE QUEEN AND PRINCE ALBERT AT HOME.

71    The royal family at home.
*Coloured lithograph, 1843.*

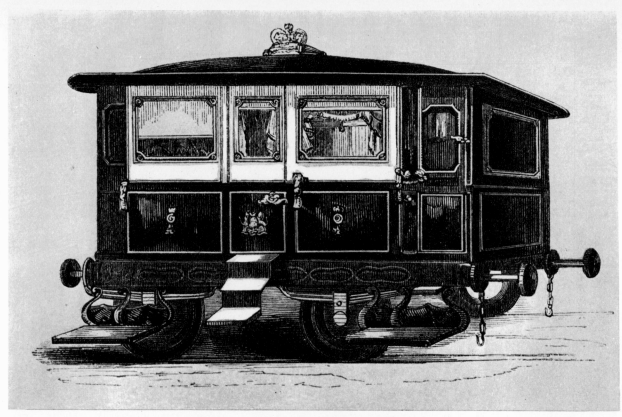

72  The first royal railway carriage.
*Woodcut, 1842.*

73  'A peep into the Royal Railroad Carriage.'
*Coloured lithograph, c. 1844.*

74 and 75 'Prince Albert driving his favourites.'
*Coloured lithograph with movable flap, c. 1843.*

76 Interior of the royal railway carriage. *Woodcut, 1842.*

77 Visit of Queen Victoria and Prince Albert to Southampton, 28 August 1843. It had been raining, and the Mayor and Aldermen emulated the gallantry of Raleigh. *Woodcut.*

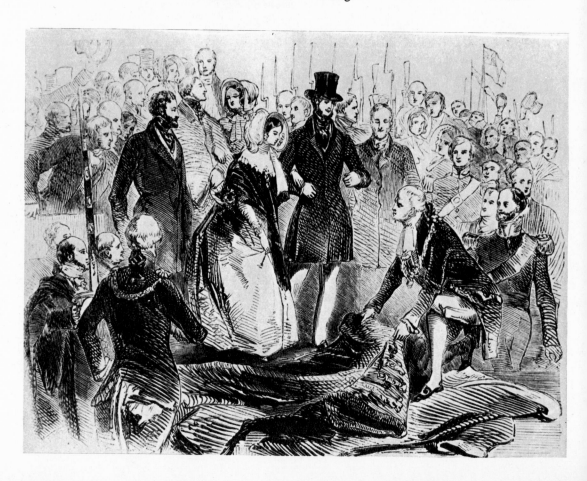

78    Reception of Queen Victoria and Prince Albert by King Louis-Philippe and his family on landing
at Tréport near Cherbourg on 2 September 1843.          *Watercolour by Eugène Lami.*

79    Arrival of Queen Victoria and Prince Albert with King Louis-Philippe and Queen Marie-Amélie
at the Château d'Eu in a char-à-banc on 2 September 1843.          *Engraving.*

80    A luncheon à l'Anglaise at the Château d'Eu, September 1843. Queen Victoria, King Louis-Philippe, Queen Marie-Amélie (back to the spectator) and Prince Albert lunching off English cheese and beer.
*Lithograph.*

81    Picnic at St. Catherine, a hunting lodge in the forest of Eu, 6 September 1843.
*Watercolour by Simeon Fort.*

82 The leave-taking of Queen Victoria and Prince Albert from King Louis-Philippe and Queen Marie-Amélie on board the royal yacht *Victoria and Albert*, 7 September 1843.
*Watercolour by François Winterhalter.*

83 The State visit to Belgium of Queen Victoria and Prince Albert, September 1843. The Queen and Prince driving with King Leopold and Queen Louise of the Belgians through Ostend on 13 September after their arrival in the royal yacht *Victoria and Albert*.
*Woodcut.*

84 Queen Victoria.
*Lithograph by Edwin Dalton from a sketch by Sir William Ross,*
*July 1843.*

85 'Royal Scotch Patronage.' Cartoon showing
the royal family's predilection for Scotland.
*Cartoon by H. H., September 1844.*

86  The royal family walking in the garden of Buckingham Palace. The Queen, Prince Albert, the Princess Royal on her pony, the Prince of Wales and Princess Alice in pram.
*Lithograph, March 1844.*

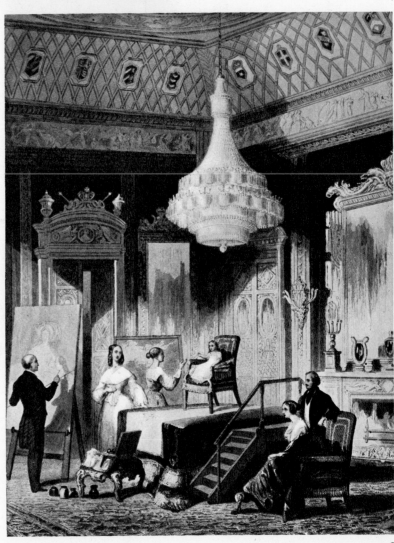

87  The Princess Royal sitting for her portrait at Buckingham Palace.
*Engraving by W. Radclyffe after a drawing by Gilbert, 1843–44.*

88 Prince Albert at the age of twenty-four, clad in mediaeval armour. Strangely enough this was the Queen's favourite portrait of her husband. The painting (or a copy) is set in a jewel-case in the form of a shrine, now at the London Museum.

*Painting by Robert Thorburn, 1843–44.*

89   Queen Victoria, aged twenty-five.
*Painting by F. Winterhalter, 1844.*

90　Queen Victoria and King Louis-Philippe setting out from Windsor Castle in the char-à-banc which he gave her. 10 October 1844. The char-à-banc is preserved at Windsor.
*Watercolour by Joseph Nash.*

91　Investiture of King Louis-Philippe with the Order of the Garter in the Throne Room at Windsor Castle, 11 October 1844.
*Watercolour by Louis Haghe.*

92  Queen Victoria and King Louis-Philippe riding in Windsor Great Park, October 1844.
*Detail from coloured lithograph by Alfred de Dreux.*

93 Queen Victoria and the Prince of Wales.
This is the first photograph of the Queen.
*Calotype 1844-45, probably by Henry Collen, miniature painter to the Queen, and the first professional calotypist.*

94 Fancy-dress ball at Buckingham Palace, 6 June 1845.
The 1,200 guests wore dresses of George II's period. Queen Victoria, Prince Albert, the Duke and Duchess of Nemours, Prince George of Cambridge and the Princess of Leiningen dancing the Minuet de la Cour.

*Watercolour by Louis Haghe.*

95   Queen Victoria's second visit to the Château d'Eu,
8 September 1845. She was landed at Tréport in a
bathing-machine because the tide was too low for the
royal barge to approach the landing-stage.
*Detail of an oil painting made later by Princess Louise,
copied from a contemporary painting.*

96   The landing of Queen Victoria and Prince Albert
at St. Pierre, Guernsey, 24 August 1846. They were on
a Channel cruise in the *Victoria and Albert*.
*Watercolour by P. J. Naftet*

97 Programme of the first Royal Command performance at Windsor Castle, by Charles Kean and his company, 28 December 1848.

98 The first Royal Command performance at Windsor Castle, in the Rubens Room, 28 December 1848. *The Merchant of Venice*, acted by Charles Kean and his company. On the dais sit Prince Albert, the Duchess of Kent, the Queen; on the steps, the four children.
*Coloured lithograph.*

99 A Scotch polka on board the *Victoria and Albert* on the way to Scotland, August 1847.
*Lithograph by H. H.*

My dear little Vic you tire me very much

Oh dear Papa it's nothing when you're used to it I like dancing aboard ship amazingly

My dear Bos you dance like a Sailor

It's the force of example dear Mother

100 Arrival of Queen Victoria and Prince Albert at Belfast during their visit to Ireland, August 1849.
*Watercolour by P. Philips.*

101   Queen Victoria's Christmas tree and presents,
Windsor Castle, 1850.
*Watercolour by J. Roberts.*

102   Queen Victoria and Prince Albert in their
dresses worn at the Stuart (Restoration) ball, Buckingham Palace, 13 June 1851.
*Watercolour by F. Winterhalter.*

103 'The First of May 1851.' It was the 82nd birthday of the Duke of Wellington, and the first birthday anniversary of his godson, Prince Arthur. The Great Exhibition had been opened that morning by the Queen, who is shown wearing the same pink dress. Prince Albert holds the plans of the Crystal Palace, which is seen in the background.

*Engraving by Samuel Cousins from a painting by F. Winterhalter.*

104 Queen Victoria opening the Great Exhibition at the Crystal Palace in Hyde Park, 1 May 1851. In the centre are the Queen and Prince Albert, the Duchess of Kent, the Princess Royal, and the Prince of Wales in Highland dress. On the left are members of the Ministry; on the right the foreign Ambassadors and a Chinaman who was only a ship's captain but pushed himself forward as an important personage and took part in the procession. *Painting by H. Selous.*

105 Queen Victoria with Princess Helena, Princess Louise (on chair) and Waldmann the dachshund. *Daguerreotype by W. E. Kilburn, Windsor Castle, 21 January 1852.*

106 Queen Victoria with her five eldest children at Frogmore, 17 January 1852. *L. to R.:* The Princess Royal, Queen Victoria, the Prince of Wales, Princess Alice, (*in front*) Prince Alfred and Princess Helena. *Daguerreotype by W. E. Kilburn.*

107 Queen Victoria and her cousin Victoire, Duchess of Nemours.
*Watercolour by F. Winterhalter, 1852.*

108 'Royal Sports.' Queen Victoria, Prince Albert, the Princess Royal with sketch-book, and the Prince of Wales in the Highlands, September 1853.
*Painting by Sir Edwin Landseer.*

109 The royal children in a dramatic version of extracts from James Thomson's *The Seasons* performed at Windsor Castle on 10 February 1854 (their parents' wedding anniversary). The Princess Royal as Spring, Princess Alice as Summer, Prince Alfred as Autumn, the Prince of Wales as Winter, Princess Helena as Britannia; also Prince Arthur and Princess Louise.

*Photograph by Roger Fenton.*

110 The Prince of Wales as Winter, and Princess Louise.
*Photograph by Roger Fenton, Windsor Castle, 10 February 1854.*

111 Prince Alfred, Dr. E. Becker (librarian to Prince Albert, and tutor), the Prince of Wales.
*Photograph by Roger Fenton, Windsor Castle, 1 February 1854.*

112 Prince Alfred as Autumn.
*Photograph by Roger Fenton, Windsor Castle, 10 February 1854.*

113 Royal family group at Windsor Castle
*L. to R.:* the Prince of Wales, the Princess Royal,
Princess Alice, Queen Victoria (wearing a chatelaine
with a pair of scissors), Prince Alfred.
*Photograph by Roger Fenton, 8 February 1854.*

114 Prince Albert.
*Photograph by Roger Fenton, Windsor
Castle, 8 February 1854.*

115 Queen Victoria in court dress and Prince
Albert in Field-Marshal's uniform after a
Drawing-room at Buckingham Palace.
*Photograph by Roger Fenton, 11 May 1854.*

116 The royal family at Buckingham Palace, in front of the
conservatory. *L. to R.:* Princess Louise, Princess Alice, Prince
Alfred, behind them the Princess Royal, Prince Arthur, Prince
Albert, Queen Victoria, the Prince of Wales, Princess Helena.
*Photograph by Roger Fenton, 1854.*

117 Queen Victoria in court dress after a Drawing-
room at Buckingham Palace.
*Photograph by Roger Fenton, 11 May 1854.*

118 Prince Albert in Field-Marshal's uniform after
a Drawing-room at Buckingham Palace.
*Photograph by Roger Fenton, 11 May 1854.*

119 A group at Osborne House. *L. to R.:* The Hon. Flora McDonald (Lady-in-
Waiting), Queen Victoria, Prince Arthur, the Marchioness of Ely (Lady-in-Waiting).
*Photograph by Dr. Becker, 21 August 1854.*

120   The royal family in front of the fountain at Osborne House. *L. to R.*: The Prince
of Wales, the Princess Royal, Princess Alice, (*in front*) Prince Arthur, Prince Albert,
Queen Victoria, Princess Louise, the Duchess of Kent, Princess Helena, Prince Alfred.

*Photograph taken by Dr. Becker on 24 May 1854, the Queen's 35th birthday.*

121   Opening of the rebuilt Crystal Palace at Sydenham by Queen Victoria, 10 June 1854. In the
centre on the dais are the Queen and Prince Albert. On the Queen's right stands the King of Portugal,
on the extreme right of the dais, Lord Palmerston. In the background is the choir which performed
Handel's *Hallelujah Chorus*.

*Daguerreotype by T. R. Williams taken during the speech of welcome.*

122   Queen Victoria and Prince Albert at Buckingham Palace on 30 June 1854.
*Photograph by Roger Fenton.*

123 Queen Victoria at Buckingham Palace on 13 July 1854. The Queen is holding a photograph of Prince Albert by Dupper (No. 124).
*Photograph by B. E. Dupper.*

124 Prince Albert.
*Photograph by B. E. Dupper, May 1854.*

125 Prince Albert's visit to the Emperor Napoleon III at St. Omer. His reception at Boulogne on 5 September 1854.
*Watercolour by George Thomas.*

126   Queen Victoria, Prince Albert, the Emperor Napoleon III and the Empress Eugénie at a
performance of *Fidelio* at the Italian Opera, Covent Garden on 19 April 1855, during the State
visit of the French Imperial couple.

*Watercolour by Louis Haghe.*

127  Visit of Napoleon III and the Empress Eugénie with Queen Victoria and Prince Albert
to the Crystal Palace on 20 April 1855.
*Photograph by P. H. Delamotte.*

128  Queen Victoria distributing the Crimean Medal in Hyde Park, 18 May 1855.
Presentation to Lieut.-Col. Sir Thomas Troubridge.
*Engraving.*

129    State visit of Queen Victoria and Prince Albert to France. Their entry into Paris with Napoleon
III and the Empress Eugénie on 18 August 1855.
*Watercolour by E. Gudrard.*

130    Review of 40,000 troops on the Champs de Mars on the occasion of Queen Victoria's and
Prince Albert's State visit to France, 24 August 1855.
*Watercolour by G. H. Thomas.*

131   Arrival of Queen Victoria and Prince Albert, Napoleon III and the Empress Eugénie
at a ball in the Hôtel de Ville, Paris, on 23 August 1855.
*Watercolour by Marc Louis Vautier.*

132  Queen Victoria.
*Watercolour by F. Winterhalter, 1855.*
Comparing this portrait with Mayall's photograph
(No. 134) taken at the same time, the great cleavage
between the reality and the ideal becomes strikingly
apparent.

133  The Princesses Helena and Louise on an African
mule, led by the groom Jones.
*Photograph by Dr. Becker, Osborne House, 1 September 1854.*

110

134 Queen Victoria.
*Photograph by J. E. Mayall, Osborne House, 28 July 1855.*

135 The royal family at Balmoral, 29 September 1855. On this day the Princess Royal (aged fourteen) became engaged to Prince Frederick William of Prussia. *L. to R.:* Prince Alfred, Prince Frederick William, Princess Alice, the Prince of Wales, Queen Victoria, Prince Albert, the Princess Royal.

*Photograph by George Washington Wilson.*

136 *Tableau vivant* of the Allies (in the Crimean War) represented by Prince Arthur (England), Princess Louise (as a French *vivandière*), Princess Helena (Turkey) at Windsor Castle on 10 February 1856.
*Photograph by Bambridge, painted over by Corbould.*

137 Queen Victoria and Prince Albert inspecting wounded Grenadier Guards returned from the Crimea, in the Marble Hall at Buckingham Palace, 1856.
*Engraving after a painting by G. H. Thomas.*

138   Queen Victoria, Prince Albert, the Prince of Wales and Prince Alfred visiting Brompton
Military Hospital, Chatham, 1856.
*Painting by Jerry Barrett.*

139   Queen Victoria laying the first stone of the Royal Military Hospital at Netley, near
Southampton, 19 May 1856. Queen Victoria, Prince Albert, the Princess Royal, Prince Alfred,
Lord Panmure (Secretary at War), Lord Winchester (Lord-Lieutenant of Hampshire).
*Watercolour by William Simpson.*

I

140   The Prince of Wales and Prince Alfred.
*Photograph by J. E. Mayall, Osborne House, August 1855.*

141   Prince Arthur.
*Photograph by Caldesi, Osborne House, 26 May 1857.*

142   The Princess Royal and Princess Alice.
*Photograph by Roger Fenton, c. 1857.*

143   Princess Helena.
*Photograph by J. E. Mayall, Osborne House, August 1855.*

144 The Princesses Helena and Louise.
*Photograph by Roger Fenton, c. 1857.*

145 Princess Alice.
*Photograph by Caldesi, Osborne House, 26 May 1857.*

146 The royal family on the terrace at Osborne House. *L. to R.*: Prince Alfred, Prince Albert,
Princess Helena, Princess Alice, (*in front*) Prince Arthur, Queen Victoria holding Princess Beatrice.
the Princess Royal, Princess Louise, (*in front*) Prince Leopold, the Prince of Wales.
*Photograph by Caldesi, 26 May 1857.*

147   *L. to R.:* Colonel (later Sir) Charles Phipps (one of Prince Albert's private secretaries), F. W. Gibbs (classical tutor to the Prince of Wales), the Prince of Wales, Prince Albert, Baron Stockmar (political adviser to Queen Victoria and Prince Albert), Dr. Becker (librarian to Prince Albert, and tutor), Baron Ernst Stockmar (son of Baron Stockmar).
*Photograph by Caldesi, Windsor Castle, April 1857.*

148   Queen Victoria and the Princess Royal.
*Photograph by Caldesi, 25 June 1857.*

149 Queen Victoria, her aunt the Duchess of Gloucester, the Prince of Wales, Princess Alice. The Duchess of Gloucester was the last of George III's children. She died ten months later at the age of 81.

*Daguerreotype by Antoine Claudet, taken at Gloucester House (now the 'In and Out' Club in Piccadilly) on 30 June 1856.*

150 The Princess Royal (with sunshade), Princess Alice, Queen Victoria, the Prince of Wales.

*Photograph taken at Windsor Castle on 10 February 1857 (17th wedding anniversary).*

151   Prince Albert
*Photograph by J. E. Mayall, Osborne House, August 1855.*

152 Princess Beatrice at the age of three weeks. The cradle was made in 1840 for the Princess Royal, and used for all the subsequent children of Queen Victoria and also for Queen Alexandra's and Queen Mary's children. It is preserved at the London Museum.

*Photograph by Caldesi, Osborne House, May 1857.*

153 A royal visit to the Crystal Palace. *L. to R.:* the Prince of Wales, Princess Alice, Prince Albert (behind the Princess Royal with sunshade), Queen Victoria, Prince Frederick William of Prussia behind her, and on the right the Archduke Maximilian of Austria (later Emperor of Mexico). The occasion is probably the first Handel Festival at the Crystal Palace, 17 June 1857, when a performance of *Judas Maccabeus* was attended by the whole court.

154 Arrival of the Emperor Napoleon III and the Empress Eugénie on a visit to Osborne, 6 August 1857. They were met by Queen Victoria and the Prince Consort.

155 Queen Victoria, the Prince Consort, and the Princess Royal, 25 January 1858, taken just before the marriage of the Princess Royal to Prince Frederick William of Prussia.

*Daguerreotype by T. R. Williams.*

156 The marriage of the Princess Royal and Prince Frederick William of Prussia (later the Emperor Frederick III of Germany) in the Chapel Royal, St. James's Palace, 25 January 1858. *L. to R.:* Prince William and Princess Augusta of Prussia, parents of the bridegroom, the Archbishop of Canterbury, Prince Frederick William, the Princess Royal; to the right of the bridesmaids Prince Alfred, behind him the Prince Consort and King Leopold, the Prince of Wales, Queen Victoria with Prince Arthur and Prince Leopold, the Princesses Louise, Helena and Alice, and behind them the Duchess of Kent and Lord Palmerston with the Sword of State.

*Painting by John Phillip.*

157 The Princess Royal's wedding cake.
*25 January 1858.*

158 The Princess Royal's bridesmaids.
*Daguerreotype by T. R. Williams, 25 January 1858.*

159 Sketch of the Princess Royal at her wedding, done from memory by Queen Victoria.

160   The Princess Royal and Prince Frederick William of Prussia on
their honeymoon at Windsor Castle.
*Photograph by Bambridge, 29 January 1858.*

161   The Prince of Wales's Confirmation photograph.
*Photograph by Bambridge, Windsor Castle, 1 April 1858.*

162   *L. to R.:* The Princesses Louise, Alice, Helena
and Prince Arthur.
*Photograph by Captain (later Lord) de Ros, Equerry,
Osborne House, July 1858.*

163   Queen Victoria and the Prince Consort, *c.* 1858.
This photograph shows very clearly the difference in their height.

164    Queen Victoria's present table at Osborne House on her fortieth birthday, 24 May 1859.

165    The royal family on the terrace at Osborne House on the Queen's fortieth birthday. *L. to R.:* Prince Leopold, Princess Louise, Queen Victoria, Prince Arthur, Princess Alice, the Princess Royal (with sunshade), Princess Beatrice, the Prince Consort, Princess Helena.    *Photograph by Bambridge.*

166   The Prince Consort's present table (with stuffed deer and numerous photographs) at Osborne House on his fortieth birthday, 26 August 1859.

167   Princess Beatrice taking her first ride at Osborne House on her second birthday, 14 April 1859.
*Photograph by Caldesi.*

127

168 *L. to R.:* Phillip, Count of Flanders (son of King Leopold), the Prince Consort, Prince Louis of Portugal (later King Louis I), the Prince of Wales, King Leopold of the Belgians, (*in front*) Queen Victoria and Princess Alice.

*Photograph taken by Captain de Ros in the garden of Buckingham Palace, 29 June 1859.*

169 *L. to R.:* Prince Leopold, Princess Louise, Prince Alfred, Princess Alice, Princess Helena.

*Photograph by Colonel de Ros, Osborne House, 9 February 1860.*

170    Queen Victoria and the Prince Consort at a military review at Aldershot, June 1859. On the
left is General Knollys in command of the troops.
*Engraving after a painting by G. H. Thomas.*

171    Queen Victoria opening the competition of the newly formed (volunteer) National Rifle Associa-
tion on Wimbledon Common. She fired the first shot from a Whitworth rifle which had been so
adjusted that she was bound to hit the bullseye, 2 July 1860
*Lithograph by A. Maclure.*

172 Queen Victoria and the Prince Consort.
*Photograph by Miss Day, Osborne House, 26 July 1859.*

174 Queen Victoria and the Prince Consort.
*Photograph by J. E. Mayall, Buckingham Palace*
*15 May 1860.*

175 Queen Victoria and the Prince Consort.
*Photograph by J. E. Mayall, Buckingham Palace,*
*15 May 1860.*

173 Queen Victoria and Princess Beatrice.
*Photograph by J. E. Mayall, Buckingham Palace,*
*15 May 1860.*

176 Queen Victoria's second visit to Coburg. *L. to R.:* Princess Alice, the Princess Royal,
Prince Frederick William of Prussia, Duke Ernest of Saxe-Coburg, Queen Victoria, the Prince
Consort, the Duchess of Saxe-Coburg.
*Photograph by Schärff, Coburg, 8 October 1860.*

130

174

175

176

131

177   Queen Victoria's present table, Windsor Castle, Christmas 1860.

178   The Prince Consort's present table, Windsor Castle, Christmas 1860.

179   Queen Victoria, with the Prince Consort, driving to the opening of Parliament, 5 February 1861.
*Watercolour by W. L. Thomas.*

180   The last Drawing-room attended by the Prince Consort, St. James's Palace, 1861.
*Painting by J. Barrett.*

182  The Duchess of Kent, who died on 16 March 1861, aged
seventy-five.
*Daguerreotype by Antoine Claudet, July 1856.*

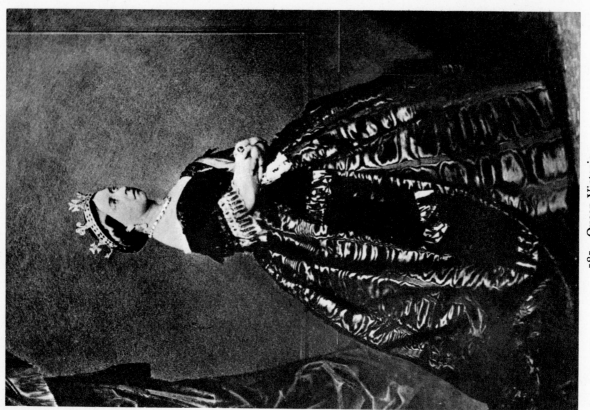

181  Queen Victoria.
*Photograph taken by Charles Clifford by order of the Queen of Spain
at Windsor Castle, 14 November 1861.*

184 The Prince Consort.
*Photograph by J. E. Mayall, 1 March 1861.*

183 Queen Victoria and the Prince Consort.
*Photograph by J. E. Mayall, 1 March 1861.*

185   An expedition in the Highlands. Queen Victoria, the Prince Consort and the Duke of Atholl
fording the Poll Tarff, 9 October 1861.
*Watercolour by Carl Haag.*

186   A picnic in the Highlands, 16 October 1861. The last Scottish expedition with the Prince
Consort. *L. to R.:* Princess Alice, her fiancé Prince Louis of Hesse, Princess Helena, the Prince
Consort, Queen Victoria.
*Sketch by Carl Haag.*

187  Queen Victoria and the Prince Consort.
*Photograph by J. E. Mayall, 1 March 1861.*

188 The Prince Consort during his last illness, holding draft memorandum on the 'Trent' question (see No. 189), December 1861.
*Painting by Thorburn. The figure has obviously been adapted from the photograph by Miss Day (No. 172).*

189 The Prince Consort's draft on the 'Trent' question, which avoided war with America, written at Windsor Castle on 1 December 1861. Below it is a note by the Queen.

190 The Prince Consort's deathbed at Windsor Castle, December 1861. The bed on which he died is probably the nearer one. There were two beds because the Prince was frequently changed from one to the other to make him more comfortable.

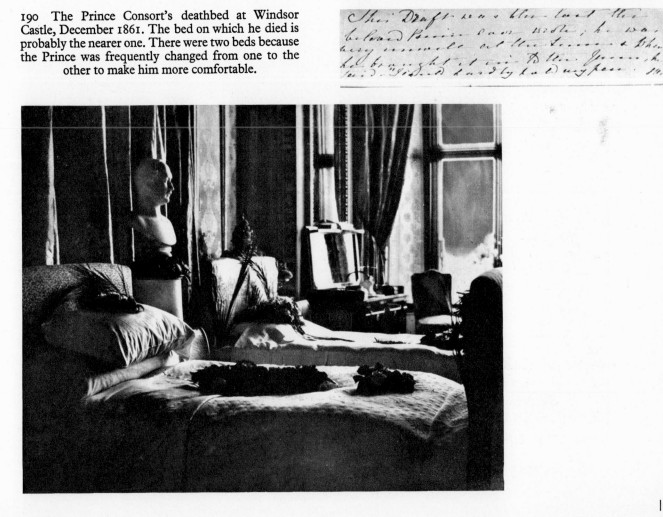

# III

# THE WIDOW
# OF WINDSOR

FOR Queen Victoria day was turned into night (Plate 191), for her it was as death in life. 'For me, life came to an end on 14 December', she wrote to the King of Prussia on 4 February 1862. 'My life was dependent on his, I had no thoughts except of him; my whole striving was to please him, to be less unworthy of him!' To the Queen of Prussia she lamented (26 May)

For me, all is over! I lived only through him, the heavenly Angel. He was my whole being, my life, my soul, yes, even my conscience! . . . Disheartened, and without interest or pleasure, I try to continue my dark and gloomy life alone, and my only wish is to join him soon. . . . I try to comfort myself by knowing that he is always near me, although invisible, and that our future union will be even more perfect and eternal! But my nature is too passionate, my emotions too fervent, and I am a person who has to cling to someone in order to find peace and comfort. The longing to see and hear him, to throw myself into his arms, to find peace and security there (as was the case for twenty-two years), is too frightful and galls me day and night.

During the first few weeks of widowhood the Queen saw no member of the Household except her friend Lady Augusta Bruce, and took her meals in her room. All communications from her Ministers and from the Household passed through Princess Alice, and at the first Privy Council meeting after the Prince Consort's death the Queen remained invisible in the next room, with the door ajar. Stunned by her loss, she performed her duties mechanically. 'The things of this world are of no interest to the Queen', she informed the Foreign Secretary, 'beyond the satisfaction she must experience if Peace is maintained, and this country is in prosperity: for *her* thoughts are *fixed* above.' The few people who saw her at Osborne—and these included Palmerston, who was moved to tears—found her aged and altered and very weak, feeling in '*utter desolation, darkness and loneliness*'.

Whereas the Prince Consort had considered it one of his duties 'to sink his *own individual* existence in that of his wife', after a few years of marriage the position in fact was reversed. The sovereign's burden was really borne by him, the Queen relying on his wisdom and guidance. She dealt with no problems and signed no papers without first discussing them with him, and he usually drafted her political memoranda and letters. No less a person than Disraeli stated: 'With Prince Albert we have buried our sovereign. This German prince has governed England for twenty-one years with a wisdom and energy such as none of our kings have ever shown.' Queen Victoria herself considered 1862 'the beginning of a new reign'.

The Queen's great sense of duty to the country, combined with her poor opinion of the Prince of Wales's ability to rule, and her firm belief in a future life, enabled her to carry on. When she returned to Windsor from Osborne early in March, it was noticed that she was a little stronger, more resigned, and courageous. She seemed uplifted by watching the progress of the Mausoleum, the foundations of which she laid, with admirable self-control, on the 15th. The Prince Consort's body was transferred here from the entrance to the royal vault in St. George's Chapel on 18 December 1862, but his monumental effigy (Plate 209) by Baron Marochetti was not completed until 1868.

At Windsor Castle, as at all the other royal residences, the Prince Consort's rooms were kept exactly as he had left them. His light-coloured top hat, gloves and cane lay on the table in the anteroom, and until the Queen's death, every day his clothes were laid out and hot water brought for his wash-basin. Wherever the Queen slept, the photograph of her husband on his deathbed hung over the empty pillow beside her (Plate 368). Nourishing her grief with this morbid romanticism comforted her as nothing else could. Her spiritual contact with her husband and absolute faith in their reunion after her death gave her courage.

When in an agony of loneliness, grief, and despair, [she told her uncle] I kneel by that bed, where he left us, decked with flowers, and pray *earnestly* to be enabled to be courageous, patient, and calm, and to be guided by my darling to *do what he* would wish; then, a calm seems to come over me, a certainty my anguish is seen and heard *not* in vain, and I feel *lifted above* this miserable earth of sorrows!

Queen Victoria's future life was dedicated to the memory of her husband. Windsor Castle and the Mausoleum at Frogmore became her 'living grave',

and soon numberless memorials to the Prince all over Britain were to remind the whole nation of 'the most perfect and the most interesting character in our history since Sir Philip Sidney'. 'Will they do him justice now?' she asked her old friend, the widowed Duchess of Sutherland, 'to whom this nation owed more than it ever can truly know.' Henceforth, all the Queen's actions were to be dictated by what she knew to be the wishes of her husband—his admirable memoranda were gospel now, he alone should guide her. His spiritual presence was always in her mind.

It is *my firm resolve*, my *irrevocable decision* [she had written to King Leopold the day after the funeral] that *his* wishes—*his* plans—about everything, *his* views about *every* thing are to be *my law*! And no *human power* will make me swerve from *what he* decided and wished—and I look to *you* to *support* and *help* me in this. . . . I am *also determined* that *no one* person, may *he* be ever so good, ever so devoted among my servants—is to lead or guide or dictate *to me*. I know *how he* would disapprove it. And I live *on* with him, for him; in fact I am only outwardly separated from him, and *only* for a *time*. . . . It is but for a short time, and *then* I go—never, *never* to part! Oh! that blessed, blessed thought! He seems so *near* to *me*, so *quite my own* now, my precious darling!

The Queen's relations with her eldest son—at no time very happy—had become painfully strained since the Prince Consort's death. She was convinced that the Prince of Wales's escapade had dealt her husband the mortal blow from which he never recovered. Her 'unconquerable aversion to the Prince of Wales', as Lord Palmerston expressed it, was a positive monomania. It quite irritated the Queen to see the Prince of Wales in the room, and she was relieved when he left on 5 February on his educational tour of Egypt and Palestine which had already been planned by his father.

Accompanied by his governor General Bruce, the Prince of Wales was met in Egypt by Dr. Stanley, later Dean of Westminster, who, though disappointed at the young Prince's preference for shooting and reading novels to exploring sites of archaeological and biblical interest, nevertheless found it impossible not to like him and to admire his astonishing memory of names and persons—a talent of first importance for royalty, and one not easily acquired.

Certain that she would soon die of a broken heart, the Queen meanwhile put her affairs in order. Requesting the return of a confidential letter, she wrote to Lord Russell, the Foreign Secretary: 'Feeling ill and weakly and longing, as the poor wretched Queen does, to join her dearly beloved and adored husband, her mind is naturally much occupied with leaving this world, and therefore with the importance of having everything in order.'

When the Prince of Wales reached home in June, forewarned against indulging in 'worldly, frivolous, gossiping kind of conversation' in his mother's presence, she was relieved to find him 'greatly improved, and most affectionate, dutiful and amiable, and only anxious to do whatever his mother and father wish'.

One of their wishes was that he should marry the seventeen-year-old Princess Alexandra, daughter of Prince Christian of Schleswig-Holstein-Sonderburg-Glücksburg, whose wife was heir to the Danish throne. Princess Alexandra had been chosen by the Prince Consort on the advice of the Princess Royal from a list of seven eligible princesses prepared by King Leopold and Baron Stockmar. Happily the young couple had liked each other when they had met in Germany in September 1861.

But first on the list of royal marriages came that of Princess Alice, who had been engaged to Prince Louis of Hesse-Darmstadt since November 1860. Owing to the mourning for her father, the wedding had been postponed for six months. It took place in the simplest possible manner on 1 July 1862 in the dining-room at Osborne House (Plate 197). It was a gloomy wedding, after which the bride and bridegroom lunched with the Queen alone.

In September the Queen travelled *incognita* as the Countess of Balmoral to Coburg, breaking the journey for a few days at King Leopold's palace at Laeken near Brussels in order to meet Princess Alexandra and her parents. From the first moment the beautiful princess endeared herself to Queen Victoria by the charm and dignity of her manner, but the Queen found it very painful to broach the subject of the engagement to her parents without

her husband, and felt immense relief when 'this most trying meeting' was ended.

In order to get to know her future daughter-in-law better, and to train her for her position, the Queen invited Princess Alexandra to her 'very sad house' for a month in November (Plate 199), during which period the Prince of Wales was sent on a Mediterranean tour. Queen Victoria disliked the idea of having to act again as chaperon during courtship. Even in the happy past, during the long engagements of the Princess Royal and Princess Alice, she had been bored, and irritated by the loss of time. She impressed on the young princess that her duty as wife of the heir to the British throne lay to England, not Denmark, and asked her to promise not to influence the Prince of Wales in favour of her native land.

To the Prince of Wales's income of over £62,000 p.a., mainly from the Duchy of Cornwall, Parliament added on his marriage an annuity of £40,000, and an annuity of £10,000 for the Princess of Wales, which was to be increased to £30,000 in the event of widowhood. Nevertheless the Prince of Wales was always short of money, partly because he had to entertain in the place of the Queen.

The marriage ceremony was performed with much pomp on 10 March 1863 in St. George's Chapel, Windsor. It was the first royal wedding to be held there since that of Henry I in 1122. A more beautiful setting could hardly be imagined than the choir with its delicate fan-vaulting and colourful banners hanging from the stalls of the Knights of the Garter. Though ladies of the royal family and the Household wore half-mourning of white, grey, mauve, or purple, the remaining nine hundred or so guests were not restricted as to colour and jewels. The Prince of Wales wore general's uniform beneath his Garter robes, and the bride a gown of Honiton lace festooned with orange-blossom (Plate 202).

Only the Widow of Windsor took no part in the ceremony. In deepest mourning, relieved by the star and blue ribbon of the Garter, she watched the magnificent scene from the Royal Closet above the chancel (Plate 200). It was noticed that she was agitated and restless, and had an expression of deep melancholy. At the blast of trumpets heralding the procession of the English princesses the Queen shook all over, terribly overcome at the sight of her fatherless children. Then the trumpets sounded again at the entry of the Prince of Wales, supported by the Duke of Saxe-Coburg and the Crown Prince of Prussia (Frederick William). The Crown Princess of Prussia burst into tears, which affected all her sisters, who wept behind their bouquets. A third fanfare announced the procession of the bride and her eight bridesmaids. While Jenny Lind sang a chorale composed by the Prince Consort, the Queen sat as if transfixed, her eyes raised to heaven. The only person not affected by the beauty and solemnity of the occasion was four-year-old Prince William of Prussia. He was in the care of his young uncles Prince Arthur and Prince Leopold, who, like himself, wore kilts. Little Willi managed to pick the cairngorm out of the handle of his dirk and flung it across the Chapel. When rebuked, he aggressively bit his uncles' knees.

Queen Victoria did not appear at the family luncheon which followed, but lunched alone with Princess Beatrice. Afterwards she joined the whole company of royalties in the Green Drawing-room to take leave of the bridal couple, and gave them her warmest blessing. Watching them drive off through enthusiastic crowds brought upsetting memories of her own and Albert's driving away twenty-three years earlier *to* Windsor amidst similar crowds and shouts of joy. To calm her feelings the Queen drove with Princess Helena to the Mausoleum, where she prayed by that beloved resting-place.

All is over and this (to me) most trying day is past, as a dream, for all seems like a dream now and leaves hardly any impression upon my poor mind and broken heart! Here I sit lonely and desolate, who so need love and tenderness, while our two daughters have each their loving husbands, and Bertie has taken his lovely, pure, sweet Bride to Osborne, such a jewel whom he is indeed lucky to have obtained. How I pray God may ever bless them! Oh! what I suffered in the Chapel, where all that was joy, pride, and happiness on January 25th, '58, [marriage of the Princess Royal] was repeated *without* the principal figure of all, the guardian angel of the family, being there. It was indescribable. At one moment, when I first heard the flourish of trumpets, which brought back to my mind my whole life of twenty years at *his* dear side, safe, proud, secure, and happy, I felt as

if I should faint. Only by a violent effort could I succeed in mastering my emotion!

Less than a month after attending her brother's wedding, Princess Alice gave birth to her first child, Princess Victoria (Plate 204). She, Prince Louis and their baby accompanied the Queen to Balmoral in May. Their presence greatly cheered her up, but after their departure the old loneliness came creeping back, tormenting the Queen with her great sorrow, desire and longing. To prevent a similar separation from Princess Helena, she decided

A married daughter *I must* have living with me, and must *not* be left constantly to look about for help, and to have to make shift for the day, which is too dreadful! I intend to look out in a year or two for a young, sensible Prince, for Lenchen [Princess Helena] to marry, who can during *my lifetime* make my house his *principal* home. Lenchen is so useful, and her whole character so well adapted to live in the house, that (unless Alice lived constantly with me, which she won't) I could *not* give her up, without *sinking* under the *weight* of my desolation. A sufficient fortune to live independently if I died, and plenty of good sense and high moral worth are the only necessary requisites. He need not belong to a reigning house.

This rather selfish streak in the Queen's character comes out again in her attitude towards the engagement of Lady Augusta Bruce, the member of the Household with whom she was on the most intimate terms, to Dr. Stanley. In her depression the Queen clung to every sympathetic person and expected that all attention should be given to her; she became possessive and resentful at having to share her friend's affection with someone else. 'My dear Lady Augusta, at *41*, without a previous long attachment, has, most unnecessarily, decided to *marry* (!!) It has been my *greatest sorrow* and trial *since* my misfortune! I thought she *never* would leave me! She will remain in my service and be often with me, but it cannot be *the same*, for her first duty is *now* to another!'

Suffering from severe nervous headaches, the Queen got into such an extreme state of weakness and worry that she began to fear for her reason and was longing for death, for only in death could she find release from the *constant sorrow* and *craving* and yearning for the *one* absorbing object of my life, and the *one only* Being who could *quiet* and *calm* me; I feel like a poor hunted hare, like a child that has lost its mother, and *so* lost, so frightened and helpless.

I *own*, beloved Uncle, that I think my life will *end more* rapidly than any of you think; for *myself* this would be the *greatest, greatest* blessing; but for the poor children I feel a *few* years more would be desirable; and for the country, I *own*, it alarms me still more.

Towards the end of 1863 a long-standing dispute concerning the rival claims of Prussia and Denmark to the Duchies of Schleswig and Holstein came to a head. Under a treaty signed in London in 1852 by all the Great Powers the independence and union of Schleswig and Holstein was guaranteed and the succession to the Duchies settled to the line of Sonderburg-Glücksburg. In November 1863, however, Denmark annexed Schleswig whilst granting independent rights to Holstein, and this arbitrary arrangement, made by King Frederick VII of Denmark, was confirmed when in the same month Princess Alexandra's father succeeded to the Danish throne as Christian IX on behalf of his wife. As Prince of Sonderburg-Glücksburg he was heir in his own right to the Duchies of Schleswig-Holstein, but since he was now King of Denmark, Holstein refused allegiance to him. This was the signal for Prince Frederick of Schleswig-Holstein-Augustenburg to claim the Duchies for himself, although in 1852 his father had renounced these rights in favour of the Sonderburg-Glücksburg line for a financial compensation. A third claimant to the disputed territory was the King of Prussia, who under Bismarck's influence saw an opportunity for annexing one if not both of the Duchies by acceding to Schleswig's petition to be 'liberated' from Denmark. The British royal family was divided from top to bottom on this question. At home and abroad Queen Victoria had relations in each of these three conflicting camps, and divided loyalties brought painful rifts. Family considerations made each party claim her active sympathy, but least the King of Prussia's party, on whose side, from purely political considerations, she nevertheless found herself. The Crown Prince and Princess of Prussia were, however, supporters of Prince Frederick, the son-in-law of Queen Victoria's half-sister, Princess Feodora of Hohenlohe-Langenburg, and so were all the Queen's other close relations in Germany, the Hesse family, and Duke Ernest of Saxe-Coburg. The Prince and Princess of Wales, on the other hand, were naturally in favour of the Danish claims, and when the Crown Prince and Princess of Prussia came to stay at Windsor Castle during November and December, such heated arguments arose that Queen Victoria had positively to forbid any mention of the Schleswig-Holstein question at table. These discussions were, of course, in German—the language the royal family always spoke among themselves.

Fritz W. [Wilhelm] is very violent, [the Queen complained to King Leopold] Vicky sensible, Feodore very anxious and at times violent, but much distressed for me, and I *miserable*, wretched, almost frantic without my Angel to stand by me, and *put* the *others* down, and in their right place! *No* respect is paid to *my* opinion *now*, and this helplessness almost drives me *wild*, and in the family *his* loss is more *dreadfully* felt than *anywhere*. It makes visits like Fritz and Vicky's *very painful* and *trying*.

Queen Victoria vigorously adhered to Prince Albert's desire for a strong, liberal Prussia; but the circumstances had changed, for Bismarck's policy was far from liberal, and right was hardly on Germany's side. The mass of the English people and Press were decidedly pro-Danish. In this they followed the traditional British characteristic of siding with the underdog, and their sympathies were certainly strengthened by the popularity of the beautiful Princess of Wales.

As some of the Ministers, and in particular Lord Palmerston, favoured Britain's active intervention on behalf of Denmark if Prussia and her ally Austria should commence warlike operations, the Queen propounded to Lord Russell that Britain should mediate to avoid bloodshed. However, Prussia, Austria and the Federal German States continued on their chosen warpath; the latter, supporting Prince Frederick, invaded Holstein on 21 January 1864, whilst Prussia and Austria invaded Schleswig on 1 February. The Queen now successfully exerted her influence to make Parliament adopt a neutral policy. She appealed not only to the Cabinet but also took the most unusual step of enlisting the support of the leader of the Opposition, Lord Derby, against her Prime Minister, Lord Palmerston, and even threatened to dissolve Parliament if her wish were not followed. Queen Victoria could be exceedingly obstinate, and on occasions like this she assumed almost autocratic power. No British monarch after her ever again matched his own will against that of the Government to such an extent; but then ours is a democratic monarchy, of which Queen Victoria refused to be Queen. 'She *cannot* and *will* not be the Queen of a *democratic* monarchy' (25 December 1880).

Without Britain's aid the Danes could offer little resistance and by July the allied armies were in occupation of both Duchies. In October, Denmark ceded them to the allies by a peace treaty signed in Vienna.

In home affairs the main event of the year 1864 was the birth of a son to the Princess of Wales on 8 January. He was christened Albert Victor in the private chapel at Buckingham Palace on the first wedding anniversary. The Queen's christening present was a gilt statuette of the Prince Consort in armour, made to her design and with inscriptions composed by herself, and supported by figures of Faith, Hope and Charity, adorned with snowdrops and white lilies for purity. A more remarkable example of Victorian taste—or tastelessness—is difficult to imagine. In discussing the name of the infant with the Prince of Wales, the Queen's mind turned to the future. 'It was beloved Papa's wish, as well as mine, that you should be called by both [Albert Edward] when you became King, and it would be *impossible* for you to *drop* your Father's. It would be monstrous, and *Albert alone*, as you truly and amiably say, would *not do*, as there can be only *one* ALBERT!' Yet these exhortations were of no avail, for in Britain it is not customary to use two Christian names as on the Continent. Apropos the naming of the Prince of Wales's second son (later King George V), Queen Victoria reminded him not to forget to add Albert at the end 'as you know we settled *long ago* that *all* dearest Papa's *male* English descendants should bear *that* name,

to mark *our line*, just as I wish all the girls to have Victoria at the end of theirs! I lay great stress on this.'

Discontent at Queen Victoria's continued absence from London and withdrawal from public and Court functions began to make itself felt in 1864. In March a placard was found hanging on the gates of Buckingham Palace announcing: 'These commanding premises to be let or sold, in consequence of the late occupant declining business.' People began to grumble that the cost of the sovereign was out of all proportion to her usefulness, and the newspapers almost unanimously declared the Queen to be failing in public duty. *The Times*, after printing a self-invented rumour that the Queen was about to break her protracted seclusion, stated that the sovereign could not expect to influence public affairs unless she appeared as a factor in them. The Queen took the unprecedented step of writing a letter to *The Times* (which was published on 6 April 1864) denying that she was 'about to resume the place in society which she occupied before her great affliction'. She was very indignant, for she was certainly not neglectful of her work. 'From the hour she gets out of bed till she gets into it again there is work, work, work—letter-boxes, questions, &c., which are dreadfully exhausting . . . her brain is constantly overtaxed.' Nothing could persuade her that the resentment was due to her refusal to appear at social and public functions, which, after all, form an essential part of the sovereign's duties. Finally she relented to the extent of holding three Courts in the season of 1864, which appeased the public, whilst the people's affection touched the Queen. Her drive to Paddington Station through the crowded Hyde Park in an open carriage was an unexpected sight for Londoners, and though this public appearance was trying for the Queen, she noted with satisfaction: 'Everyone said that the difference shown, when *I* appeared, and [when] Bertie and Alix drive, was not to be described. Naturally for *them* no one stops, or *runs*, as they always did, and *do* doubly now, for me.'

But a few Courts were not enough to satisfy *The Times*, which returned to the attack on the third anniversary of the Prince Consort's death, reminding the Queen that the living have their claims as well as the dead. Giving way to a certain extent, the Queen held six Courts during the 1865 season.

In August she made yet another journey to Coburg, this time to unveil on the Prince Consort's birthday a ten-foot-high gilded bronze statue of him by William Theed (Plate 213). Twenty-four relations were present. 'Never since Vicky's marriage', lamented the Queen, 'had our nine children been assembled together; and now they were all together, and the *Head* of *all* was missing!'

Queen Victoria arranged a meeting in Coburg with Prince Christian of Schleswig-Holstein, younger brother of the unsuccessful claimant to the Duchies. Though thirty-nine and rather bald, he was the 'young, sensible Prince' destined for Princess Helena. The Princess, even before she knew anything of her mother's design, spontaneously said that she thought Prince Christian amiable and agreeable, whilst he, having no country of his own, was very content to live in England. The Queen's plan therefore suited everyone admirably, particularly as she did not insist on Prince and Princess Christian actually residing with her. They lived at Frogmore House after their marriage in the private chapel at Windsor Castle on 5 July 1866 (Plates 215, 216). To provide her son-in-law with some slight occupation, the Queen appointed him Ranger of Windsor Home Park.

The sudden death of Lord Palmerston at his desk at 10 Downing Street two days before his eighty-first birthday in October 1865 relieved Queen Victoria of future anxieties and battles. 'I *never* liked him, or could even the least respect him, nor could I forget his conduct on certain occasions to my Angel.'

Two months later the Queen lost her dearly loved Uncle Leopold, who had taken care of her like a father and been the greatest influence in her life prior to her marriage. His death, which had been expected for some time, was the heaviest blow that had fallen on the Queen since the loss of her husband, and she felt stunned. 'It is dreadful; and again at this time of year, so close to that painful anniversary of the 14th.' As on all occasions when she was particularly upset, the Queen sought calm at 'the dear peaceful Mausoleum, and the two dear ones

who loved each other in this life seemed strangely mingled together'. The Queen knew that her uncle wanted to be interred beside his first wife in St. George's Chapel, Windsor, and was grieved when this rather unreasonable desire met with a flat refusal from the Belgian people, who understandably wished that the King who had ruled over them for thirty-four years should have his last resting-place in their country.

Meanwhile, agitation against the Queen's seclusion continued, and reluctantly giving way to what she considered cruel persecution, she agreed to open Parliament on 6 February 1866, after a lapse of five years. The traditional ceremony, significant for its demonstration of the position of the sovereign in the Constitution, had rarely been omitted except for reasons of health, and Queen Victoria was in fair health, though depressed in spirits. She bitterly resented the lack of feeling on the part of those who demanded 'this dreadful ordeal'—which she could 'only compare to an execution'—and wrote to Lord Russell, who had succeeded Lord Palmerston as Prime Minister,

To *long* to *witness* the spectacle of a poor, broken-hearted widow, nervous and shrinking, dragged in *deep mourning, alone* in *state* as a *Show*, where she used to go supported by her husband, to be gazed at, without delicacy of feeling, is a thing *she cannot* understand, and she never could wish her bitterest foe to be exposed to! . . . It is hard, when she works and slaves away all day and till late at night, not to be spared at least such trials.

The Queen refused to drive in the State coach or to wear the Robes of State, which were draped over the throne. Nor did she consent to read the speech from the throne herself. When she entered the House she felt on the point of fainting, and during the reading of the speech by the Lord Chancellor she sat rigid, staring in front of her and feeling all eyes fixed upon her. Next day she was 'terribly shaken, exhausted, and unwell from the violent *nervous* shock' the effort had cost her.

Events on the Continent during the next few months, from which Prussia emerged as the head of the whole of northern Germany, filled Queen Victoria with misgivings, for although she saw her own and Prince Albert's hopes of a strong Prussia fulfilled beyond expectation, she now realized that it was an illiberal Prussia that was emerging, led by a dangerous fire-brand. Her disillusionment was great.

Seeking an excuse for compelling Austria to give up her hitherto leading rôle in the German Confederation, Bismarck set the whole of Germany aflame by various warlike acts in an attempt to unify the German States under Prussia's leadership. In June the Prussians invaded Holstein (which under the treaty of Vienna was occupied by Austria) and a week later Prussia demanded the dissolution of the German Confederation. A lightning war ensued, in which the Prussians defeated the Austrians as well as the various armies of the German Confederation. Within seven weeks the war was over and Prussia's leadership of a new North German alliance established. The King of Hanover, Queen Victoria's first cousin, who had supported Austria, had his kingdom annexed by Prussia, whilst the Grand Duke of Hesse had to cede the northern part of Hesse-Darmstadt.

At home, the British public first became aware at about this period of the importance of John Brown (Plate 210). Originally one of Prince Albert's gillies, and from 1858 onward the Queen's regular attendant in the Highlands, John Brown had taken part in all the happy excursions from Balmoral. He led the Queen's pony, helped her to clamber over rough ground, insisted that she put on her shawl or mackintosh when necessary, boiled the kettle for tea (and put whisky in it), and served at table during *incognito* visits to country inns. When in the weeks following the Prince Consort's death the Queen refused to leave the house, John Brown and her favourite pony Lochnagar were sent for from Scotland to Osborne, and this had the desired effect. Because of his associations with the Prince and with Balmoral, for which the Queen was permanently homesick, she now became still more attached to her Highland servant, whom she found 'a *real* comfort, for he is *so* devoted to me—so simple, so intelligent, *so unlike* an *ordinary* servant, and so cheerful and attentive'. Brown had, in the Queen's opinion, 'all the independence and elevated feelings peculiar to the Highland race, and is singularly straightforward, simple-minded, kind-hearted, and disinterested; always ready to oblige; and of a discretion rarely to be met with'. Whilst Brown's completely natural behaviour and lack of awe in the presence of royalty amused the Queen by its novelty, his tearful habits endeared him to her own emotional nature, and in February 1865 he was promoted to be her regular outdoor attendant everywhere.

The Queen's enthusiasm for her personal attendant was shared neither by her children nor by the Court, the general opinion being that he was, according to mood, either over-familiar, or rude and surly, and that he sometimes smelt of whisky. Her undisguised affection for and dependence on John Brown caused the most absurd rumours to circulate, such as that she was mad and Brown her keeper; she was a spiritualist and Brown her medium for contacting the Prince Consort's ghost; even the rumour that they were secretly married found circulation through a scurrilous pamphlet entitled *Mrs. John Brown*. Jokes spread from society to the general public via *Punch*. The royal family, members of the Household, friends and Ministers all considered this friendship most unwise, inexpedient, and embarrassing, but secure in the innocence of their relations, the Queen ignored 'the wicked and idle lies about poor, good Brown' and let it be known that 'the Queen will not be dictated to, or *made* to *alter* what she has found to answer for her comfort'. And that was that.

On the last day of November 1866 Queen Victoria visited Wolverhampton, accompanied by Prince and Princess Christian (Helena) and Princess Louise, to unveil an equestrian statue of the Prince Consort by Thomas Thornycroft. Nothing could give the Queen greater satisfaction than the dedication of memorials to her Angel, and on such occasions she raised no objection to a public appearance, however much it distressed her. 'It seemed so strange being amongst so many, yet feeling so *alone*, without my beloved husband! Everything so like former great functions, and yet so unlike! I felt much moved, and nearly broke down when I saw the dear name.' After the ceremony the Queen on a sudden impulse decided to pay a special tribute to Wolverhampton—the first English municipality to honour her husband's memory in this way. She knighted the Mayor, John Morris (Plate 218), who was quite bewildered when Lord Derby informed him of the Queen's intention.

On 20 May of the following year Queen Victoria laid the first stone of the Royal Albert Hall (Plate 220), originally intended for scientific and artistic congresses as well as performances of music and exhibitions of various kinds. In a short speech the Queen reminded the audience that it had been Prince Albert's intention to establish here (on this large plot of land purchased out of the profits of the Great Exhibition) a centre of institutions for the promotion of art and science. (Several of these had already been founded.) 'I have been sustained by the thought that I should assist by my presence in promoting the accomplishment of his great designs.' Amidst the flourish of trumpets and the booming of twenty-one guns in Hyde Park, the polished block of granite was lowered into place, the Queen declaring it to be well and truly fixed. The ceremony closed with a short prayer by the Archbishop of Canterbury and a performance of *L'Invocazione all'Armonia* composed for orchestra and chorus by Prince Albert.

In July the Sultan Abdul Aziz of Turkey paid a State visit to England. He had been splendidly entertained in Paris by Napoleon III, and Lord Derby, the Prime Minister, impressed upon Queen Victoria the political necessity of receiving the Sultan soon after his arrival and not waiting—as she wished—until the naval review at Spithead arranged for the fifth day of his visit. At this the Queen was exceedingly annoyed, for it entailed postponement of her intended journey to Osborne by three days. She bitterly complained to Lord Derby of

the want of consideration shown by the *public* for her health and strength, and she foresees ere long a *complete breakdown* of her nervous system. . . .

It is very wrong *not* to say that the Queen *is incapable* of those fatigues and of this excitement, working and drudging as she does from *morning* till *night*, and weighed down by the responsibility and cares of her most unenviable position, and with the anxieties consequent upon being the widowed mother of so large a family. Often has she wished that the time might come when she could go to that world 'where

the wicked cease from troubling and the weary are at rest'.

Having made her protest, the Queen did her duty. She received the Sultan, who was staying at Buckingham Palace, at Windsor Castle the day after his arrival, and at the naval review on 17 July she entertained him on board the *Victoria and Albert*. Unfortunately there was a howling gale and the Sultan was continually retiring below, but in an interval between his attacks of seasickness the Queen managed to confer on him the Order of the Garter, which he had set his heart upon. This was a last-minute change of plan, for the Queen had intended giving him the Star of India which she considered more suitable for non-Christians, and she had to borrow the Garter insignia from Prince Arthur and Prince Louis of Hesse.

The publication in January 1868 of *Leaves from a Journal of our Life in the Highlands* did much to restore the old affection the public had felt for the Queen before her seclusion. Dedicated to the memory of the Prince Consort, the *Leaves* consisted of extracts from the Queen's journal relating to their holidays in Scotland, and elsewhere. The simple descriptions of the domestic life of the royal family in Scotland, the spontaneity of her diary entries and absence of any pretentiousness, enchanted the public and made the book a best-seller. The Queen was thrilled by its success and collected reviews as eagerly as most authors do.

Ever since she came in, at a quarter past five [she wrote to (Sir) Theodore Martin] she has done nothing but read the reviews in the newspapers. She is very much moved—deeply so—but not uplifted or 'puffed up' by so much kindness, so much praise. She sends one [review] that is very gratifying, which Mr. Martin has *probably* not seen. Pray, let the Queen have it back.

In the first year after publication the *Leaves* brought in over £4,000 profit which was devoted to charitable purposes.

In February Queen Victoria accepted a new Prime Minister for the seventh time, Lord Derby having resigned owing to frequent bad attacks of gout. Benjamin Disraeli (1804–1881) had been Chancellor of the Exchequer in Lord Derby's three

Conservative governments, and the Second Reform Bill of 1867 was recognized as his personal achievement.

In the 'forties and 'fifties Queen Victoria had strongly disapproved of Disraeli's violent attacks on Sir Robert Peel for repealing the Corn Laws in 1846. After the Prince Consort's death her opinion softened, for Disraeli's fine tributes to him caused her deep gratification. Phrases such as 'the Prince is the only person whom Mr. Disraeli has ever known, who realized the Ideal' were sweet music in the Queen's ears.

On accepting office Disraeli expressed his devotion and craved the guidance of one whose judgment 'few living persons, and probably no living Prince, can rival'. He admitted to laying on flattery with a trowel, but it pleased the Queen and made collaboration with her much easier than if he had constantly reminded her of her duty towards the country as Gladstone later did. Disraeli had the gift of making politics interesting, amusing even, and the Queen enjoyed his witty descriptions of what went on in the House.

When after barely three months the Government was defeated on Gladstone's motion for the disestablishment of the Irish Protestant Church, the Queen refused to accept Disraeli's resignation. The dissolution of Parliament was deferred for about six months on account of the formation of new constituencies, the Bills for which had not yet passed their final stages. During this short time the Queen's relationship with Disraeli became more intimate than it had been with any Prime Minister since Lord Melbourne. 'She opened all her heart and mind to me, and rose immediately in my intellectual estimation,' wrote Disraeli. 'Free from all shyness, she spoke with great animation and happy expression.' Disraeli sent all his novels to the Queen and she reciprocated with a copy of *Leaves*. Henceforth discussions on literature were held on a level of equality. 'We authors, Ma'am' was a phrase often on Disraeli's lips.

Every week Queen Victoria sent her Prime Minister wild flowers from the grounds at Windsor or Osborne, and during his stay at Balmoral in September gave him some very personal presents, including a box full of family photographs, and a portrait of the Prince Consort. Carrying on the Government 600 miles from the metropolis doubled the labour for Disraeli, but he knew how to handle the Queen. His method was as wise as it was simple: 'I never refuse; I never contradict; I sometimes forget.'

Unfortunately this happy state of affairs was abruptly ended when the Government was defeated at the general election after only nine months in office. The Queen offered Disraeli a peerage on resignation, but preferring to stay in the House of Commons he asked that his wife alone be given the title. This request the Queen found 'very embarrassing', fearing that the proposed arrangement would expose both Mr. and Mrs. Disraeli to ridicule, but she acceded to his wish and Mary Anne became Viscountess Beaconsfield in her own right.

Queen Victoria's eighth Prime Minister, William Ewart Gladstone (1809–1898), had entered Parliament at the age of twenty-three on the Conservative side but had become a Liberal in 1859. In character, personality and political views Gladstone was the complete antithesis of Disraeli, and it is not surprising that the Queen's feelings for him were the very opposite to those she held for her ex-Prime Minister. Unfortunately it was not in Gladstone's nature to follow his wife's advice to pet the Queen sometimes, and he entirely failed to inspire her with confidence. He showed little interest in her private affairs, lacked sympathy for her abnormal distress and hypochondriacal concern for her health, and treated her as though she were a public department, whereas Disraeli treated her as a woman. Moreover, Gladstone was inclined to lecture the Queen, and his obstinacy matched hers. Thus antipathy made their collaboration difficult and unpleasant, and as time went on, the Queen found Gladstone even harsh and dictatorial, and his 'overbearing obstinacy and imperiousness . . . most disagreeable'. She complained later that he would have liked to rule her as Bismarck ruled the Emperor of Prussia.

Gladstone's first ministry undertook more legislative activity than any other Government of the reign. The first measure was naturally the disestablishment of the Irish Church on which the Conservative Government had fallen. But even in matters which did not displease the Queen as this

Bill did, Gladstone's verbose and far from lucid memoranda exhausted her and made her sigh for Disraeli's lighter touch.

In March 1869 Queen Victoria went to a cultural tea-party at the Deanery, Westminster, where her friend Lady Augusta Stanley had gathered together some celebrities in the way Prince Albert had wanted to thirty years earlier. Sir Charles Lyell, the geologist, Browning, Carlyle, and others were invited. At first, mutual shyness made conversation with the Queen rather difficult, but the celebrities relaxed over tea and then 'talked very entertainingly'. Carlyle, 'a strange-looking eccentric', held forth in a drawling melancholy voice with a broad Scottish accent upon the utter degeneration of everything. Browning, 'a very agreeable man', learnt of the Queen's admiration for his late wife's poetry, but was left wondering about her opinion of his own.

The Poet Laureate Tennyson, whose *In Memoriam* had given Queen Victoria comfort in her grief, had already met her shortly after the Prince's death.

Though having little time for recreational reading, the Queen admired the novels of Sir Walter Scott, Charlotte Brontë, George Eliot, and above all Charles Dickens, whom she sought for some time to meet. An opportunity arose when she learned that Dickens possessed some photographs of the American Civil War, for being herself a great collector of photographs she desired to see them. During the ninety minutes' interview which took place at Buckingham Palace in March 1870 the Queen remained standing to honour her famous visitor, as etiquette did not permit him to sit down. Dickens was touched when on taking leave the Queen gave him a copy of her book inscribed 'From the humblest of writers to one of the greatest.'

With the coming of age of Princess Louise in March 1869 the question of a suitor engaged the Queen and other members of the royal family. Recent history ruled out a suggested Prussian alliance, for 'what could be more painful', argued the Queen, 'than the position in which our family were placed during the war with Denmark, and between Prussia and Austria? Every family feeling was rent asunder.' Princess Louise was equally anxious to avoid the divided loyalties which caused such mental conflict to her sister, the Crown Princess of Prussia, who was—according to the Prince of Wales—'too German in England and too English in Germany'. It was fortunate that Princess Louise's wish to marry in her own country coincided with her mother's feelings in this matter, for it avoided a domestic problem which under the political stresses of recent years the Queen had come to look upon as an inconvenience rather than a blessing. 'Nothing is more unpopular here or more uncomfortable for me and everyone', she complained to the Prince of Wales, 'than the long residence of our married daughters from abroad in my house, with the quantities of foreigners they bring with them, and the foreign view they entertain on all subjects.' A British nobleman of high rank and fortune would, moreover, infuse new and healthy blood into the royal family, whereas all the eligible foreign Protestant princes were related to it. When the Marquis of Lorne proposed to Princess Louise in October of the following year (Plate 230) the Queen gave her approval the more readily since the Franco-Prussian War had only confirmed her previous fears. It was not since 1515, when Henry VIII's sister married Charles Brandon, Duke of Suffolk, that the sovereign had sanctioned the marriage of a princess to a subject. The wedding took place with much pomp on 21 March 1871 at St. George's Chapel, Windsor. Unfortunately the Queen's desire for new blood in the royal family remained unfulfilled, for Princess Louise was the only one of her nine children who remained childless.

Queen Victoria, who had constantly counselled peace between France and Prussia, found herself again in sympathy with Prussia when, after considerable provocation, France declared war in July 1870. Overwhelmed with anxiety for the Crown Princess and Princess Alice, whose husbands had taken the field, and for 'the country she loves best next to her own', she had, nevertheless, to tell her eldest daughter, 'We must be neutral *as long as we can*, but no one here conceals their opinion as to the *extreme iniquity* of the war, and the unjustifiable conduct of the French!' The Crown Princess was constantly blaming Britain for remaining neutral, which upset her mother. 'These divided interests in royal families are quite unbearable. Human nature is not made for such fearful trials, especially not mothers' and wives' hearts.'

When the news of Napoleon III's surrender at Sedan on 2 September reached Paris a Republic was proclaimed, and the Empress, who was acting as Regent, fled to England. Queen Victoria appealed to King William of Prussia to shape his demands in such a way that the French could accept them without utter humiliation, and pleaded that Paris should be spared bombardment. Bismarck determined that the fulfilment of German designs should not be impeded by 'petticoat sentimentality'. The fulfilment of his designs demanded the bombardment of Paris as a prelude to the proclamation of King William of Prussia as Emperor of Germany in the Galerie des Glaces at Versailles. On 18 January 1871 Bismarck's ambitious plan for the unification of Germany under Prussia's leadership, to which the other German kings and princes had been persuaded or coerced, found fulfilment. Thinking only in terms of the *next* Emperor, Queen Victoria concluded that 'a powerful Germany can never be dangerous to England, but the very reverse, and our great object should therefore be to have her friendly and cordial towards us'. Alas, she could not foresee that her son-in-law was fated to reign for only ninety-nine days, and that little Willi would one day become Britain's bitterest enemy.

Despite Queen Victoria's pleading, the peace treaty imposed on France on 26 February was more vindictive than the most pessimistic had anticipated. France had to cede Alsace-Lorraine, pay 5,000 million francs (then 200 million pounds) indemnity, and submit to the token occupation of the capital by German troops for forty-eight hours.

Always generous when misfortune befell others, Queen Victoria reaffirmed her old friendship for the ex-Emperor and Empress in their darkest hour. The ex-Empress and her fourteen-year-old son had reached England, separately, in September 1870 and settled at Camden Place, Chislehurst, which was placed at their disposal by a sympathizer. Queen Victoria visited Eugénie in November and found her bearing her misfortunes with dignity and patience. 'There was an expression of deep sadness

in her face, and she frequently had tears in her eyes. She was dressed in the plainest possible way, without any jewels or ornaments, and her hair was simply done.' On the ex-Empress's return visit to Windsor Castle on a dreary and pouring wet December afternoon Queen Victoria 'entertained' her by taking her down to the Mausoleum. 'What a fearful contrast to her visit here in '55!' she felt, and no doubt the same thought crossed Eugénie's mind, who was 'so touching in her gentleness and submission', still waiting for her husband's release from detention at Wilhelmshöhe.

The establishment of the Third Republic led to an increase of republicanism in England, and in 1871 Queen Victoria's popularity sank to its lowest ebb. People sometimes turned their backs when she drove past, or even called out against her. Though constantly urged by Gladstone and by members of the royal family to stay in London and perform public duties, she would not heed their advice.

The unrest in Ireland was largely blamed on the Queen's neglect. It was certainly a contributory factor in the rise of the Fenians—a powerful and violent secret brotherhood founded in 1867 to fight for Irish independence. In two hundred years the sovereign had spent only twenty-one days in Ireland. As Queen Victoria herself could not be persuaded to pay more frequent visits there, both Disraeli and Gladstone repeatedly urged her to let the Prince of Wales take up residence in Ireland as Lord-Lieutenant or Governor. This, they thought, would please the Irish and provide a useful occupation for the Prince. But each time the plan was brought up the Queen opposed it. She also vetoed the proposal for a royal residence in Ireland on the grounds that nobody would ever go there for health or pleasure, and 'to have a residence in Ireland and *not* be there, would be *worse*'. Thus Queen Victoria's neglect of Ireland is said to have led to the Irish Free State, whilst the Prince of Wales's complete lack of employment led him to waste his time at the races, at the gambling table, and in society. Not until ten years after his father's death was he for the first time allowed to play a small part at Court (an investiture), for the Queen 'could not bear the thought of anyone helping me and standing where my dearest one had always stood'. Another twenty-one years were to pass before she could bring herself to implement her intention 'to lift up my son and heir and keep him in his place near me'.

During her usual autumn stay at Balmoral the Queen was laid up with acute rheumatic gout which made her quite helpless, unable to walk or even to feed herself. In addition, a swelling six inches in diameter had to be cut from her arm. This severe illness caused a friendly reaction in the Press, but the Queen thought it very hard that she must suffer physically before people could feel for her and understand her. Gladstone, in particular, she could not forgive for his failure to make the public realize that 'the Queen could not do more than human strength could bear'.

Sympathy was universal when soon after her own illness the Prince of Wales was stricken with typhoid fever—the disease that had caused his father's death. Queen Victoria went to Sandringham, the Prince of Wales's newly-completed country house, where she learned that the attack was far more violent than her husband's ten years before. From the 11th to the 13th December the Prince of Wales was expected to die at any moment. The Queen, the Princess of Wales and Princess Alice kept constant watch, supporting each other in their despair as best they could.

> Alice and I said to one another in tears, 'there can be no hope'. I went up to the bed and took hold of his poor hand, kissing it and stroking his arm. He turned round and looked wildly at me saying, 'Who are you?' and then, 'It's Mama'. 'Dear child', I replied. Later he said, 'It is so kind of you to come,' which shows he knew me, which was most comforting to me.

As the 'dreadful anniversary' of the 14th December returned again, the Queen expected that this fatal day would dawn upon another deathbed; she could hardly fathom it when the doctors gave her the wonderful news that her son had passed the crisis. In private conversation she sadly remarked: 'Had *my* Prince had the same treatment as the Prince of Wales, he might not have died'—an indication perhaps that she did nourish doubts about Sir James Clark's ability, although publicly she had never failed to defend him.

The whole nation, including many republicans, had shown so much loyalty and affection during the Prince of Wales's illness that it was felt judicious to hold a public Thanksgiving Service at St. Paul's Cathedral, though the royal family would have preferred not to make an outward show of their solemn feelings. On 27 February 1872 the Queen (Plate 231), the Prince and Princess of Wales drove in semi-State through gaily decorated streets and amidst deafening cheers from enthusiastic crowds to St. Paul's Cathedral, which the Queen thought 'a *most* dreary, dingy, melancholy and undevotional church'.

Two days later brought emotions and excitement of a less pleasant kind. The Queen with Prince Arthur, Prince Leopold and a lady-in-waiting were just preparing to leave the carriage at Buckingham Palace after an afternoon drive

> when suddenly someone appeared at my side, whom I at first imagined was a footman, going to lift off the wrapper. Then I perceived that it was someone unknown, peering above the carriage door, with an uplifted hand and a strange voice, at the same time the boys calling out and moving forward. Involuntarily, in a terrible fright, I threw myself over Jane C., [Churchill] calling out, 'Save me', and heard a scuffle and voices! I soon recovered myself sufficiently to stand up and turn round, when I saw Brown holding a young man tightly, who was struggling, Arthur, the Equerries, etc., also near him. They laid the man on the ground and Brown kept hold of him till several of the police came in. All turned and asked if I was hurt, and I said, 'Not at all'. . . . Cannon, the postilion, called out 'There it is', and looking down I then did see shining on the ground a small pistol! This filled us with horror. All were white as sheets, Jane C. almost crying, and Leopold looked as if he were going to faint.
>
> It is to good Brown and to his wonderful presence of mind that I greatly owe my safety, for he alone saw the boy rush round and followed him!

The youth, Arthur O'Connor, was an Irish Independence fighter who wanted to force the Queen to sign a document in connection with Fenian prisoners. The pistol was found not to be loaded. This frightening though harmless attack, added to the effect of the Thanksgiving, rallied the people to their Queen in renewed manifestations of cordial sympathy and loyalty which not even republican hotheads in Parliament could seriously disturb.

Thus these events brought to an end the several years' period of the Queen's unpopularity, during which rumours of her abdication were frequent. Deeply affected by the change in the public's mood, she responded by more frequent public appearances. She was especially touched by her hearty reception from the poorest of the poor on paying her first visit to the East End to open Victoria Park at Bethnal Green, for there she had expected jeering rather than cheering.

In June 1873 the Shah of Persia paid a State visit to England. This fabulously rich and mysterious Oriental potentate had aroused intense curiosity in all the capitals he had visited on his European tour, and many rumours concerning his personal habits preceded his arrival in London. It was known that his three favourite wives had been sent back from Moscow because they aroused too much interest, but the lack of female company caused the Shah to frequent disreputable places in Berlin and his Minister at Constantinople had been cabled for the immediate dispatch of a couple of female slaves. Reports of his uncouth table manners at the Court of Berlin also gave rise to misgivings, for he showed his immense interest in European food by examining it after it had been partly chewed, throwing it under the table if it failed to come up to expectations.

During his fortnight's stay at Buckingham Palace the Shah visited Queen Victoria three times at Windsor Castle. The first occasion was on the thirty-sixth anniversary of her accession.

Felt nervous and agitated at the great event of the day, the Shah's visit. All great bustle and excitement. . . . Was much surprised at seeing no troops lining the hill, as was done when the Sultan came here. Sent for Colonel Ponsonby [the Queen's private secretary] who ran down to give some directions, in hopes of getting them still, and some makeshift was arrived at, just as we heard the Shah had arrived at the station.

After watching with her daughters the gradual approach of the twelve carriages, from her room,

the Queen received the Shah at the main entrance (Plate 232). He was covered from head to foot with diamonds, rubies, and emeralds, even his buttons were rubies, and in his high black astrakhan cap was an aigrette of diamonds. After decorating the Shah with the Garter and receiving from him Persia's highest orders, the party sat down to luncheon to the skirl of the bagpipes. The Shah was enchanted and told the Queen how eager he was to see Scotland after reading her *Leaves*, which he had had translated into Persian. It was noted that he consumed large quantities of fruit and iced water, but silence reigns as to whether he repeated at Windsor his startling performance at table which had so shocked the Court at Berlin.

The beginning of 1874 saw the end of the first Gladstone Government. The country went to the polls and swept the Conservatives back into power with a triumphant majority. It was with the utmost satisfaction that Queen Victoria received back Disraeli, who knelt down and kissed hands, saying: 'I plight my troth to the kindest of mistresses!' After the austerity of Gladstone, Disraeli's fantastic personality acted like a tonic on her spirits. The Queen's position and whole way of life did not permit her to be very womanly. She had little time for ordinary feminine occupations, and saw comparatively little of her children. Perhaps the more, she felt the need for masculine support, for the society of a man whose charm and brilliant conversation would help her overcome the mental loneliness she had suffered since the Prince Consort's death. Disraeli fulfilled these needs with consummate tact. On one occasion the Queen's welcome was so hearty that for a moment Dizzy really thought she was going to embrace him. She actually offered him a chair because of his gout, but he thought it better to decline. Eventually, however, the time came when he sat through their private talks, tactfully replacing the chair against the wall so that it should not bear witness to the breach of etiquette.

During the general election the Queen's mind had often wandered from Westminster to Petersburg, where on 23 January her second son Prince Alfred, Duke of Edinburgh, married the Grand Duchess Marie (Plates 233, 234). She was the only daughter of Czar Alexander II, whom the Queen had imagined herself to be 'a little in love with' thirty-five years before. The young couple were welcomed by the Queen at Windsor on 7 March, and five days later London got its first glimpse of the Duchess when, despite a heavy snowstorm, the Queen drove with the Edinburghs to Buckingham Palace in an open landau (Plate 235).

When the Duchess of Edinburgh found that the Princess of Wales—the daughter of a petty king—took precedence over herself—the daughter of a powerful Emperor—she withdrew from society. In May the Czar came to England on a State visit, and he agreed with the Queen's contention that she could not confer on the wife of her second son the right to take precedence over the wife of the heir-apparent, but the Russian Grand Duchess was to have precedence over Queen Victoria's daughters. Immediately afterwards another awkward situation arose. The Czar wanted to stay two days beyond the date fixed by the Queen for going to Balmoral, and as usual she refused to alter her plans. Lord Derby, Lord Aberdeen and the Prince of Wales vainly argued against this insult to the Czar, but when Disraeli begged the Queen to postpone her journey as a personal favour she complied 'for Mr. Disraeli's sake and as a return for his great kindness'. It was also Disraeli who, feeling that the Prince of Wales's talents were being wasted, with much difficulty persuaded the Queen to agree to his State tour of India in 1875–1876.

In November 1875, the opportunity arose to buy from the Khedive of Egypt nearly half the shares in the Suez Canal which had been opened six years earlier. The Khedive had already given an option to a French syndicate, and over four million pounds had to be found immediately if Britain were to seize the chance. So large a sum could not be paid without the approval of Parliament, which was not in session, but by a bold stroke Disraeli borrowed the money from Rothschild's bank, giving as security 'the British Government'. When Queen Victoria received Disraeli's note saying, 'It is just settled. You have it, Madam', she was overjoyed. 'It is *entirely* the doing of Mr. Disraeli, who has *very large ideas*, and *very lofty views* of the position this country should hold. His mind is so much greater, larger, and his apprehension of things great and small so

much quicker than that of Mr. Gladstone', who had declined the shares when some years earlier they had been offered by de Lesseps. Still more incredible, in view of Britain's possessions in and vital trade links with the East, appears Lord Palmerston's objection to the construction of the Suez Canal in 1855.

Now that Britain had obtained so large a share of control over the highway to India, Queen Victoria coveted the title of Empress of India. Besides, the fact that the Duchess of Edinburgh took precedence over her children rankled, and before long, she thought, her eldest daughter would be an Empress and take precedence over herself. Disraeli's first feelers in this direction were not encouraging. Some people argued that 'Empress' was not a higher title than 'Queen'; others, more puritanical in outlook, objected to the imperial title on the grounds that it 'evokes the images of conquest, of persecution, and even of debauchery'. However, thanks to Disraeli's diplomatic handling of the matter, the Bill was approved by the House in April 1876 after a stormy passage, and Queen Victoria was proclaimed Empress of India in London on 1 May, and at a great Durbar in Delhi on 1 January 1877 (Plates 236, 237). That evening the new Empress celebrated the assumption of her title with a dinner party at Windsor, to which the Prime Minister, now Earl of Beaconsfield, was invited. He found the small dignified figure, usually so sombrely attired, blazing from head to foot with magnificent Oriental jewellery—presents from Indian princes which the Prince of Wales had brought back. When Dizzy enquired whether the Queen-Empress were wearing *all* the jewels she replied with immense satisfaction 'Oh, no', and sent for a number of small portmanteaux, the contents of which she spread out before his admiring eyes.

If the Queen had strong imperialistic tendencies, one must at the same time admit that she was not a jingoist, and that her views on the treatment of natives and coloured races were beyond reproach. They should be treated, she informed the Colonial Secretary, Lord Carnarvon in December 1874, 'with every kindness and affection, as brothers, not—as alas! Englishmen too often do—as totally different beings to ourselves, fit only to be crushed and shot down!' To ensure that her feelings should not be merely construed as a pious hope but as the country's policy, she commanded '*All* her Colonial Governors should *know* her feelings on this *subject* of the *native* races.'

Since 1875 war had been threatening to engulf the Near East once more. A situation had arisen rather similar to that leading to the Crimean War. The Balkan Christian subjects of the Sultan were in revolt, and Russia expressed her intention of aiding the insurgents, who were members of the Greek Church, as she had in 1853. Russia's real motive now as then was, of course, to use the situation as an excuse to get control of Constantinople, which would be her gateway to the West, and to unite the Slav peoples.

Gladstone, deeply shocked by the atrocities committed by Turkish irregular troops in Bulgaria, emerged from retirement and with all his eloquence crusaded against Britain's giving Turkey any support. Possibly encouraged by the favourable reception given to Gladstone's polemics in Britain, the Czar declared war on Turkey on 24 April 1877, the Russian armies simultaneously invading the Turkish Balkan dominions. Lord Derby, the Foreign Secretary, declared Britain's strict neutrality, but Queen Victoria bombarded Lord Beaconsfield with letters and telegrams urging a firm stand against Russia. The Queen had always distrusted Russia's intentions and now desired war against her as vehemently as she had advocated neutrality in the wars waged by Prussia—and on each occasion she found herself in disagreement with her Government and the feeling of the country. In spite of her constant entreaties and threats to abdicate, Beaconsfield found no support in the Cabinet for involving Britain in war with Russia.

After a decisive defeat of the Turks on 10 December, however, Beaconsfield favoured limited support for Turkey and decided to act, if necessary even without the Foreign Secretary's co-operation. To demonstrate her wholehearted approval of the Prime Minister's policy, Queen Victoria visited him on the 15th (Plate 238) at his country house, Hughenden Manor in Buckinghamshire, and stayed to luncheon. Her gesture created a powerful impression both in Britain and abroad, for no Prime Minister had been honoured in this way since the days of Lord Melbourne.

Following reports of the swift Russian advance on Constantinople, the Queen again threatened to resign if Britain were 'to kiss the feet of the great barbarians'. Beaconsfield was now actively preparing for intervention, and this led to the resignation of the Secretary of State for the Colonies and soon afterwards of the Foreign Secretary. But by the time the British fleet entered the Dardanelles 'to protect British life and property' in Constantinople, the war was practically over, and on 3 March 1878 Russia and Turkey signed a peace treaty at San Stefano, a few miles outside Constantinople. Though this treaty established *inter alia* independence or autonomy for most of the Turkish provinces in Europe, it was generally feared that they would become Russian satellites. British interests in particular were threatened by the possibility that Russia might thus gain an outlet to the Mediterranean through Bulgaria, which up to 1919 had an Aegean coastline. Early in June Beaconsfield negotiated a secret agreement with Turkey whereby England obtained Cyprus in return for a promise to defend Turkish interests. Since none of the European Powers except Russia liked the treaty of San Stefano, Bismarck called together a congress at Berlin to revise its terms, at which Germany, Britain, France, Austria, Italy, Russia, and Turkey were represented. The Conference opened in Berlin on 13 June 1878 under Bismarck's chairmanship, and lasted a month. Before setting out, Beaconsfield warned Queen Victoria that hostilities would result if Russia did not give way on certain points affecting British interests. His firmness in ordering a special train for the departure of the British delegation when Russia remained obstinate had the desired effect. 'What is the use of power if you don't make people do what they don't like?' he once wittily remarked. Willing to take risks, and not merely bluffing, his doctrine was certainly effective on this occasion, and Beaconsfield returned with the new Foreign Secretary, Lord Salisbury, in triumph bringing 'peace with honour', and assuring Queen Victoria that she would soon be mistress of Europe. 'High and low', she told him, 'the whole country is delighted, except

Mr. Gladstone, who is frantic.' She wanted to reward his achievement with a dukedom, but Beaconsfield accepted only the Garter. The Queen's high esteem and friendship for her Prime Minister had already found expression in her correspondence with him. Dropping all formality she wrote in the first person, signing 'Yours affectionately, Victoria R.I.', and had authorized him too to drop the usual formulas.

To what extent Beaconsfield had succeeded in dispelling the gloom of the Widow of Windsor and inspiring her with a new pleasure in life is illustrated by an incident that occurred at Osborne some months before the Berlin Congress. To everyone's great surprise the Queen one evening joined the ladies and gentlemen of the Household in a dance. 'We had five dances, and I danced a Quadrille, and a valse (which I had not done for eighteen years) with dear Arthur, who valses extremely well, and I found I could do it as well as ever!'

The Queen's comparative happiness was again clouded over in November when once more illness attacked those she loved. This time bad tidings came from Darmstadt. Four of Princess Alice's children and her husband had diphtheria, and one little girl died. While nursing her children the devoted mother caught the disease and died within six days, on the fatal 14 December, the eighteenth anniversary of her father's death.

> That this dear, talented, distinguished, tender-hearted, noble-minded, sweet child, who behaved so admirably during her dear father's illness, and afterwards, in supporting me, and helping me in every possible way, should be called back to her father on this very anniversary, seems almost incredible, and most mysterious! To me there seems something touching in the union which this brings, their names being for ever united on this day of their birth into another, better world!

Grief for the Grand-Duchess of Hesse was not allowed, however, to interfere with the preparations for the marriage of Prince Arthur, Duke of Connaught, to Princess Louise Margaret (Plate 244), daughter of Prince Frederick Charles of Prussia and great-niece of the Emperor. Prince Arthur was Queen Victoria's favourite son, '*dearer* than any of

the others put together', and though she had previously pronounced against another Prussian alliance, she gave way when after six years' search for a wife Prince Arthur fell in love with a Prussian princess. The wedding took place in St. George's Chapel, Windsor, on 13 March 1879.

Two months later news was received that Princess Charlotte, eldest daughter of the Crown Princess of Germany and wife of the Hereditary Prince of Saxe-Meiningen, had been safely delivered of a daughter. It is unusual to welcome the third generation of descendants before completing one's sixtieth year, but Queen Victoria was delighted at becoming a great-grandmother, and Lord Beaconsfield in congratulating her remarked, 'Your Majesty has become "the mother of many nations".'

In March of the following year Beaconsfield dissolved Parliament in the belief that the situation would be favourable to the Conservatives. He had miscalculated, however, for largely owing to Gladstone's Midlothian electioneering campaign—an innovation introduced into British political life by the great Liberal leader—the country returned a Liberal Parliament.

Queen Victoria was staying at Baden Baden when she received the totally unexpected news of this 'great calamity for the country and the peace of Europe'. Her first reaction was grief at losing Beaconsfield. 'What your loss to me as a Minister would be', she telegraphed, 'it is impossible to estimate. But I trust you will always remain my friend, to whom I can turn and on whom I can rely.' Her second thought was how to avoid Gladstone. Six months earlier, she had assured Lady Ely, 'I never could take Mr. Gladstone as my Minister again, for I never *could* have the slightest *particle* of confidence in Mr. Gladstone *after* his violent, mischievous, and dangerous conduct during the last three years.' Now she told her private secretary, Sir Henry Ponsonby, 'She will sooner *abdicate* than send for or have any communication with *that half-mad fire-brand* who would soon ruin everything, and be a Dictator.' Ponsonby tried to calm the Queen and convince her that Gladstone was at least loyal and devoted to her. Indignantly she replied with her own brand of passionate invective: 'He is *neither*; for *no one can* be, who spares no means . . . to *vilify,—attack—*accuse of *every* species of iniquity a Minister, [i.e. Beaconsfield] who had most difficult times and questions to deal with—and who showed a most unpardonable and disgraceful spite and personal hatred to Lord Beaconsfield who restored England to the position she had lost under Mr. Gladstone's Government. Is this *patriotism* and devotion to the *sovereign*? . . . Such conduct is *unheard of* and the *only* excuse is—that he is not quite *sane*.'

Gladstone's opposition to the Zulu War in 1879 which he rightly denounced—like the Afghan War of 1880 and the first Boer War of 1881—as imperialist wars, had incensed the Queen even more than his opposition during the late Russo-Turkish War. For in this struggle for power between Britain, Germany and Russia, the Queen had become a dedicated Imperialist, and anyone who opposed Imperialism was considered by her unpatriotic. 'If *we are* to *maintain* our position as a *first-rate* Power . . . we must, with our Indian Empire and large Colonies, be *prepared* for *attacks* and *wars*, *somewhere* or *other*, *continually*. The *true economy* is *to be always ready*.' And with the same conviction as present-day statesmen she added the same fallacious argument, 'It will *prevent war*.'

Queen Victoria still hoped that she could persuade Lord Hartington, to whose hands Gladstone had temporarily entrusted the leadership of the Opposition, to head the Government. However, Gladstone not surprisingly refused to serve under anyone, and *nolens volens* the Queen had to accept him as Prime Minister once more. After that she argued against practically every member of the Cabinet he suggested (Plate 247) but again she achieved no compromise. That defiance which had once succeeded against Sir Robert Peel left Gladstone unmoved. His own obstinacy matched the Queen's when the occasion demanded it.

The Queen's offer to Lord Beaconsfield of a dukedom was refused for the second time. Instead, he requested a peerage for his private secretary, Montagu Corry, who became Lord Rowton—an unprecedented honour which caused Gladstone to scoff that nothing like it had been heard of since Caligula made his horse a consul.

Lacking all confidence in Gladstone, Queen Victoria looked to her ex-Prime Minister and trusted friend for advice and assistance, and unconstitutionally they carried on a secret correspondence. No wonder Gladstone found his office very trying and complained to Lord Rosebery that 'the Queen alone is enough to kill a man'. Judging from her New Year's resolution for 1881, the Queen was aware of her own failings. 'I feel how sadly deficient I am, and how over-sensitive and irritable, and how uncontrollable my temper is, when annoyed and hurt. But I am so overdone, so vexed, and in such distress about my country that that must be my excuse. I will daily pray for God's help to improve.'

The following spring Lord Beaconsfield lay on his deathbed. The Queen wrote or telegraphed to him every day, and sent regular supplies of his favourite spring flowers, primroses—a strange emblem for that flamboyant personality. 'You are very constantly in my thoughts, and I wish I could do anything to cheer you and be of the slightest use or comfort.' She enquired whether he were well enough to see her, but witty to the last, he murmured, 'Better not; she would only give me a message for Albert.' On 19 April he died. Queen Victoria was quite overwhelmed at the loss of the friend whose devotion, unselfishness and kindness had eased her burden and cheered her life during the last dozen years as no one else could. In or out of office she could turn to her dear friend for advice and help. 'Her gratitude is everlasting . . . his dear memory will ever live in her heart! The Queen can think of little else and the bitter tears will flow again and again.'

Beaconsfield was buried, as he wished, beside his wife in the little church at Hughenden. Next to his heart was placed a signed photograph of the Queen of whom he had said 'she is the sovereign not only of my person, but of my heart'.

On 2 March 1882 another attempt was made on the Queen's life as she got into her landau at Windsor station.

. . . there was the sound of what I thought was an explosion from the engine, but in another moment I saw people rushing about and a man being violently hustled, people rushing down the street. I then realised that it was a shot, which must have been meant for me, though I was not sure, and Beatrice said nothing, the Duchess, [of Roxburghe] who was also in the carriage, thinking it was a joke. No one gave me a sign to lead me to believe anything amiss had happened. Brown however, when he opened the carriage, said, with a greatly perturbed face, though quite calm: 'That man fired at your Majesty's carriage.'

The next day the Queen examined the revolver and bullets with interest, and then walked with Princess Beatrice to the Mausoleum to offer up prayers of thanksgiving for her preservation. This was the seventh attack on the Queen. The would-be assassin —a grocer's assistant—was pronounced insane; he had in fact already spent two years in a lunatic asylum.

Easter was spent at Menton with Princess Beatrice and Prince Leopold, Duke of Albany. It was the first of the Queen's many spring holidays on the Riviera. Her youngest son, debarred from an active life by haemophilia, had fortunately inherited his father's studious habits and cultivated tastes, which made him 'a link between Court and culture'. He was noted as an accomplished speaker, and the only member of the royal family who could speak English without a German accent. 'How thankful we must be that he has been preserved to us!' wrote the Queen on his twenty-ninth birthday, at Menton. 'How often has his poor young life hung on a thread! Though the idea of his marrying makes me anxious, still, as he has found a girl, so charming, ready to accept and love him, in spite of his ailments, I hope he may be happy and carefully watched over.' The wedding of the Duke of Albany to Princess Helena Frederica of Waldeck-Pyrmont (Plate 245) took place on 27 April 1882 at St. George's Chapel, Windsor. In the evening a State banquet (Plate 246) was held in St. George's Hall; among the guests were King William III and Queen Emma of the Netherlands, elder sister of the bride. The Queen gave Claremont, which she had purchased after the death of King Leopold, to the newly-married couple.

On 29 March of the following year the Queen 'again sustained one of those shocks like in '61 when every link has been shaken and torn'. The loss of John Brown was 'irreparable, for he deservedly possessed my entire confidence; and to say that he is daily, nay, hourly, missed by me, whose lifelong gratitude he won by his constant care, attention, and devotion, is but a feeble expression of the truth:

> A truer, nobler, trustier heart,
> More loyal and more loving, never beat
> Within a human breast.'

None less than the Poet Laureate wrote the inscription for the tombstone which the Queen placed to Brown's memory in Crathie churchyard, Balmoral:

> Friend more than Servant, loyal, truthful, brave,
> Self less than duty even to the grave.

A statue was erected to him at Balmoral, and memorial seats were placed on the royal estates, but—like the numerous photographs of Brown which cluttered up the Queen's private rooms—they were destroyed when the Prince of Wales, who heartily detested the former gillie, became King.

It was only by the firm disapproval of the Dean of Windsor who threatened to resign, that Queen Victoria was dissuaded from publishing a memoir she had written on John Brown, but she had her own back by dedicating 'to the memory of my devoted personal attendant and faithful friend, John Brown' a further selection of extracts from her journal, entitled *More Leaves from the Journal of a Life in the Highlands, from 1862 to 1882.* This book was published in February 1884. On the copy she sent to Tennyson, Queen Victoria described herself as 'a very humble and unpretending author, the only merit of whose writing was its simplicity and truth'.

Exactly a year after the death of John Brown, the sudden death of the Duke of Albany from cerebral haemorrhage brought fresh grief to the Queen. He had been married less than two years and left an infant daughter, Princess Alice (now the Countess of Athlone).[1] The Queen felt badly shaken by this new misfortune. 'I am a poor, desolate old woman, and my cup of sorrow overflows! Oh! God, in

---

[1] A posthumous son, Charles Edward, was born the following July. He inherited his father's title, and subsequently became Grand Duke of Coburg.

His mercy, spare my other dear children.' Yet no other loss, not even of her dearest children, ever affected her as much again as the death of her husband. It was as though Albert's loss had made such a hole in her heart that all later sorrows slipped through.

Adding to the Queen's personal grief was anxiety concerning the vacillating and inconsistent policy of the Government over the situation in the Sudan. The Sudanese, under the fanatical Mahdi who claimed to be a prophet, were in rebellion against Egypt, then practically administered by Britain. The Government, with the Queen's unwilling acquiescence, had advised the Khedive to abandon the Sudan to the rebels, but at the same time Britain undertook to rescue some Egyptian garrisons and settlers in the Sudan by sending the influential ex-Governor of the Sudan, General Gordon, to negotiate their withdrawal. Queen Victoria's grave doubts as to whether he could execute his mission single-handed were soon confirmed: in March 1884 Gordon was besieged in Khartoum, the capital of the Sudan, by the Mahdi's forces. Though the Queen constantly urged that an expedition be sent to rescue Gordon, the Government declined to send help. When at last an expeditionary force was sent, it arrived two days after Khartoum had been taken and its defenders massacred. Burning with indignation, Queen Victoria placed the responsibility for General Gordon's murder on the Government. 'Mr. Gladstone and the Government *have*—the Queen feels it *strongly*—Gordon's innocent, noble heroic blood on their consciences. *No one* who reflects on *how* he was *sent* out, how he was *refused*, can deny it! . . . May they *feel* it, and may they be *made to do so!*'

Soon after the funeral of the Duke of Albany the Queen, accompanied by Princess Beatrice, left for Darmstadt to attend the wedding of her grand-daughter Princess Victoria (eldest daughter of the late Grand Duchess of Hesse) to Prince Louis of Battenberg (first cousin of the Grand Duke of Hesse). This visit turned out to have far-reaching consequences for both the Queen and her youngest and only unmarried child, for during their stay Princess Beatrice fell in love with Prince Henry of Battenberg, a brother of the bridegroom.

Since Princess Louise's marriage, Princess Beatrice had been her mother's constant companion. She was 'the flower of the flock', 'the little Baby my darling one loved so much, to whom he almost gave his last smile', the one child, therefore, whose presence comforted the Queen most, and whom she had decided should never marry. Marriage, in fact, was not allowed to be mentioned in the presence of the Princess—as though a girl would not think of it for herself! The Queen found Prince Henry 'very amiable, very unassuming and sensible, and in addition very good-looking', and since he had neither estates nor money, he agreed to the Queen's condition that he and his wife should live with her. Princess Beatrice's eldest sister and brother were both hostile to the match, for Prince Henry was not only an unimportant prince, but also the offspring of a morganatic union. The engagement therefore caused a family rumpus. The Prince of Wales sent no congratulations, and in retaliation the Queen, Princess Beatrice and her fiancé did not attend the coming-of-age celebrations at Sandringham of Prince Albert Victor of Wales.

The relative unimportance of the bridegroom, and family objections, called for a quiet wedding, which took place in Whippingham Church, Osborne, on 23 July 1885. Most of the close relations, including the Prince of Wales and his family, were present, but the absence of the Crown Prince and Princess of Germany and their children was commented upon. 'Though I stood for the ninth time near a child and for the fifth time near a daughter, at the altar, I think I never felt more deeply than I did on this occasion, though full of confidence. When the Blessing had been given, I tenderly embraced my darling "Baby"' (aged twenty-eight). The wedding luncheon (Plate 254) was served in a marquee on the lawn at Osborne House. Afterwards, all the royal guests and the bridal group (Plate 255) were photographed on the terrace for the picture of the wedding which Caton Woodville was to paint.

When Queen Victoria conferred the Order of the Garter on her new son-in-law, there were renewed objections. The other royal Knights considered that the Order of the Bath would have been sufficient.

**TABLEAUX VIVANTS,**

**✦ FRIDAY, JANUARY 24, 1890. ✦**

**I.**

**❧ ESTHER. ☙**

| | |
|---|---|
| Queen Vashti | H.R.H. the Duchess of Albany. |
| Queen Esther | Miss McNeill. |
| King Ahasuerus | Mr. Muther. |
| Ladies | The Hon. Ethel Cadogan. Miss Cowell. |
| Attendants | Munshi Hafiz Abdul Karim. Saiyad Ahmad Husain. Mirza Yusuf Beg. |

**II.**

**❧ FOTHERINGAY. ☙**

| | |
|---|---|
| Mary, Queen of Scots | H.R.H. Princess Louise, Marchioness of Lorne. |
| The Duchess of Argyll | H.R.H. Princess Beatrice, Princess Henry of Battenberg. |
| Mary Beaton | H.R.H. the Duchess of Albany. |
| Mary Seaton | Countess Feodore Gleichen. |
| Sister Veronica | Miss Alberta Ponsonby. |
| Secretary | Lt.-Colonel A. Collins. |
| Queen's Confessor | Mr. Victor Biddulph. |

**III.**

**THE ✦ SURRENDER ✦ OF ✦ CALAIS.**

| | |
|---|---|
| Queen Philippa | H.R.H. Princess Louise, Marchioness of Lorne. |
| Edward III. | Gen. Sir Henry Ponsonby. |
| The Earl of Derby | The Marquis of Lorne. |
| The Earl of Shrewsbury | Major the Hon. H. C. Legge. |
| Lord Cobham | Mr. A. Cowell. |
| Sir Walter Manny | Lt. the Hon. S. Fortescue, R.N. |
| Eustache de St. Pierre | Mr. Muther. |
| Jehan d'Aire | Dr. Reid. |
| Jacques de Wisant | Major Bigge. |
| Dominican Friar | Mr. Victor Biddulph. |

Programme of Tableaux Vivants at Osborne.

Finally, her bestowal on Liko, as he was known in the family, of the title of Royal Highness was not recognized by the Courts of Berlin, Vienna and Petersburg, who insisted on treating the marriage as a morganatic one. Yet in the face of so much opposition from every quarter, Prince and Princess Henry of Battenberg remained very cheerful. Their support and companionship meant more to the ageing Queen than all her other children together. Prince Henry, in particular, quite transformed her dull domestic life with his affectionate and gay disposition, giving her more happiness than she had experienced since the death of the Prince Consort. Before long, the Battenbergs, supported by the ladies and gentlemen of the Households, and occasionally by Princess Louise and her husband and the Duchess of Albany, staged elaborate

tableaux vivants (Plate 266) and plays to amuse the Queen, who took the greatest interest in these theatrical activities and on occasion acted as self-appointed censor. It would not do, for instance, that Princess Louise playing the villainess in a French comedy was to be reproached as 'a degraded woman' by the assistant private secretary Major Bigge!

Early in 1891 the Waterloo Chamber at Windsor was fitted up as a theatre for a performance of *The Gondoliers* by the D'Oyly Carte Opera Company. It was the first professional dramatic production in any of the royal palaces for thirty years. *Cavalleria Rusticana*, performed a few months later, the Queen enjoyed so much that she asked Mascagni for a signed photograph for her album. *Il Trovatore, Carmen, Lohengrin* and *Faust* (the Queen's favourite opera at that period) and many other productions of a lighter nature were staged at Windsor Castle. In 1893 the Comédie-Française gave several performances there. Sarah Bernhardt, Eleanore Duse, Beerbohm Tree, Ellen Terry and Henry Irving all played before Queen Victoria.

These entertainments were looked forward to by the Household as much as by the Queen, for the Court was very dull. Especially was this the case at Balmoral, where life has been compared to that at a strictly-disciplined school, or worse. (Sir) Henry Campbell-Bannerman, when a member of Gladstone's Cabinet, told his wife: 'It is the funniest life conceivable: like a convent. We meet at meals, and when we are finished, each is off to his cell.' Communications were by letter rather than by word of mouth, for the Household was infected with the Queen's habit of writing notes. No one was allowed to leave the Castle until the Queen had gone out, which was often not before four o'clock. Attendance at church on Sundays was obligatory. The rooms were frightfully chilly and draughty, because the Queen entertained the view that cold was healthy. She abominated tobacco. Smoking was allowed only in a small room which was reached by crossing the open kitchen courtyard, and austerely furnished like a guardroom with a wooden table and chairs. The Queen looked upon it as a kind of opium den. A distinguished member of the Government is said to have been found by a friend lying on his bedroom floor puffing cigar smoke up the chimney, for the Queen had a keen nose. She once complained to her private secretary that the papers he had been working on smelt of tobacco. After Princess Beatrice's marriage, Prince Henry (who, like Prince Christian, was a great smoker) persuaded the Queen to provide a properly furnished room which could be reached without going out of doors. At Osborne and Windsor smoking was only allowed in the billiard room—far away from the Queen's apartments.

Wherever Queen Victoria resided there were four dinners—the Queen's, the Household's, the upper and the lower servants'. The Queen's dinner, to which a few members of the Household were invited, was usually, according to Sir Henry Ponsonby, 'appallingly dull', though when animated the Queen could be very entertaining, relating amusing reminiscences. Queen Victoria was by no means lacking in a sense of humour. She appreciated a good joke and, when in the right mood, could see the fun of an amusing episode or misunderstanding. When Admiral Seymour lunched with her shortly after the capsize of the *Sea Mew*, she enquired 'How is Miss Seymour?' The reply of the Admiral, who was rather deaf, startled everyone within hearing. 'All right, thank you, Ma'am. We've got her on her side, and tomorrow we are going to scrape her bottom.' Uncertain of the Queen's reaction, members of the royal family present controlled their mirth until she burst out in a hearty laugh, which made her quite breathless.

Even when grown up, Queen Victoria's children stood so much in awe of her that they were afraid to approach her direct and used Ponsonby as an intermediary. Every morning after breakfast those members of the Queen's family who were staying with her waited in fear and trembling lest they should receive one of her famous notes, in which anyone who had aroused her displeasure the day before was informed of it. Not infrequently some little punishment was inflicted, such as withdrawing the use of the Queen's horses. At so early a date as 1872 the Queen had complained that her children 'become more and more strangers to her and no longer seem to fit in with her ways and habits (which she thinks are simple and good) when they once go

Programme of the first Royal Command Cinema performance.

out a great deal into Society'. But in spite of the large number of children she had brought into the world her feelings cannot exactly be described as maternal. It was observed that the presence of several of her children together gave her little pleasure and not infrequently led to rows.

Shortly before Princess Beatrice's wedding the Government was unexpectedly defeated on the Budget and Gladstone resigned, relieved that his painful relations with the Queen were at an end, and aware that she felt the same. The Queen 'in very civil terms' offered him a peerage which was with equal civility declined. Considering that Gladstone was nearly as old as Beaconsfield had been at the time of his death, the Queen hoped that Gladstone would retire from politics, but when the Conservative Government headed by Lord Salisbury lost the confidence of the House after only six months in office, she was fated to have the Grand Old Man back once more. The great leader of the Liberals was, in fact, Prime Minister longer than any other in Queen Victoria's reign—twelve and a half years—though his third ministry lasted for only eight months, falling on the Home Rule for Ireland Bill. When the retiring Prime Minister came to Osborne in July 1886 to surrender the seals of office, he actually found himself for once in agreement with the Queen, when their conversation turned to the question of education. The Queen complained that it was carried too far, and to her surprise the G.O.M. agreed, remarking that 'it ruined the health of the higher classes uselessly, and rendered the working classes unfitted for good servants and labourers'. Emancipation of women was another subject on which both had equally unprogressive views. 'This mad, wicked folly of Women's Rights', railed the Queen, 'with all its attendant horrors, on which her poor feeble sex is bent, forgetting every sense of womanly feeling and propriety.' It was a subject on which the Queen could not contain herself. On learning that Lady Amberley (Bertrand Russell's mother) was one of the leading agitators, she burst out: 'Lady Amberley ought to get a good whipping. God created men and women different—then let them remain each in their own position. Woman would become the most hateful, heartless, and disgusting of human beings were she allowed to unsex herself, and where would be the protection which man was intended to give the weaker sex?' This is an extraordinary opinion to be held by a female sovereign.

No tension existed between the Queen and Lord Salisbury, who in 1886 became Prime Minister once more. Before long, a copy of Salisbury's portrait by Richmond joined Beaconsfield's portrait by von Angeli in the vestibule to the Queen's private apartments at Windsor Castle. In return she gave him an enamelled photograph and a bronze bust of herself.

At the opening of the Indian and Colonial exhibition at the Albert Hall on 4 May 1886 (Plate 258) the Queen expressed her pleasure at the leading part the Prince of Wales had taken in its organization, which she saw as a development of her husband's ideas. To mark the occasion, the second verse of the National Anthem was sung in Sanskrit. It was one of those eccentricities so beloved by the Victorians, for none of those present except Professor Max Müller who had made the translation had the faintest notion of the ancient language of the Hindu priests.

Immensely curious about the peoples of her Empire, the Queen held a reception at Windsor for eighty representatives of the countries participating in the exhibition. Amongst Indians, Cingalese, Kaffirs, pigmy Bushmen, Malays, and Chinese, all in native costume, five Cypriots seemed almost commonplace. Needless to say, they were all photographed afterwards on the terrace for the Queen's albums.

The first tangible sign of the Jubilee spirit which was soon to seize the whole country was a New Year's present to the Queen from the Prince of Wales—a Jubilee inkstand. On the inside of the crown which acted as lid was a portrait of the Queen. 'Very pretty and useful', she commented. Far stranger Jubilee offerings were the patent automatic musical bustle which played the National Anthem whenever the wearer sat down, and a walking-stick made of 10,923 compressed postage stamps, which is preserved at the London Museum.

The nation's rejoicing at Queen Victoria's long reign was demonstrated at numerous public engagements, which filled two and a half months, but above all at the culmination of the celebrations on 20 and 21 June 1887. On the 20th, the actual fiftieth anniversary of her accession, Queen Victoria came up to Buckingham Palace from Windsor and was hostess at a luncheon party (Plate 259) to many visiting royalties from all over Europe, the Middle and Far East. In the evening there was a large family dinner party.

The following day Queen Victoria, her sons and daughters, grandsons and granddaughters, and their wives and husbands, attended a Thanksgiving service in Westminster Abbey. In the procession were thirty-two princes of the Queen's own house. The most impressive figure was by general consent the Crown Prince of Germany in a white cuirassier's uniform and silver helmet with the imperial eagle, looking like Lohengrin. In vain had the royal family tried to persuade Queen Victoria to ride in the State coach wearing the Robes of State and the crown. She insisted on driving in an open landau (Plate 260), wearing a black silk dress and an ordinary bonnet, trimmed with white lace (Plate 261), but her lack of display in no way damped the extraordinary enthusiasm of the vast multitudes which lined the route of the royal progress to and from the Abbey. London had been transformed beyond recognition by triumphal arches, garlands, and inscriptions (Plate 263), and a cloudless sky added to the festival spirit. In a separate procession were the Kings of Belgium, Greece, Denmark and Saxony and the Crown Princes of Austria, Portugal, Sweden and Greece, Prince Ludwig of Bavaria (later King Ludwig III), the Duke of Aosta, the Queen of Hawaii, and princes from India, Persia, Siam and Japan. It was a magnificent spectacle such as London had not seen since the coronation.

In the Abbey, where the Queen had not attended a service for fifty years, the procession re-formed and passed slowly up the nave, crowded with dignitaries of the Empire and people eminent in the arts, literature, and science. The Prince Consort's *Te Deum* and *Chorale* were performed during the service, at the conclusion of which all the members of the royal family filed past the Queen as she sat on Edward I's coronation chair, with the Robes of State draped over it. Here ceremonial pageantry gave way to family affection, and discarding etiquette the Queen embraced them all without reserve.

When the royal family at last got back to Buckingham Palace it was nearly three o'clock, but before sitting down to luncheon the Queen gave Jubilee brooches to all princesses and tie-pins to all princes. After luncheon the Queen watched a march past of the naval guard of honour, and received numerous presents, sumptuous, beautiful, and eccentric, which were later publicly exhibited at St. James's Palace. Quite exhausted, she was pushed in her wheel-chair to her room, where she lay on the sofa opening countless telegrams until it was time to change for the Jubilee banquet into a dress embroidered with roses, thistles and shamrocks in silver, and large diamonds. Apropos the oft-repeated statement that Queen Victoria wore

mourning for Prince Albert for the rest of her life, many illustrations in this book prove that this was not the case. It is true that she usually wore black, but that was the accepted colour for middle-aged and elderly ladies. After the banquet, at which sixty-four royal personages were present, the Queen felt half dead with fatigue and was wheeled back to her room in the hope of seeing something of the illuminations.

The following day was also packed with engagements. After driving to St. James's Palace to visit her eighty-nine-year-old aunt the Duchess of Cambridge, and a big luncheon party at Buckingham Palace, the Queen gave Jubilee medals to the kings and princes, and received more presents, including a Jubilee offering of £75,000 from the Women of the British Empire—most of which was spent on a nurses' institute. Leaving Buckingham Palace for Windsor in the late afternoon, Queen Victoria was acclaimed by enormous crowds on Constitution Hill, and again in Hyde Park, where 26,000 elementary school children were entertained and provided with refreshments at the instigation of the *Daily Telegraph*. Each child received a Jubilee cup with the Queen's portrait on it, and a little girl handed her a bouquet tied up in ribbon on which was embroidered: 'God bless our Queen, not Queen alone, but Mother Queen and Friend.' Then a big balloon with the name 'Victoria' painted on it was released, and one of the children exclaimed, 'Oh, look! There's the Queen going up to heaven!'

Eton and Windsor were one mass of flags and decorations, and at the bottom of Castle Hill yet another loyal address was read, to which the Queen replied. After this, her statue was unveiled (Plate 264) amidst great jubilation, the ringing of bells, and bands playing. This ceremony was not, however, the last of the day's activities, for just when dinner was ending a torchlight procession of Eton boys came into the Castle Quadrangle singing college songs and cheering the Queen. The royal family (Plate 262) went out to the Quadrangle and the Queen thanked the boys. The Round Tower was illuminated with electric light, and so were other parts of the Castle and the town, but the Queen was too tired to go and see it, and retired to her room to write in her diary: 'These two days will ever remain indelibly impressed on my mind, with great gratitude to that all-merciful Providence, who has protected me so long, and to my devoted and loyal people. But how painfully do I miss the dear ones I have lost!'

The following weeks were crowded with official openings, military reviews and other functions. After that the Queen retired to Osborne exhausted, but 'amply repaid for my great exertion and fatigue, by the unbounded enthusiastic loyalty and devotion evinced from all parts of my vast Empire, by high and low, rich and poor, from far and near, which has sunk deep in my heart!'

191 Mourning the Prince Consort. Royal family group with the bust of the Prince Consort.
*L. to R.:* The Princess Royal, Princess Helena, the Queen holding a photograph of the Prince, the
Prince of Wales. Beneath this group photograph the Queen wrote 'Day turned into night.'
*Photograph by Bambridge, Windsor Castle, 28 March 1862.*

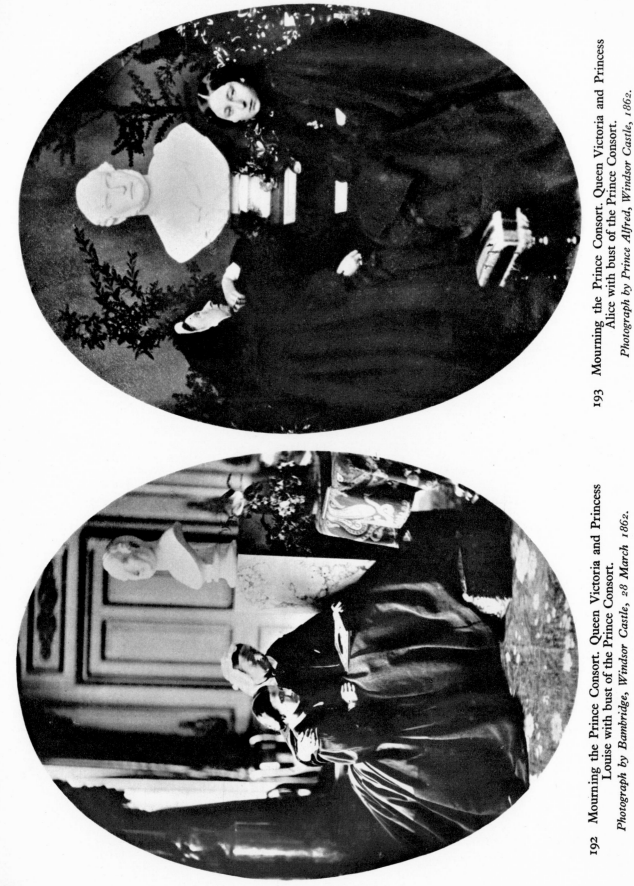

192 Mourning the Prince Consort. Queen Victoria and Princess
Louise with bust of the Prince Consort.
*Photograph by Bambridge, Windsor Castle, 28 March 1862.*

193 Mourning the Prince Consort. Queen Victoria and Princess
Alice with bust of the Prince Consort.
*Photograph by Prince Alfred, Windsor Castle, 1862.*

195  The Widow of Windsor.
*Photograph by Ghémar Frères, Brussels, September 1862.*

194  Queen Victoria with her first grandson Willy (later Kaiser Wilhelm II), 1862.

196 Princess Alice and her husband Prince Louis of Hesse in Garter Robes (worn at the Prince of Wales's wedding).
*Photograph by J. E. Mayall, May 1863.*

197 The marriage of Princess Alice to Prince Louis of Hesse in the dining-room at Osborne House, 1 July 1862. In the left background is Queen Victoria with the Prince of Wales, Prince Alfred and Prince Leopold. In front of them Duke Ernest of Saxe-Coburg who gave the bride away. On the right are the parents and brother of the bridegroom.
*Painting by G. H. Thomas.*

198 Queen Victoria planting a memorial oak to the Prince Consort in Windsor Great Park, 25 November 1862. The Queen was accompanied by Princess Alice (Princess Louis of Hesse) and Princess Alexandra of Denmark (both behind the tree) and her Lady-in-Waiting, the Countess of Caledon (behind the Queen, to the left). The group on the right consists of Prince Louis of Hesse, Prince Leopold, Princess Louise and Count Gleichen (son of Princess Feodora of Hohenlohe-Langenburg).

199   Queen Victoria with Princess Alexandra of Denmark and the Countess of Caledon (Lady-in-Waiting).
*November 1862.*

200 The marriage of the Prince of Wales to Princess Alexandra in St. George's Chapel, Windsor Castle, 10th March 1863. The Queen observed the ceremony from the Royal closet.
*Engraving after a painting by W. P. Frith.*

201 The Prince and Princess of Wales's wedding cake, a masterpiece of Gothic architecture weighing 80 lbs.

202   Wedding photograph of the Prince and Princess of Wales, 10 March 1863.
The Prince is wearing the robes of the Garter.
*Photograph by J. E. Mayall.*

203 *L. to R.:* Princess Helena, Princess Alice and her husband Prince Louis of Hesse, Queen Victoria and Princess Beatrice; behind the bust of the Prince Consort is the Prince of Wales, the Princess of Wales showing a picture of the Prince Consort to Prince Arthur; (*behind*) Princess Louise.
*Photograph by J. E. Mayall, April 1863.*

204 Queen Victoria with her granddaughter, Princess Victoria Mary of Hesse, eldest child of Princess Alice and grandmother of the present Duke of Edinburgh.

*Photograph taken at Balmoral by George Washington Wilson, October 1863.*

205    Queen Victoria with Princess Helena (*left*) and Princess Louis of Hesse (Princess Alice) (*right*),
grouped in front of a painting of the Prince Consort, in the drawing-room at Balmoral.
*Photograph by G. W. Wilson, October 1863.*

206 The building of the Royal Mausoleum at Frogmore. The Mausoleum is a cruciform building in Romanesque style, to which the Prince Consort's body was transferred from St. George's Chapel a year after his death. The interior was not completed until 1868.
*Photograph by Horatio Nelson King, February 1864.*

207 Interior of the Royal Mausoleum, Frogmore. On the granite sarcophagus lies Marochetti's marble effigy of the Prince Consort, beside which was placed in 1901 the effigy of Queen Victoria which had been sculptured by Marochetti at the same time as that of the Prince (No. 330).
*Photograph by H. N. King, February 1864.*

208 Staircase at Osborne House, with statue of the Prince Consort in Roman armour.

209 Detail of Baron Marochetti's effigy of the Prince Consort.

211   Queen Victoria. Both at Balmoral Castle and at Osborne House are spinning wheels used by the Queen.
*Photograph by J. E. Mayall, c. 1863.*

210   Queen Victoria with Princess Louise and John Brown, her favourite attendant.
*Photograph by C. Jabez Hughes, Osborne House, April 1865.*

213   Queen Victoria at the unveiling of a memorial statue of the Prince Consort at Coburg on his birthday, 26 August 1865.

212   Queen Victoria and John Brown.
*Photograph by G. W. Wilson, Balmoral, 1863.*

214   Queen Victoria, aged forty-seven, 1866.

215 Wedding photograph of Princess Helena and Prince Christian of Schleswig-Holstein.
*Photograph by J. E. Mayall, 5 July 1866.*

216 The marriage of Princess Helena and Prince Christian of Schleswig-Holstein in the private chapel at Windsor Castle, 5 July 1866. The Queen, who gave the bride away, and the Prince of Wales, can be seen to the left of the bride.
*Painting by C. Magnusson.*

217 Queen Victoria.
*Photograph by W. & D. Downey, 1866.*

218 Queen Victoria knighting John Morris, the Mayor of Wolverhampton, after her unveiling of a memorial statue of the Prince Consort, 30 November 1866. The Queen was accompanied by Princess Helena and Princess Louise. Behind the Mayor can be seen Lord Derby.

*Composite photograph and drawing by R. W. Thrump.*

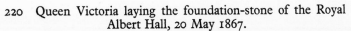

219  Engraving of Queen Victoria, 1866, with her autograph corrections. The engraving was copied from the photograph by Downey (No. 217) and used as frontispiece to the Queen's book, *More Leaves from the Journal of a Life in the Highlands*, 1884.

220  Queen Victoria laying the foundation-stone of the Royal Albert Hall, 20 May 1867.

221 Queen Victoria and Queen Augusta of Prussia (later Empress of Germany), mother-in-law of the Princess Royal.
*Photograph taken at Frogmore, 9 July 1867.*

222 Visit of the Empress Eugénie to Osborne, July 1867. Queen Victoria, the Empress, Prince and Princess Louis of Hesse going for an afternoon drive.

223　Queen Victoria at the age of forty-eight, with her dog Sharp.
*Photograph by W. & D. Downey, Balmoral, 1867.*

224 Queen Victoria going for a drive at Balmoral with Princess Louise and Princess Beatrice. On the box, John Brown and the coachman Bourner.
*Photograph by Whitlock, September 1867.*

225 Interior of the tent erected at Balmoral for the gillies' ball given by Queen Victoria on Princess Christian's birthday, 25 May 1868. *L. to R.:* on the dais: the Duchess of Atholl, Princess Beatrice, Queen Victoria, Princess Louise, the Prince of Wales, Prince Leopold, Prince Arthur.
*Photograph by W. & D. Downey.*

226 Queen Victoria and Prince Christian Victor, eldest child of Prince and Princess Christian. *Photograph by W. & D. Downey, June 1868.*

227 The royal family at Balmoral, 25 May 1868. *L. to R.:* Prince Leopold, Queen Victoria, Princess Beatrice, Prince Arthur, Princess Louise, the Prince of Wales. On the steps, the Duchess of Atholl. *Photograph by W. & D. Downey.*

229 Queen Victoria with the children of the Prince and Princess of Wales. *L. to R.*: Prince Albert Victor, Queen Victoria, Prince George (later King George V), Princess Victoria, Princess Maud (later Queen of Norway). *Photograph by W. & D. Downey, November 1871.*

228 The royal family at Osborne House. *L. to R.*: Princess Beatrice, Prince Leopold, in front of him Prince Albert Victor (elder son of the Prince of Wales), behind him to the right his brother Prince George, Queen Victoria, behind her Princess Louise, the Princess of Wales with her daughter Princess Louise. *Photograph by C. Jabez Hughes, April 1870.*

231 Queen Victoria in the dress she wore at the National Thanksgiving Service at St. Paul's Cathedral for the recovery of the Prince of Wales, 27 February 1872.
*Photograph by W. & D. Downey.*

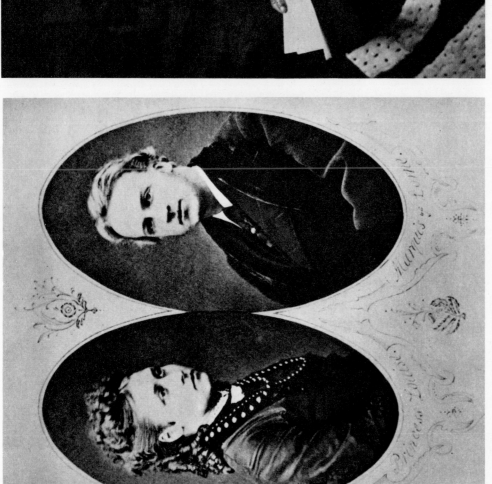

230 Engagement photograph of Princess Louise and the Marquis of Lorne (later Duke of Argyll) on 24 October 1870. The marriage took place on 21 March 1871.

232  Visit of the Shah of Persia to Windsor Castle, 20 June 1873. *L. to R.:* Prince Leopold, Prince Arthur, Prince Christian, the Shah, Queen Victoria, Princess Christian, Princess Louise, Princess Beatrice.
*Watercolour by N. Chevalier.*

233  The marriage of Prince Alfred, Duke of Edinburgh, and the Grand Duchess Marie of Russia, daughter of Czar Alexander II, in the chapel of the Winter Palace, St. Petersburg, 23 January 1874. The Greek Orthodox service was preceded by an Anglican service performed by Dean Stanley in the Salle d'Alexandre in the Winter Palace on 11 January.

234 The Duchess of Edinburgh wearing a Russian Uhlan uniform. 1874.

235 Arrival of Queen Victoria with the Duke and Duchess of Edinburgh at Buckingham Palace on 12 March 1874.
*Watercolour by John O'Connor.*

236 Queen Victoria as Empress of India on an ivory throne, presented by the Rajah of Travancore, and shown at the Great Exhibition.
*Photograph by W. & D. Downey, 1876.*

237 Proclamation of Queen Victoria as Empress of India at Delhi by the Viceroy, Lord Lytton, 1 January 1877.
*Photograph by Bourne & Shepherd, Calcutta.*

238  Queen Victoria and Disraeli at the railway station, High Wycombe,
after her visit to Hughenden Manor on 15 December 1877.
*Woodcut by J. Durand.*

240 The royal family at Balmoral, September 1878.
*L. to R.*: Princess Louise, Prince Leopold, Queen
Victoria, the Marquis of Lorne, Princess Beatrice.
*Photograph by G. W. Wilson.*

239 Queen Victoria with Prince Arthur, Duke of Connaught,
Princess Beatrice, and Spot.
*Photograph by G. W. Wilson, Balmoral, October 1876.*

192

242 Queen Victoria with the children of Princess Alice, Grand Duchess of Hesse, who had died two months earlier. *L. to R.*: Princesses Irene, Elizabeth, the Queen, Ernest, Hereditary Grand Duke of Hesse, Princess Victoria Mary, in front Princess Alix (later the Czarina). *Photograph by W. & D. Downey, February 1879.*

241 Queen Victoria and Princess Beatrice. An indoor pose, in spite of the umbrella. *Photograph by A. J. Melhuish, c. 1879.*

244 The Duchess of Connaught (Princess Louise Margaret of Prussia) on her wedding day, 13 March 1879.

243 The wedding cake of the Duke (Prince Arthur) and Duchess of Connaught, 13 March 1879.

246 Menu card of the State Banquet in St. George's Hall, Windsor Castle, on the occasion of the marriage of the Duke of Albany to Princess Helena of Waldeck-Pyrmont, 27 April 1882.

245 Prince Leopold, Duke of Albany, and his fiancée Princess Helena of Waldeck-Pyrmont.
*Photograph by J. Thomson, February 1882.*

247 'Cabinet Making.' Head carpenter (Gladstone): 'I hope your Majesty likes the new Cabinet. It's been hard work—such a quantity of material!' The Queen: 'I see most of it is well seasoned—let us hope the new wood will stand well!'.
*Cartoon in* Punch, *8 May 1880.*

248 Queen Victoria at a review of 52,000 volunteers in Windsor Great Park, 9 July 1881. In the carriage with the Queen is the Princess of Wales. Standing beside it, *L. to R.*: the Duke of Connaught, the Prince of Wales, Prince George (later King George V).

249 Queen Victoria holding Princess Margaret of
Connaught (later Crown Princess of Sweden).
*Photograph by Alexander Bassano, April 1882.*

250 A royal group at Balmoral, 21 October 1882. *L. to R.:* the Grand Duke of Hesse (Prince Louis),
Princess Beatrice, Queen Victoria, Princess Alix of Hesse, the Hereditary Grand Duke of Hesse, the
Duchess of Connaught and her daughter Princess Margaret. The dogs Wat, Gay Girl and Spot.

251 Queen Victoria investing the Duke of Connaught with the Order of the Bath, 24 November 1882. *Watercolour by William Simpson.*

252 Visit of the Crown Princess of Germany to Balmoral, September 1884. *L. to R.:* the Duchess of Edinburgh and (in front) her daughters the Princesses Marie (later Queen of Roumania), Victoria Melita and Alexandra, Queen Victoria, Princess Victoria of Prussia, her mother the Crown Princess of Germany (the Princess Royal), Princess Beatrice.
*Photograph by Watson.*

253   Queen Victoria at the age of sixty-six.
*Photograph by Alexander Bassano, 1885.*

255　Wedding group of Princess Beatrice and Prince Henry of Battenberg, Osborne House, 23 July 1885. The bridesmaids were all nieces of the bride.

*L. to R. front row*: the Princesses Victoria Melita, Marie and Alexandra of Edinburgh, Princess Beatrice, Prince Henry of Battenberg. *Middle row*: the Princesses Maud of Wales, Alix of Hesse, Marie-Louise and Victoria of Schleswig-Holstein. *Back row*: Prince Alexander of Battenberg (then Prince of Bulgaria), the Princesses Louise of Wales, Irene of Hesse, Victoria of Wales, Prince Francis Joseph of Battenberg (brother of Prince Henry).

*Photograph by G. Mullins.*

254　Menu card of the banquet on the occasion of Princess Beatrice's marriage to Prince Henry of Battenberg, Osborne, 23 July 1885.

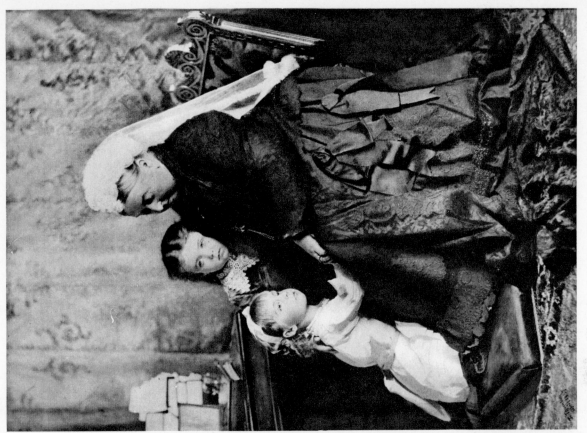

257  Queen Victoria with two of her grandchildren, Princess Alice of
Albany (*left*) and Princess Margaret of Connaught.
*Photograph by J. Thomson, Windsor Castle, April 1887.*

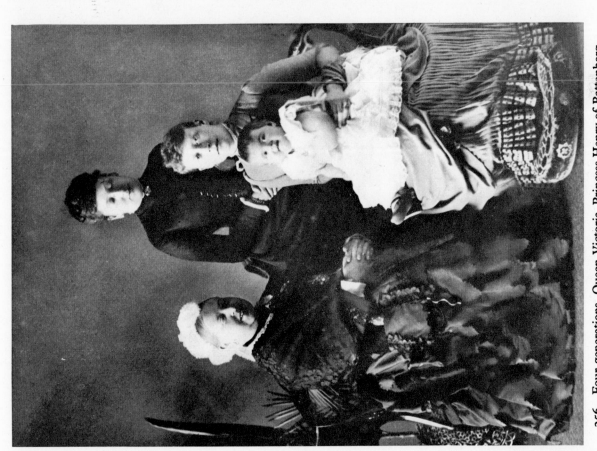

256  Four generations. Queen Victoria, Princess Henry of Battenberg,
Princess Louis of Battenberg (Victoria of Hesse) and her daughter
Princess Alice (mother of the present Duke of Edinburgh). One of the
few pictures of the Queen smiling.
*Photograph by G. Mullins, April 1886.*

258 Queen Victoria opening the Indian & Colonial Exhibition in the Albert Hall, 4 May 1886. *Watercolour by R. T. Pritchett.*

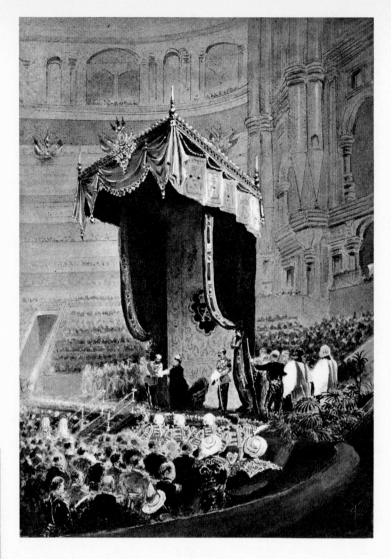

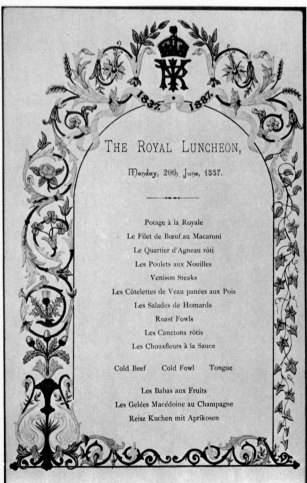

THE ROYAL LUNCHEON,

Monday, 20th June, 1887.

Potage à la Royale

Le Filet de Bœuf au Macaroni

Le Quartier d'Agneau rôti

Les Poulets aux Nouilles

Venison Steaks

Les Côtelettes de Veau panées aux Pois

Les Salades de Homards

Roast Fowls

Les Canetons rôtis

Les Chouxfleurs à la Sauce

Cold Beef    Cold Fowl    Tongue

Les Babas aux Fruits

Les Gelées Macédoine au Champagne

Reisz Kuchen mit Aprikosen

259 Menu of Queen Victoria's Jubilee luncheon at Buckingham Palace, 20 June 1887.

260 Queen Victoria's Jubilee procession, 21 June 1887. The royal carriage passing the Treasury on the return journey from the Thanksgiving Service in Westminster Abbey. The Queen is beaming with delight. With her in the carriage are the Crown Princess of Germany and the Princess of Wales.

*Photograph by Yorke & Co.*

261 Queen Victoria in the dress she wore for the Jubilee procession.
*Photograph taken at Osborne House by Gustave Mullins, August 1887.*

262 Queen Victoria with her children, grandchildren, their wives and husbands, at Windsor Castle on 22 June 1887. Facing the Queen is the widowed Duchess of Albany with her daughter Princess Alice; near the sofa on the right sit the Crown Princess of Germany and Princess Christian; standing, in a white uniform, the Crown Prince of Germany; on the extreme right Princess Louis of Battenberg (daughter of Princess Alice) with her child Princess Alice (grandmother and mother, respectively, of the present Duke of Edinburgh). In the centre stands the Prince of Wales, facing him the Duke of Connaught and the Princess of Wales. By the window are Prince George of Wales (later King George V) and Prince William of Germany (later the Kaiser).
*Painting by Lauritz Tuxen.*

263   Street decorations for Queen Victoria's Jubilee procession—Piccadilly Circus, facing Lower Regent Street.
*Photograph by Yorke & Co., June 1887.*

264 Queen Victoria at the unveiling of her Jubilee statue by Sir Edgar Boehm at Windsor, 22 June 1887.
*Watercolour by E. T. Pritchett.*

265 Royal family group at Balmoral, September 1887. *L. to R.:* Prince Albert Victor of Wales, Princess Alix of Hesse (later the Czarina), Queen Victoria, Princess Henry of Battenberg, Princess Irene of Hesse, and Bosco, the dog of Prince Henry of Battenberg.
*Photograph by Watson.*

266 'Homage to Queen Victoria.' Ladies of the Household in a *tableau vivant* arranged by Prince and Princess Henry of Battenberg at Osborne House, January 1888.
*Photograph by Hughes and Mullins.*

267 Queen Victoria (wearing the small Imperial crown and her wedding veil and lace flounce) with the Prince and Princess of Wales.
*Photograph by Alexander Bassano, 1887.*

266

267

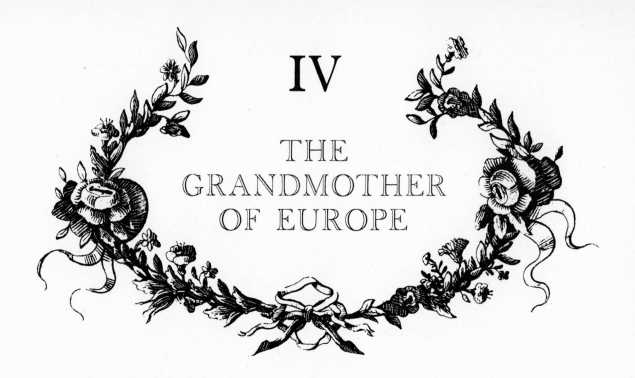

# IV

# THE GRANDMOTHER OF EUROPE

A DEEP shadow was cast upon the last months of the brilliant and eventful Jubilee year, and forebodings of the sorrow 1888 might bring weighed heavily on Queen Victoria. Forewarned since May that a growth in the throat of the Crown Prince of Germany might be malignant, she learned on 12 November of the diagnosis of cancer which would lead to death at an early date. Despite the doctor's report, the Queen with characteristic optimism tried to delude herself into thinking that they might be wrong. Although Sir Morel Mackenzie, the leading throat specialist in Europe, had signed the report, he strengthened the Queen in this belief, and contrary to the opinion of the German surgeons, was against taking the risk of the dangerous operation which might have saved the patient's life. When tracheotomy became imperative three months later it gave relief, but the cancerous growth which the German surgeons had wanted to remove in the first place remained. Yet the Queen still did not heed the warnings of the German specialists but clung to the continued hopeful reports of Mackenzie, whose extraordinary behaviour in this matter is very reminiscent of that of Sir James Clark during the Prince Consort's last illness.

The death on 9 March 1888 of the ninety-year-old Emperor Wilhelm I, who had been for many years Bismarck's feeble tool, brought a dying man to the throne. The period of a liberal reign in a Germany linked to Britain by the closest ties of kinship and friendship was doomed to be of short duration. The great moment to which the new Emperor Frederick III, his wife, and Queen Victoria had been looking forward during the last thirty years had come too late. The twenty-nine-year-old Crown Prince, who treated his parents with contempt, was only waiting to step into his father's position to revert to the reactionary, dictatorial and militaristic policy of Bismarck, the enemy of the liberal-minded Emperor, and still more so of the Empress. She, who had irritated everyone by her constant praise of the British way of life, had always remained an outsider in Germany, and there were many intrigues against her. The disputes of the doctors had led to newspaper attacks on the Crown Princess who, it was said, in her Anglophilia had disregarded German medical opinion.

Determined to see her beloved son-in-law once more, Queen Victoria made a detour to Berlin on her homeward journey from Florence, where she had spent a month's holiday in the spring. After stopping at Innsbruck to meet the Emperor Franz Joseph, who had specially travelled from Vienna, the Queen, with Prince and Princess Henry of Battenberg, arrived at Berlin on 24 April, and stayed with her daughter and son-in-law at Charlottenburg Palace. 'Fritz was lying in bed, his dear face unaltered, and he raised up both hands with pleasure at seeing me and gave me a nose-gay. . . . Vicky is very sad, and cried a good deal, poor dear. Besides her cruel anxiety about dear Fritz, she has so many worries and unpleasant-nesses.'

A serious quarrel was dividing the Imperial family at that time. The second daughter, Princess Victoria, had for five years been secretly engaged to Prince Alexander of Battenberg—Princess Beatrice's brother-in-law—but the proposed marriage was denounced by Bismarck as a sinister plot of Queen Victoria's to embroil Germany with Russia. As ruler of Bulgaria, following the Congress of Berlin, Prince Alexander had incurred the distrust of Czar Alexander III, was kidnapped by Russian officers and forced to abdicate at pistol-point in 1886. The Empress considered only her daughter's happiness; Crown Prince William, soon to be head of the family, violently opposed the union, for snobbish as well as for political reasons. Queen Victoria viewed the engagement with sympathy but wanted to avoid any conflict of views which would harm her and the Empress's relations with the future Kaiser. Fearing that the Queen, who had a reputation for match-making amongst relations, would use all the influence of her strong personality and family ties in favour of the alliance, Bismarck sought an audience with her. The man of blood and iron was 'unmis-takably nervous and ill at ease' when he arrived, but he emerged 'deeply gratified' for he found that he had been mistaken. The Queen 'was agreeably surprised to find him so amiable and gentle'. In July, Prince Alexander was obliged to break off the engagement. The following year he married an opera singer and retired into private life as Count Hartenau. The disappointed princess in 1890 made

an unhappy marriage with Prince Adolf of Schaumburg-Lippe.

On 26 April 1888 Queen Victoria's sad visit came to an end. Six weeks later she received a telegram at Balmoral announcing that all was over.

I cannot, cannot realise the dreadful truth—the awful misfortune! It is too, too dreadful! My poor dear Vicky, God help her! . . . Feel very miserable and upset. None of my own sons could be a greater loss. He was so good, so wise, and so fond of me! . . . The misfortune is awful. My poor child's whole future gone, ruined, which they had prepared them-selves for for nearly thirty years!

Frederick III had reigned for only ninety-nine days. The new Emperor—'the Kaiser' of the Great War—was, with all his faults, genuinely devoted to his grandmother, and what is more, stood in awe of her. However angry, the Queen always handled the Kaiser with tact, writing to him in the calmest, most persuasive vein, quite contrary to her usual emphatic style. Hoping to smooth out the unhappy relations with his mother, she now begged him 'to bear with poor Mama if she is sometimes irritated and excited. She does not mean it so; think what months of agony and suspense and watching with broken and sleepless nights she has gone through, and *don't mind it*. I am so anxious that all should go smoothly, that I write thus openly in the interests of both.' At the same time she telegraphed to Lord Salisbury, the Prime Minister, 'Trust that we shall be *very cool*, though civil, in our communications with my grandson and Prince Bismarck, who are bent on a return to the oldest times of government.' Speaking soon afterwards to the British Ambassador in Berlin, the Kaiser blamed the estrangement from his mother on 'that good stubborn English blood which will not give way in both our veins. The consequence is that, if we do not happen to agree, the situation becomes difficult.'

Kaiser Wilhelm II was so conceited and hot-headed that he upset not only his mother and grandmother but also his uncle, the Prince of Wales. He refused to meet him in Vienna that autumn although their visits to the Emperor Franz Joseph coincided, and the Prince of Wales had to avail himself of the hospitality of the King and Queen of

Roumania during his nephew's stay in Vienna. The cause of the Kaiser's annoyance is ascribed to the Prince of Wales's roundabout and unwise enquiry whether the late Emperor had intended to restore to France the provinces of Alsace and Lorraine, and to Denmark, Schleswig-Holstein. The Kaiser also resented being treated by his uncle as a nephew, instead of as the Emperor by the heir apparent of a kingdom. Queen Victoria was furious when she heard of this, and complained to Lord Salisbury (15 October 1888) 'This is really too *vulgar* and too absurd almost *to be believed* . . . to pretend that he is to be treated *in private* as well as in public as "His Imperial Majesty" is *perfect madness*! . . . *If he has such notions, he had better never come here.* The Queen will not swallow this affront.'

In November the widowed Empress Frederick (Plate 269) came on a three months' visit to Britain with her daughters. Weeping behind her thick crêpe veil, the Empress's story of persecution by Bismarck and by her own son made the Queen's blood boil. Mindful of the Kaiser's touchiness, she made her daughter take precedence over herself wherever they went.

The attempts of Prince Christian, uncle of the Kaiserin, at mediation between the Kaiser and the Prince of Wales in the hope of extracting an apology, were breezily dismissed by the Kaiser. Some months later, however, in view of the Kaiser's intended visit to England in the summer of '89—a visit which was by no means welcome—he disclaimed the Vienna episode as a misunderstanding—an excuse which did not bear examination but was nevertheless accepted as the Kaiser was making the round of foreign Courts. The indecent haste with which he set out for St. Petersburg a month after his father's funeral had also called forth Queen Victoria's disapproval.

On her seventieth birthday Queen Victoria saw for the first time the old ceremony of the Trooping of the Colour, in the Quadrangle at Windsor Castle. She had been awakened first thing in the morning by Princess Beatrice's little son 'Drino' (Alexander) and daughter Victoria Eugenia, called Ena (later the Queen of Spain), bringing flowers for 'Gangan'. A third child, Leopold, had been born three days earlier, much to the disgust of the others, who protested, 'Won't kiss that.'

Because of the recent upset with the Kaiser, Queen Victoria did everything possible to put him in a good humour before his visit to England. The rank of a British admiral, which she bestowed on him, gratified his vanity and he declared with delight that wearing the same uniform as Nelson made him 'quite giddy'. The Kaiser arrived at Cowes on 2 August in his large steam yacht the *Hohenzollern*, escorted by a squadron of twelve warships. He was amiable, seemed genuinely delighted with his visit, and showed devotion to his grandmother. Nevertheless, when he departed on 8 August, leaving as parting gift his bust in a helmet with the Imperial eagle, Queen Victoria breathed a sigh of relief: 'Thank God! All went off well.' On the surface this was the case, but the Prince of Wales, who ignored his previous snubbing and constantly escorted the Kaiser to reviews and the Cowes Regatta, was immensely irritated by his nephew's arrogant and tactless behaviour. From now on until 1895 the Kaiser made a visit to England a regular annual habit, but the superficial cordiality wore thinner on each occasion on account of his objectionable behaviour: interference, proffering of unwanted advice and criticism, and extreme rudeness both to Lord Salisbury and to his uncle, to whom he referred as 'the old peacock'. But with the Queen, the Kaiser was always the devoted grandson. His friend Fürst Philipp zu Eulenburg-Hertefeld was astonished at the complete change in his behaviour. The Kaiser, usually so jolly and talkative at dinner parties, seemed to hesitate to address the Queen, and his answers to her remarks showed almost childlike devotion.

The beginning of 1892 brought Queen Victoria deep grief. On 14 January Prince Albert Victor, Duke of Clarence, the elder son of the Prince of Wales, died at the age of twenty-eight of influenza which had developed into pneumonia. Only the previous month he had become engaged to Princess May (Mary), daughter of the Queen's first cousin, the Duchess of Teck (Princess Mary of Cambridge) and their wedding had been fixed for February. It was a terrible blow for his parents, fiancée and grandmother to see this promising young life cut short. The Duke of Clarence had been devoted to Queen Victoria, for whom his loss was 'more sad and tragical than any but one that had befallen her'. Before she had time to recover from this blow came the news of the death of her son-in-law the Grand Duke of Hesse on 13 March.

It was a bad year for the Queen. Following these two griefs came a great annoyance. In August Lord Salisbury resigned, a majority pledged to support Gladstone's Irish Home Rule Bill having been returned to Parliament. The prospect of having 'that dangerous old fanatic thrown down her throat' filled the Queen with horror. Putting the government of the country into 'the shaking hand of an old, wild, and incomprehensible man of 82½' she considered dangerous. Gladstone, equally uncomplimentary about the Queen's infirmities, thought her intellect sluggish and her judgment impaired.

By the following spring Queen Victoria's zest for life had reasserted itself, and on her seventy-fourth birthday she expressed the wish that it were the sixty-fourth instead.

Prince George of Wales succeeded to the Duke of Clarence's position as next heir to the crown after his father, and became engaged to his fiancée. The engaged couple made their first public appearance together at the opening of the Imperial Institute by Queen Victoria on 10 May 1893. It was the most brilliant State ceremony since the Jubilee. Indian and Colonial troops rode in the procession escorting the Queen to the building. On her declaring the Institute open (Plate 282) the Prince of Wales turned a golden key in the door of a miniature model of the Institute, which, by an electric contact caused the bells in the tower to peal.

The marriage of the Duke of York (as Prince George had been created on his grandmother's seventy-fourth birthday) took place in the Chapel Royal at St. James's Palace on 6 July 1893 (Plate 279) in the presence of Queen Victoria (wearing her wedding lace and veil) and other members of the royal family, the King and Queen of Denmark (grandparents of the bridegroom), the Czarevitch, Prince and Princess Henry of Prussia, the Crown Prince of Belgium, the new Grand Duke of Hesse, and several of the princes of India. During the wedding festivities some amusing mistakes were caused by the striking likeness between the bridegroom and his cousin the Czarevitch.

Gladstone's fourth and final Ministry lasted for only eighteen months. Unable to agree to accept increased naval estimates, the Grand Old Man offered the Queen his resignation on 3 March 1894, giving as reason, increasing deafness and failing sight. Staying at Windsor Castle for his last Council, he came to realize at last the extent of the Queen's dislike. There was no pretence of regret for his retirement from the premiership and from political life altogether, though the Queen did bring herself to show some sympathy for its cause. Yet not one word of gratitude for Gladstone's long services to the country passed her lips, only cool approval of his wish 'to be relieved at his age of these arduous duties', coupled with the hope that he would be able to enjoy peace and quiet with his devoted wife, and that his sight might improve. She did not offer him a peerage again, knowing that he would not accept it. But Gladstone had expected a more valuable parting gift than her photograph, 'but there was nothing of the kind, for I cannot reckon as anything, what appeared to be a twopenny-halfpenny scrap, photographic or other, sent during the forenoon of our departure by the hand of a footman'.

Mrs. Gladstone, weeping, assured the Queen of her husband's devotion, and begged to be allowed to tell him that the Queen believed it. To this she agreed, adding (in her journal) 'though at times his actions have made it difficult to believe', and she kissed Mrs. Gladstone farewell. Animosity blinded Queen Victoria to Gladstone's greatness, and lack of hypocrisy made her cruel. They met once more for the last time three years later at Cannes, at the instigation of Princess Louise. Gladstone found the Queen 'decidedly kind'; she actually shook hands with him, 'a thing which had never happened with me during all my life'. When Gladstone died the following year, the Queen's first reaction was, 'I never liked him: how can I say I am sorry?' But she did like Mrs. Gladstone, and managed to write kindly of her husband's devotion, and distinction as a statesman, without in any way committing herself as to his political services, which she considered served his party more than the country.

Lord Rosebery, who had succeeded Gladstone, headed the Government until June 1895 when

Lord Salisbury resumed power for the third time, staying in office during the remaining years of Queen Victoria's reign.

On the death of Duke Ernest of Saxe-Coburg in August 1893, his nephew Prince Alfred, Duke of Edinburgh, succeeded to the Duchy. On 19 April of the following year his second daughter, Princess Victoria Melita, married her first cousin the Grand Duke of Hesse, son of Princess Alice and the Grand Duke Louis who had died in 1892. Queen Victoria, who had planned the inter-marriage of her grand-children, visited Coburg for the wedding on her way back from her third holiday in Florence, and was the focal point of a large gathering of European royalties (Plates 283, 284). The day after the wedding the Queen gave her approval to the engagement of another granddaughter, Princess Alix of Hesse, to the Czarevitch (son of the Princess of Wales's sister Dagmar and Czar Alexander III), who succeeded his father as Nicholas II less than a month before his marriage on 26 November 1894. This was the most imposing match of any of Queen Victoria's children or grandchildren, apart from that of her eldest daughter, the Empress Frederick.

Unfortunately the marriage of Princess Victoria Melita and the Grand Duke of Hesse turned out unhappy, and, learning of the domestic discord, Queen Victoria vowed with tears, 'I will never try and marry anyone again.' For some years the couple stayed together through awe of 'Grandmama Queen', but shortly after her death they were divorced on grounds of 'natural antipathy', and the Grand Duchess married another cousin, the Grand Duke Cyril of Russia, whom she had been fond of since childhood.

On 23 June 1894 the birth of a son to the Duke and Duchess of York added an heir in the fourth generation in direct succession (King Edward VIII). Queen Victoria was present at the christening three weeks later at White Lodge, Richmond, the residence of the Duke and Duchess of York, and herself handed to the Archbishop the baby wearing the Honiton lace robe made for the Princess Royal's christening and worn by all the Queen's children and English grandchildren. After tea, 'we were photographed, I, holding the baby on my lap,

Bertie and George standing behind me, thus making the four generations' (Plate 286).

The Duke and Duchess of York's second son (King George VI) was born on the worst possible day—the anniversary of the Prince Consort's death (14 December 1895). His father affirmed that Queen Victoria regarded his arrival on that day of mourning as 'a personal affront'.

A week earlier, Prince Henry of Battenberg left with an expeditionary force for Ashanti, where the natives were in revolt against British rule. Prince Henry set his heart on this opportunity to serve his adopted country, for though on most happy terms with his wife and mother-in-law, he had often smarted under his enforced inactivity as a hanger-on at Court and arranger of amateur theatricals. However, his good intentions were ill-fated, for almost immediately after arrival in West Africa he was attacked by fever and sent home. His death during the voyage on 20 January 1896 quite stunned Princess Beatrice and Queen Victoria, who lamented: 'I have lost a dearly beloved and helpful son, whose presence was like a bright sunbeam in my home.' Soon after the military funeral on 5 February in Whippingham Church, where Princess Beatrice had been married ten and a half years before, she went with her three children to Cimiez. The Queen joined them in March, but a heavy cloud hung over the house, and the familiar southern landscape had lost its charm compared with previous visits.

In addition to this personal grief, tension between Britain and Germany was causing the Queen great anxiety. The unofficial raid of Dr. Jameson, administrator of the British South Africa Company, into the Transvaal and his surrender to the Boers on New Year's Day 1896 had prompted the Kaiser, with his notorious flare for mischief-making, to telegraph his congratulations to President Kruger on restoring order against the 'armed bands' and 'disturbers of the peace . . . safeguarding the independence of the country against attacks from outside'. The intended dispatch of German colonial troops from German East Africa to assist President Kruger was only prevented by the refusal of the Portuguese Government to allow them transit through Mozambique. War would inevitably have resulted from armed intervention. As it was, the Kaiser's provocative telegram had already roused the British nation to fury, and to settle the incident quickly and peacefully Queen Victoria thought it wiser to use her personal influence with her grandson rather than run the risk of raising the pitch of national feelings by recriminatory Foreign Office dispatches. Her calm and tactful letter explaining that the Jameson Raid was made without the knowledge of the British Government completely deflated 'impetuous and conceited' Willi, who made various feeble excuses which Lord Salisbury advised the Queen to accept at their face value. This incident, and other interferences, made further visits of the Kaiser to England impossible until 1899. To improve relations between the two countries, Sir Theodore Martin on behalf of the Queen in January 1898 requested the editors of the national Press to modify their tone towards the Kaiser and the German people.

On 22 July 1896 Princess Maud, youngest child of the Prince of Wales, married her cousin Prince Charles of Denmark (later King Haakon of Norway) and Queen Victoria attended their wedding in the chapel at Buckingham Palace. Indeed, the recurring cycle of births, weddings, deaths and family gatherings are of necessity the chief events in the closing years of the private life of the Grandmother of Europe.

On 23 September 1896 Queen Victoria had ruled longer, by one day, than any other British sovereign, the previous longest reign having been that of her grandfather George III. The day before, 'Nicky and Alicky', the new Czar and Czarina, arrived at Balmoral with their baby daughter the Grand Duchess Olga (Plate 293). Lord Salisbury joined the Queen at Balmoral for informal talks with the Czar, after taking the necessary precaution of specifying that on doctor's orders the temperature of his room must not be less than 60°F. The Czar entirely agreed with the Queen and her Prime Minister on the importance of friendly relations between Russia and Britain, the most powerful empires, and disclaimed any unfriendly intentions against India. He would not commit himself, however, on several other important matters on which he was sounded, such as General Kitchener's expedition for the

reconquest of the Sudan—a move which was looked upon with suspicion by Russia and France—and the British occupation of Egypt. Though the Czar was far more amiable than the Kaiser, the Queen and Lord Salisbury felt that they had achieved little.

The Czar's and Czarina's visit was made the occasion for a big family gathering. With the Duke and Duchess of York and their children, who came over to Balmoral from nearby Glen Muick, there were four generations of the royal family. 'If only dear Liko were still with us', sighed the Queen. Every day after luncheon the Duke of York's two-year-old son Prince Edward, called David (the present Duke of Windsor) used to try to pull his great-grandmother up out of her chair, saying 'Get up, Gangan', and failing, ordered her Indian attendant: 'Man, pull it', which made everybody laugh very much.

During the 'nineties Hafiz Abdul Karim, one of the Indian attendants employed by Queen Victoria since the Jubilee, went some way towards filling the place of John Brown. Originally a clerk, Karim soon became dissatisfied with waiting at table, and expressed his wish to return home. The Queen then promoted him to 'Munshi' (teacher, or clerk), and photographs showing him holding dishes were destroyed. The Munshi taught the Queen Hindustani, besides being her personal attendant (Plates 287, 309). He also took part in amateur theatricals (see page 160) and, being intelligent and educated, he was occasionally shown by the Queen confidential documents concerning India, and it is possible that the Munshi's views on the British in India are incorporated in Queen Victoria's letter of 29 May 1898 to Lord Salisbury regarding the future Viceroy, Lord Curzon.

The future Viceroy must really shake himself more and more free from his red-tapist, narrow-minded Council and entourage. He must be more independent, must *hear for himself* what the *feelings* of the Natives really are, and do what he thinks right, and not be guided by the *snobbish* and vulgar overbearing and offensive behaviour of many of our Civil and Political Agents, if we are to go on peacefully and happily in India, and to be liked and beloved by high and low, as well as respected as we ought to be, and not trying to trample on the people and continually reminding them and make them feel that they are a conquered people. They must of course *feel* that we are masters, but it should be done kindly and not offensively, which alas! is so often the case.

The Munshi's influence annoyed the Queen's Household, and the Secretary of State for India objected to his being shown State papers. The Queen gave way on this point, but at the same time showed her confidence in the Munshi by conferring on him the nominal title of 'Indian Secretary'.

In 1897 Queen Victoria had a long spring holiday at Cimiez near Nice to set her up for the exertions of her sixty years' Jubilee celebrations. On these Riviera holidays she was always accompanied by Princess Beatrice; sometimes she was also joined by Princess Christian and other of her children, when the royal family's suites and servants might amount to as many as a hundred people.

The sixtieth anniversary of Queen Victoria's accession fell on a Sunday. The Queen was at Windsor, and during the service which she attended at St. George's Chapel with her family (Plate 295) the Prince Consort's *Te Deum* was rendered. The following day she came up to London for the Jubilee procession on 22 June. Queen Victoria's appearance in the capital was a rare event, and her drive from Paddington Station to Buckingham Palace became a triumphal entry. The people gave their Queen a heartfelt and rousing welcome as she drove in hot sunshine through the decorated streets. 'Our hearts thy Throne' read the inscription on a triumphal arch near Paddington, and this was the Jubilee mood throughout the next few days. At Buckingham Palace crowds of relations awaited the royal matriarch with presents. In the afternoon she received foreign princes, ambassadors and envoys until she felt quite exhausted.

After a hot and restless night, disturbed by the noise of the crowds in the parks, Queen Victoria watched part of the procession passing Buckingham Palace while she breakfasted. Before leaving the Palace at a quarter past eleven, she pressed an electric button, which cabled her message to all parts of the Empire: 'From my heart I thank my beloved people. May God bless them!'

The main difference between this and the pre-vious Jubilee lay in the fact that this Diamond Jubilee was a festival of Empire, to which no European crowned heads were invited, much to the chagrin of the Kaiser. Instead, fifteen Colonial premiers had assembled in London, and during the festivities the first Imperial Conference was held under the presidency of the Colonial Secretary, Joseph Chamberlain.

Each Colony had sent a detachment of troops (Plate 299), so that the Colonial procession was of immense length and variety, a veritable living anthropological museum. The royal procession proper was a dazzling kaleidoscope of colour and gold, and finally, with the Prince of Wales and the old Duke of Cambridge riding on either side, came an open landau (Plate 298) drawn by eight cream-coloured horses. In it was a little old lady dressed in black relieved with a touch of white, and silver embroidery, sitting very still and looking as though she were trying not to cry. Indeed, at times tears were seen to roll down her cheeks as the crowds spontaneously broke into 'God save the Queen'. Opposite her sat the Princess of Wales and Princess Christian. Her eldest daughter could not drive with her, for the Queen must sit alone to be seen, and etiquette would not permit an Empress to drive with her back to the horses.

It was the proverbial 'Queen's weather' again, and the crowds cheered the Queen with the utmost enthusiasm along the entire six-mile route. At St. Paul's Cathedral an open-air Thanksgiving service (Plate 300) formed the climax of the procession. Crippling rheumatism prevented the Queen from getting out of her carriage, and a plan to pull the carriage into the Cathedral had been abandoned because she would not hear of removing the obstructing statue of Queen Anne outside St. Paul's, remarking: 'They will want to remove *my* statues next.' On the steps of the west front were gathered the two Archbishops in purple coronation copes, the Bishop of London, the Dean and Chapter of St. Paul's and of Westminster Abbey, other Church dignitaries, the Prime Minister and members of the Government, and a choir 500 strong. After the service the Archbishop of Canterbury called for 'Three cheers for the Queen', and the procession of troops and carriages continued to the Mansion

House and thence over London Bridge (Plate 299) and through the poor districts on the south side of the Thames back to Buckingham Palace.

In the evening there was a large dinner party at the Palace. On the Queen's table stood an 8½-foot-high trophy of orchids in the form of a crown, composed of between 50,000 and 60,000 blooms from all over the Empire. The day's events had been exhausting for the aged Queen, but after retiring at eleven she still dictated her diary entry, even to the details of the dresses she wore on that 'never-to-be-forgotten day'. 'No one ever, I believe, has met with such an ovation.... The crowds were quite indescribable, and their enthusiasm truly marvellous and deeply touching. The cheering was quite deafening and every face seemed to be filled with real joy. I was much moved and gratified.'

The next afternoon, 'feeling dreadfully hot and sleepy', the Queen received addresses from both Houses of Parliament and from county councils and mayors in the ballroom at Buckingham Palace. It was all rather much at seventy-eight, and the journey back to Windsor in the heat of the late afternoon was an ordeal, with addresses all the way (Plate 304). Nevertheless, five days later the Queen returned to Buckingham Palace to hold a garden party at which, in addition to royalty and society, there was a unique attendance of leading actors and actresses, musicians and artists. The Queen drove round the garden in her victoria, speaking to as many of her guests as possible. Then, putting on a white apron in the homeliest fashion to protect her dress, she had tea and strawberries in a marquee.

In the closing years of the century many of the aged Queen's public engagements were connected with the army, for British troops saw service on several military expeditions besides the Boer War. Inspecting troops (Plate 305), presenting regimental colours and visiting Netley Hospital (Plate 311) became far more frequent occurrences, and in spite of poor sight—she was suffering from cataract—the Queen made quilts for wounded soldiers, and scarves and caps for men serving, and was most annoyed when she discovered that some of them had been given to officers.

The Battle of Omdurman on 2 September 1898 ended the long rebellion in the Sudan. Two days later British and Egyptian flags were hoisted at Khartoum, where General Kitchener held a memorial service for General Gordon, thirteen and a half years after his death. 'Surely he is avenged!' triumphed Queen Victoria.

The Queen's most important public appearance not concerned with the army was the laying of the foundation-stone of the new Victoria and Albert Museum building, formerly called the South Kensington Museum, on 17 May 1899 (Plate 315).

As the years went by the Queen inevitably lost many old friends and valued servants who were also friends. 'All fall around me. I become more and more lonely.' Never did she cease to miss her husband, though the longing to join him now admitted of postponement. On her eightieth birthday she thanked God 'for having preserved me so long to my dear children, all my friends, and the whole nation', and prayed to be preserved still. Nearly 3,000 congratulatory telegrams arrived—many more than at the Jubilee—and in the afternoon the Queen drove to the Mausoleum and laid at the foot of the 'dear tomb' one of the innumerable bouquets of flowers that had been sent to her. 'How much my dear Albert would have rejoiced to see all these marks of love and loyalty!' For the family dinner party the Queen put on one of her Jubilee dresses, embroidered with silver, and the diamond chain her children had given her on that occasion. The day was crowned gloriously by a performance of *Lohengrin* in the Waterloo Chamber, with the de Reszke brothers, which created a deep impression on the Queen. 'It was a fine ending to this memorable day.'

Throughout the long and critical negotiations with the Government of the Transvaal Republic in the summer of 1899 the Queen hoped that armed conflict could be avoided. No agreement was reached, however, regarding suzerainty and the demand of the foreign settlers—mostly British—for the franchise, which they felt they should have, considering that numerically they were four times as strong as the Dutch farmers, the Boers, and had developed the mineral wealth of the country. President Kruger was willing to give settlers the vote after seven years' residence, but not retrospectively and after five years as the British Government demanded. The very moderate Boer ultimatum requesting arbitration and the withdrawal of British troops from the frontier within forty-eight hours was rejected by Britain, and another unnecessary imperialistic war began on 11 October.

During September and October, 70,000 men were dispatched to South Africa—the largest number so far sent to any war—and they were joined by contingents from India, Canada, Australia and New Zealand. For the first few months of the war Britain suffered heavily. Mafeking, Kimberley and Ladysmith were besieged, and one military disaster followed another, yet Queen Victoria did not lose heart. Her classic remark to A. J. Balfour, 'Please understand that there is no one depressed in *this* house; we are not interested in the possibilities of defeat; they do not exist' became a famous war slogan in the Second World War. Though confident in public, the Queen grieved deeply over the casualty lists, and the weakness of age led to much weeping. Her journal entry for 1 January 1900 starts on a troubled note: 'I begin today a new year and a new century, full of anxiety and fear of what may be before us!'

In the spring the tide turned; one after another Kimberley, Ladysmith and Mafeking were relieved. Shortly after the relief of Ladysmith, Queen Victoria came to London on 8 March 1900 for a three days' visit (Plate 319). Dense crowds greeted her with unprecedented enthusiasm exceeding even that shown at the Jubilee, and quite spontaneously as there was no preparation or pageantry. Jubilant Britain stood in isolation, however, for world opinion condemned her war in South Africa as unjustified and imperialistic.

With both France and Italy hostile, Queen Victoria decided to take her spring holiday in Ireland, where she had not been for forty years, particularly as by this visit she could also show her appreciation of the Irish regiments which had especially distinguished themselves in South Africa. In April she sailed in the *Victoria and Albert* to Kingstown, where she was wheeled ashore wearing a bunch of shamrock pinned on her dress and carrying a sunshade embroidered with the same emblematic plant.

The Queen spent three weeks at Viceregal Lodge,

Dublin (Plate 322). As usual, the Whitehall boxes were attended to every morning, and letters were read and answered. Then came a short drive in a bathchair drawn by a white Egyptian donkey, and after luncheon a carriage drive of about twenty miles. The tired old lady often dozed during these long drives, and in order that she might not be seen nodding, one of the equerries would make his horse prance at the approach of a village as a signal for Princess Beatrice to awaken her mother. Contrary to her expectations, the Queen really enjoyed her stay in Ireland, finding the people 'warm-hearted and sympathetic'.

The burden of years of constant hard work and worry had weakened the Queen's ability to bear further grief which was soon to befall her. In July she made herself quite ill over unfounded reports of 400 European victims of the Boxer riots, in the British Embassy in Pekin. Later the same month she was shocked to learn that her second son, the Duke of Saxe-Coburg, was suffering from cancer of the throat (for the truth about his illness had been withheld from her), and his death on the 31st came as a great shock. 'Oh, God! My poor darling Affie gone too! My third grown-up child, besides three very dear sons-in-law. It is hard at eighty-one! . . . One sorrow, one trial, one anxiety, following another. It is a horrible year, nothing but sadness and sorrows of one kind and another.' The Duke's only son had also recently died, and the succession to the Duchy now passed by a special arrangement to his nephew the young Duke of Albany, posthumous son of Prince Leopold.

During her autumn stay at Balmoral more distressing news arrived. Her grandson, Prince Christian Victor of Schleswig-Holstein, had died of fever in South Africa. Her daughter, the Empress Frederick, was a victim of cancer. The Queen was very depressed, and when she left Balmoral she seemed to feel that she would never see her beloved Scotland again. Her health now showed signs of breaking down under the weight of her grief and her years. She completely lost her appetite, suffered from insomnia, and found it very annoying when she overslept in the morning, and felt drowsy during the day. On occasion even her remarkable memory failed her.

The Queen's last Christmas day, spent as usual at Osborne, was a sad one. The news was carefully broken to her, in instalments, that Jane, Lady Churchill, her only surviving intimate friend, had died in the night. Lady Churchill had been a member of the Household for nearly fifty years.

Sadness darkened the Queen's last weeks, which were spent on her island home. Gradually her worn-out body and mind sank into a state of hopeless weakness. Bad nights, sleeping late, resting, dozing, taking a short drive, meals consisting only of a little milk or Benger's food, signing papers, dictating to a daughter or granddaughter, followed each other in monotonous succession. On 2 January 1901 she received Lord Roberts, the Supreme Commander in South Africa, on his return, and conferred on him the Garter and an earldom for his services in saving the situation in the Boer War—a little prematurely, perhaps, considering that the war continued to drag on for another seventeen months. The Queen was in harness almost until the end. Her condition gave rise to no immediate anxiety until 17 January, and even the first bulletin published on the 19th gave no real indication of the seriousness of her state. Her children were, however, summoned to Osborne, but when the Queen rallied on the 19th the Prince of Wales went back to London, to return on the 22nd with the Kaiser, who had broken off the bicentenary celebrations of the foundation of the Prussian monarchy to be at his grandmother's deathbed. Only the Empress Frederick could not be present on account of her own mortal illness.

The Queen was unconscious save for brief moments when the flickering flame of life burnt up and she recognized her children. Her last articulate word was 'Bertie'. Surrounded by her family, her life slowly ebbed away in the arms of the Kaiser. To the Duke of Argyll it seemed like the last moments of a great three-decker ship sinking. Queen Victoria died at half past six on the evening of 22 January 1901 (Plate 325) in the sixty-fourth year of her reign, thirty-nine years of which had been spent 'on a dreary, sad pinnacle of solitary grandeur'.

What has been the essential of our very existence—the first thought in our daily life, has gone. [wrote Sir Arthur Bigge, the Queen's private secretary, to Lord Esher two days later] The Queen was an incomparable example of strict fulfilment of duty, tenacity of power, fearlessness in wielding it, marvellous capacity for work, and with all these gifts which made her great— the tenderness and simplicity of a girl—the unfailing thought for others which inspired in all hearts true love and affection.

For ten days Queen Victoria lay in State in the dining-room at Osborne House, which was converted into a mortuary chapel. She was dressed in white, wearing her widow's cap and wedding veil. The small Imperial crown and the Order of the Garter lay on the coffin, which was covered with the Queen's Robes of State. Four officers of the 1st Grenadier Guards mounted guard with a member of the late Queen's Household.

Queen Victoria left precise instructions for her funeral. As head of the Army, she wished to have a military funeral.

On the sunny afternoon of 1 February 1901 the coffin was brought from Osborne House to Cowes Pier, followed by the royal mourners on foot (Plate 326). At three o'clock the royal yacht *Alberta*, which had so many times transported the Queen to and from her island home and now bore her body, steamed slowly from Cowes to the mainland, passing along a ten-mile line of battleships and cruisers of the British fleet on the northern side, and on the southern, warships from Germany, France, Portugal, and Japan. She was preceded by a flotilla of eight destroyers, and a salute was fired from one man-of-war after another as the little yacht came level with them. Behind the *Alberta* steamed two larger yachts, the *Osborne* and the *Victoria and Albert* with King Edward on board, and then the great *Hohenzollern* of the Kaiser.

That night the coffin remained on board in Portsmouth harbour; early the next morning it was taken by train to London. Whereas the previous day the Navy had honoured the dead sovereign, in London detachments of the Army marched in the funeral procession and lined the route from Victoria Station past Buckingham Palace, St. James's Palace and Piccadilly, to Hyde Park, Marble Arch and finally Paddington Station. Vast silent crowds, the largest that had ever been seen in London, and most of whom had known no other sovereign than Queen Victoria, watched the funeral cortège slowly pass by to the solemn strains of Chopin's funeral march. Black clothes were almost universal, and even the poorest wore some sign of mourning. The streets were draped with royal purple, however, not black, at the Queen's own wish. State officials and troops preceded the gun carriage drawn by eight of the Queen's favourite cream-coloured horses. On it rested the white coffin, covered with the Imperial banner, the Queen's Standard, and the sparkling crown and orbs of her sovereignty. Behind it rode King Edward, on his right the Kaiser, on his left the Duke of Connaught. They were followed by the Kings of Greece, Belgium and Portugal and forty imperial and royal princes representing all European and several Eastern dynasties. Then came six carriages containing Queen Alexandra, the royal princesses, three aged field-marshals, and some of the ladies of Queen Victoria's and Queen Alexandra's Households.

On arrival at Windsor by train soon after two o'clock the coffin was placed once more on a gun carriage, and the procession had already started to move off when two of the horses, which had become restive during their long wait, kicked over the traces and plunged and reared dangerously. To the great chagrin of the Artillery, the naval guard of honour were put in place of the horses, and using the communication-cord of the royal train in place of the cut traces, dragged the gun carriage along the processional route through Windsor (Plate 327) and part of the Long Walk, through the Upper, Middle and Lower Wards of Windsor Castle, to the west door of St. George's Chapel. After the burial service the Queen was moved once more to a temporary resting-place before the altar of the Albert Memorial Chapel. Here she lay in State all that night and the following day and night. At each of the four corners of the bier an officer of the Guards mounted guard once more (Plate 328).

On Monday, 4 February, Queen Victoria was carried to her last resting-place, the Mausoleum at Frogmore (Plate 329). This final funeral ceremony took place in the privacy of the royal family, visiting sovereigns and princes, and the royal Household. After a short and simple burial service the coffin was lowered into the grey granite sarcophagus and placed beside that of the Prince Consort (Plates 207, 330). So, after thirty-nine years, Queen Victoria was at last reunited with her husband, according to her intention carved over the door of the Mausoleum: 'Farewell, most beloved! Here at last I will rest with thee; with thee in Christ I shall rise again.'

268　Queen Victoria at the age of seventy-five.
*Photograph by Russell & Sons, Windsor, 1894.*

269  Queen Victoria and her eldest daughter the widowed Empress Frederick of Germany.
*Photograph by Byrne, February 1889.*

270  The marriage of Princess Louise of Wales and the Duke of Fife in the private chapel at Buckingham Palace, 27 July 1889. The Queen and the Princess of Wales are on the left, the Prince of Wales in the centre.
*Photograph probably by Alexander Henderson.*

271 Queen Victoria, Prince and Princess Henry of Battenberg and their children, Prince Alexander, Princess Victoria Eugenie (later the Queen of Spain) and Prince Leopold.
*Photograph by Watson, November 1889.*

272 Queen Victoria on holiday at Aix-les-Bains. *L. to R.:* Princess Margaret of Connaught (later the Crown Princess of Sweden), Queen Victoria, Prince Henry of Battenberg, Princess Patricia of Connaught (now Lady Patricia Ramsay), Prince Arthur of Connaught, the Marquis of Lorne, Princess Henry of Battenberg.
*Photograph by Georges Brun, at the Maison Mottet, 10 April 1890.*

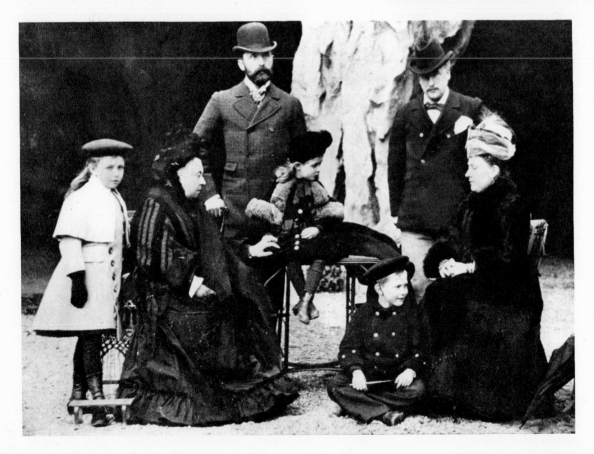

273   Queen Victoria with the Prince of Wales at a
garden party at Marlborough House, 14 July 1890.
*Woodcut from* The Illustrated London News.

274   Queen Victoria launching the cruiser *Royal
Arthur* at Portsmouth, 26 February 1891.
*Watercolour by R. T. Pritchett.*

275 Queen Victoria's visit with the Empress Frederick to the Horse Show, Islington, 5 March 1891.
*Watercolour.*

276 A Drawing-room at Buckingham Palace, 1894. On the right stand the Prince of Wales, the Duchess of York (later Queen Mary) and her mother, the Duchess of Teck. The Princess of Wales is on the Queen's left.
*Wash drawing by W. Hatherell.*

277  Queen Victoria and her granddaughter Princess Helena Victoria, elder daughter of Prince and Princess Christian of Schleswig-Holstein.
*Photograph by G. Mullins, Osborne, 29 July 1892.*

278  Queen Victoria's visit to the Church of the Santissima Annunziata, Florence, 11 April 1893, during a holiday in Florence.
*Drawing by A. Forestier.*

279  The marriage of the Duke and Duchess of York
(later King George V and Queen Mary) in the Chapel
Royal, St. James's Palace, 6 July 1893. On the left
stands the bride's mother, the Duchess of Teck. The
Prince of Wales is near the Archbishop of Canterbury.
On the Queen's left, the Grand Duke Ernest Louis of
Hesse, on her right, the Queen of Denmark, the
Princess of Wales and the King of Denmark. Behind
Queen Victoria's chair stand Princess Henry of Batten-
berg, the Marquis and Marchionness of Lorne and
Prince Henry of Battenberg nearest the curtain.
*Watercolour by A. Forestier.*

280  Queen Victoria with the Duke and Duchess
of York.

*Photograph by G. Mullins, Osborne House,*
*12 August 1893.*

281 Queen Victoria at the unveiling of Princess Louise's statue of her in Kensington Gardens, on 28 June 1893. It was erected as a Jubilee memorial by the inhabitants of Kensington.
*Woodcut.*

282 Queen Victoria opening the Imperial Institute, South Kensington, 10 May 1893. Sitting on either side of the Queen on the dais are the Prince of Wales (*left*) and the Duke of Edinburgh (*right*). In front of the Prince of Wales is a model of the Institute.
*Photograph by Russell & Sons.*

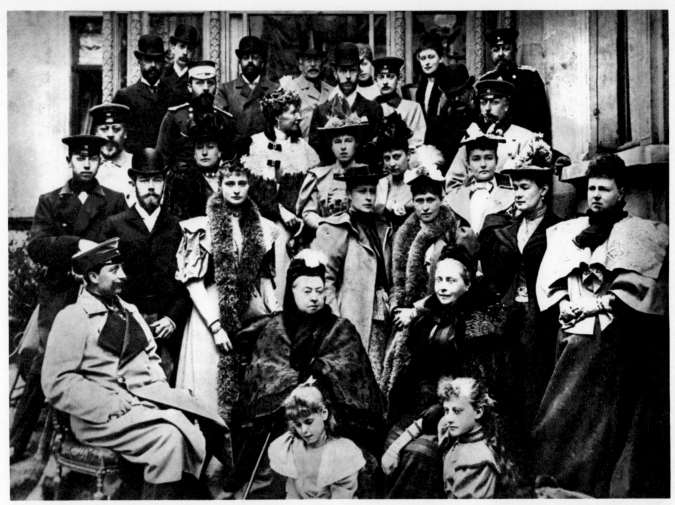

283   Family reunion at Coburg, for the marriage of two of Queen Victoria's grandchildren—Princess Victoria Melita (daughter of Prince Alfred, Duke of Saxe-Coburg-Gotha (formerly Edinburgh) and the Grand Duke of Hesse (son of Princess Alice)—on 19 April 1894. Photograph taken on 21st. *L. to R., seated:* Kaiser Wilhelm II, Queen Victoria, the Empress Frederick of Germany. *2nd row:* Prince Alfred of Saxe-Coburg-Gotha, the Czarevitch, his fiancée Princess Alix of Hesse, her sisters Princess Louis of Battenberg and Princess Henry of Prussia, the Grand Duchess Vladimir of Russia, the Duchess of Saxe-Coburg-Gotha. *3rd row:* the Prince of Wales, Princess Henry of Battenberg, Princess Philip of Saxe-Coburg-Gotha, and at the right end of this row the Duchess of Connaught, and behind her the Duke of Connaught. *Back two rows:* Prince Louis of Battenberg, the Grand Duke Paul of Russia, Prince Henry of Battenberg (in uniform), Prince (later King) Ferdinand of Roumania, Count Mensdorff, the Grand Duke Serge of Russia, almost hidden behind him Princess Ferdinand of Roumania, Prince Henry of Prussia, the Grand Duchess Serge of Russia, Grand Duke Vladimir of Russia, Duke of Saxe-Coburg-Gotha.

284   Queen Victoria and the Empress Frederick. Standing behind, *L. to R.:* the Duke of Connaught, the Duke of Saxe-Coburg-Gotha, Kaiser Wilhelm II, the Prince of Wales.

*Coburg, 21 April 1894.*

285 The christening photograph of Prince Edward of York (the present Duke of Windsor), 16 July 1894. Queen Victoria holding Prince Edward, with the Princess of Wales and the Duchess of York.

286 Four generations of British sovereigns. Queen Victoria holding Prince Edward of York (King Edward VIII), behind her are standing the Prince of Wales (King Edward VII) and the Duke of York (King George V).

*Nos. 285 and 286 taken by W. & D. Downey at White Lodge, Richmond Park, after the christening of Prince Edward of York, 16 July 1894.*

287 Queen Victoria and her Indian attendant the Munshi Hafiz Abdul Karim listening to a despatch read by her private secretary Major (Sir) Arthur Bigge, 1896.
*Watercolour by J. Begg.*

288 Royal family group at Ballater, Scotland. *L. to R. back row:* Princess Helena Victoria of Schleswig-Holstein, Prince Henry of Battenberg, Count Mensdorff, Princess Henry of Battenberg, the Duke of York. *Seated:* Queen Victoria and the Duchess of York holding Prince Edward. *In front:* Princess Victoria Eugenie of Battenberg, Prince Waldemar of Prussia (son of Prince Henry of Prussia), Prince Alexander of Battenberg.
*Photograph by Milne, September 1895.*

289   Queen Victoria at breakfast with Princess Henry of
Battenberg and Princess Helena Victoria of Schleswig-
Holstein (facing camera) at Nice, April 1895. The Indian
attendants are Ghulam Mustafa and Chidda.

*Photograph by Alexander Henderson.*

290   Queen Victoria and the widowed Princess Henry
of Battenberg.

*Photograph by G. Mullins, Osborne House, May 1896.*

291  Queen Victoria receiving the Chinese Ambassador Li Hung Chang at Osborne House, 5 August 1896.

292  Queen Victoria at the age of seventy-seven.
*Photograph by W. & D. Downey, 1896.*

293 Visit of the Emperor and Empress of Russia to Balmoral. *L. to R.:* the Czarina Alexandra Feodorovna (formerly Princess Alix of Hesse) holding the Grand Duchess Olga, Czar Nicholas II, Queen Victoria, the Prince of Wales.

*Photograph by W. & D. Downey, 29 September 1896.*

294 Visit of the Emperor and Empress of Russia to Balmoral. *L. to R.* Francis Clark (gillie), the Duke of Connaught, Czar Nicholas II, Princess Patricia of Connaught (sitting on step of carriage), Queen Victoria, Princess Helena Victoria of Schleswig-Holstein, the Czarina, the Duchess of Connaught, Princess Margaret of Connaught.

*Photograph by W. & D. Downey, 3 October 1896. On this occasion Downey took the first ciné-film of Queen Victoria and the Czar.*

233

295  The Diamond Jubilee. Queen Victoria entering St. George's Chapel, Windsor Castle, for the Thanksgiving Service on 20 June 1897. Behind her is the Empress Frederick with Sir Arthur Bigge.
*Watercolour by J. Begg.*

Vᴿ

**OFFICIAL PROGRAMME.**

OF THE

**DIAMOND JUBILEE**

**✦PROCESSION✦**

*Which will take place*

**On Tuesday, June 22ₙd, 1897**

*To celebrate the event of*

**Her Most Gracious Majesty's**

**✦RECORD REIGN✦**

*1837 ✦✶✦ 1897*

**PRICE SIXPENCE.**

By permission of the Lord Chamberlain.

296  Programme of Queen Victoria's Diamond Jubilee procession.

297   Queen Victoria at the time of her Diamond Jubilee, June 1897. The Queen is wearing her wedding veil, and a bracelet containing a miniature photograph of the Prince Consort, and holding a photograph of him.

*Photograph by Gunn & Stewart.*

298   Queen Victoria driving to St. Paul's Cathedral for the Thanksgiving Service, 22 June 1897. At the City boundary. Immediately behind the carriage, on horseback, are the Duke of Cambridge and, on the left, the Prince of Wales. In the carriage with the Queen are the Princess of Wales and Princess Christian.

*Photograph by E. P. Robson.*

299 The Diamond Jubilee procession crossing London Bridge—contingent of Queensland Mounted Rifles.
*Photograph by the London Stereoscopic & Photographic Co.*

300 The *Te Deum* outside St. Paul's Cathedral on 22 June 1897. At the foot of the steps is drawn up the royal carriage containing the Queen, the Princess of Wales and Princess Christian. The Archbishops of Canterbury and York, the Bishop of London and other church dignitaries are standing opposite the carriage. Mounted, and facing it, are the Prince of Wales and the Duke of Cambridge.

301 The Lord Mayor of London, George F. Faudel-Phillips, receiving a baronetcy from Queen Victoria, June 1897.
*Watercolour by W. Hatherell.*

302 Invitation to the Diamond Jubilee ball at the Guildhall. A remarkable example of Victorian decorative design, recording incidents of the Queen's reign.

303 Queen Victoria's official Diamond Jubilee portrait by W. & D. Downey. She is wearing her wedding veil and lace.

*Victoria R I*
*1837  1897*

239

304   Queen Victoria receiving an address of congratulation and welcome from the Mayor and Corporation of Windsor, 23 June 1897. The ceremony took place opposite her statue, which then had a stone canopy.                                    *Photograph by Hills & Saunders, Windsor.*

305   Among the Jubilee ceremonies, the Queen as head of the army held a big military review at Aldershot on 1 July 1897. Passing in front of the royal carriage are the bands of the cavalry regiments present.                                    *Photograph by Wyrall & Son, Aldershot.*

306    The Mayor and Corporation of Newport, Isle of Wight, the Queen's neighbours on her island
home, present an address of congratulation on 24 July 1897.
*Photograph by Hughes & Mullins, Ryde.*

307    The Queen's afternoon drive at Balmoral. *L. to R.:* George Gordon (gillie), the pony Bella, the
Duchess of Roxburghe, Queen Victoria with her dog Turi, and Mohammed Ismail.
*Photograph by Milne, September 1897.*

308 Queen Victoria with (*L. to R.*) Princess Victoria Eugenie of Battenberg, Princess Francis Joseph of Battenberg (Princess Anna of Montenegro), the Duchess of York.
*Photograph by Milne, Balmoral, September 1897.*

309 Queen Victoria signing State papers at Frogmore, *c.* 1898. With her is the Munshi.

310   Queen Victoria and Prince Edward of York (later King Edward VIII).
*Photograph by Hughes & Mullins, Osborne House, July 1897.*

311 Queen Victoria's visit to Netley Hospital on 14 May 1898, accompanied by Princess Henry of Battenberg and Princess Christian. The Queen presents the V.C. to Private Vickery and Piper Findlater. This is the first picture of the Queen wearing spectacles.

312 Queen Victoria in her donkey carriage at Cimiez on the Riviera, April 1898.
*Photograph by Alexander Henderson.*

244

313 That rare smile of Queen Victoria caught by a photographer, Charles Knight, 15 February 1898.

314 Three Victorias: the Queen with her grand-daughters Princess Victoria of Wales (standing) and Princess Helena Victoria of Schleswig-Holstein.
*Photograph by Milne, Balmoral, June 1898.*

315 Queen Victoria accepting a bouquet from a
student of the Royal Female School of Art when she
laid the foundation-stone of the Victoria and Albert
Museum on 17 May 1899.

*Pen drawing by Boyd.*

316 Queen Victoria leaving the Hotel Regina,
Cimiez, for her afternoon drive. She stayed there
from 12 March to 2 May 1899 and at other times.

*Watercolour by Reginald Cleaver.*

317  Queen Victoria with the Prince of Wales, Princess Victoria of Wales, and Prince Edward of York.

*Photograph by Milne, Balmoral, September 1898.*

318    Royal family group at Osborne, August 1898. *L. to R.:* Prince Leopold of Battenberg, Princess Aribert of Anhalt (Princess Marie Louise); in front of her, Prince Edward of York, the Duchess of York holding her second son Prince Albert (later King George VI); *(in front)* Prince Alexander of Battenberg; *(behind)* Princess Margaret of Connaught, next to her the Duke of York holding his daughter Princess Victoria (called Mary, the present Princess Royal); Queen Victoria with her dispatch boxes, Prince Arthur of Connaught, the Duchess of Connaught, Princess Henry of Battenberg; sitting with dog Princess Patricia of Connaught, behind her Princess Ena (Victoria Eugenie) of Battenberg (later Queen of Spain), Princess Helena Victoria of Schleswig-Holstein, Prince Maurice of Battenberg.

*Photograph by G. Mullins.*

247

319   Queen Victoria's drive to the City, 8 March 1900, shortly after the relief of Ladysmith.
The royal carriage in Holborn.

320   Queen Victoria at the age of eighty.
*Photograph by Hughes & Mullins, Osborne House, 25 August 1899.*

321 Queen Victoria.
*Woodcut by Sir William Nicholson, c. 1899.*

322 Queen Victoria's visit to Dublin, 4–26 April 1900. The archway—
a facsimile of the entrance to Beggotsath Castle—had been specially
erected.

*Watercolour by Percy French.*

324 The last photograph of Queen Victoria, 12 December 1900. The Queen was visiting the Irish Industries Exhibition at Windsor Town Hall. With her in the carriage are Princess Henry of Battenberg and the Duchess of York.
*Photograph by W. F. Seymour.*

323 Queen Victoria with Prince Edward of York and the baby Prince Henry of York (now the Duke of Gloucester).
*Osborne, July or August 1900.*

325 Announcement of Queen Victoria's death in a special issue of the *London Gazette*, which appeared the same evening, 22 January 1901.

326 Queen Victoria's funeral procession from Osborne House to the Trinity Pier, Cowes, Isle of Wight, 1 February 1901. The royal mourners.
*Photograph by Russell & Sons, Southsea and Windsor.*

327 The funeral procession of Queen Victoria at Windsor, 2 February 1901. Behind the gun carriage drawn by sailors walk Kaiser Wilhelm II (*left*), King Edward VII (*centre*) and the Duke of Connaught.
*Photograph by Bender & Lewis, Croydon.*

328 Queen Victoria's Lying-in-State in the Albert Memorial Chapel, Windsor Castle, 2–3 February 1901.
*Photograph by Russell & Sons, Windsor.*

329   Queen Victoria's funeral procession at Windsor Castle, from the Albert Memorial
Chapel to the Mausoleum at Frogmore, 4 February 1901.
*Photograph by Russell & Sons, Windsor.*

330 Effigy of Queen Victoria by Baron Marochetti for the Mausoleum, Frogmore, made at the same time as the Prince Consort's effigy (No. 209).

# V
# QUEEN VICTORIA'S PHOTOGRAPH ALBUMS

MOST drawn or painted portraits of the youthful Queen Victoria bear little resemblance to her real appearance. The most fanciful of all are unquestionably those of the Court painter Alfred Chalon, who in his craving to please made the sitter quite unrecognizable by his excessive flattery. His best portrait shows the young sovereign in her Coronation robes (Plate 41). Most of the others reduce her to a simpering doll and have been purposely omitted from this book. Understandably, Chalon did not fear competition from the realistic art of photography. The Queen enquiring one day in 1841 or 1842, when daguerreotype portraits were still a novelty, whether he were not afraid that photography would ruin his profession of miniature painter, Chalon confidently replied in his peculiar mixture of French and English, 'Ah non, Madame; photographie can't flattère.'

The charming Winterhalter portraits of Queen Victoria in the late 'forties and 'fifties (Plates 89, 102, 103, 107, 132) stand out from the sea of inferior works. Winterhalter was most successful in the balance he achieved between resemblance and expression, and the flattery often associated with a

royal portrait. Though the Queen looks years younger in his paintings than in reality (compare Plates 132 and 134), the likeness is certainly there. Winterhalter was gifted with a 'photographic' memory and occasionally also reassured himself with actual photographs, for the more Queen Victoria became accustomed to photographic portraits, the less was she deceived by flattering paintings. Truth she also insisted on in topographical views and pictures of animals. With that love of accuracy which was an outstanding trait of Queen Victoria's character, it was only natural that a good likeness should mean more to her than artistic merit, and to emphasize her attitude she frequently pressed photographs on the artists she employed. If a painter still strayed from what the Queen considered the truth, she would not hesitate to point out the deviation immediately.

Queen Victoria was in the habit of having favourite family portraits copied again and again as presents for relations and friends, or to hang in the various royal residences. Usually engravings of these pictures were published, and when the proofs were submitted for the Queen's criticism she frequently made some pertinent comment in the margin, as for example in the engraving after a photograph by Downey (Plates 217 and 219) which was used as frontispiece to the second volume of *Leaves*.

In her insistence on an exact likeness the Queen was as much concerned about portraits of friends as those of herself and her family. When Sir John Millais was painting for her a smaller copy of his portrait of Disraeli after the statesman's death, the Queen sent him three photographs as a guide, pointing out which features needed alteration compared with the first version.

Among the many hundreds of photographs of Queen Victoria, few show her as sovereign. She preferred to be portrayed as wife and mother. Only three have preserved for posterity her charming smile (Plates 256, 260, 313), which was commented upon by all who knew her well. During her happy married life, photographic materials were not sensitive enough to allow of instantaneous exposures, and a smile would have looked frozen and artificial, even if self-consciousness during the rather long exposure had not caused that smile to disappear. Disraeli, and later Prince Henry of Battenberg, brought a little sunshine into her life again, and occasionally a smile would enliven the drooping features of the Queen, making her look years younger. But it was only after fast gelatine dry plates had made snapshots possible in the 'eighties that one day a photographer happened to snatch a rare moment (Plate 313) when the Queen's face was radiant with happiness. 'Those who never saw the Queen's smile', said Lady Ponsonby, 'can have little idea of the marvellous way in which it brightened and exhilarated the lines of the Queen's features in advancing years. It came very suddenly, in the form of a mild radiance over the whole face, a softening and a raising of the lines of the lips, a flash of kindly light beaming from the eyes.'

It was in the year of Queen Victoria's accession that L. J. M. Daguerre succeeded in making pictures by the first practicable process of photography—the daguerreotype. The Queen followed the rapid development of the new art with keen interest from the moment the first daguerreotypes imported into England from France were laid before her on the morning she proposed to Prince Albert—15 October 1839 (see page 15). Shortly after their marriage the Queen and Prince, 'expressing their highest admiration of this wonderful discovery', accepted some views of Paris, Rome, and other continental cities from Antoine Claudet, pupil of Daguerre and first licensee of the process in England, where the daguerreotype was protected by a patent.

At this time it was not yet possible to take photographic portraits on account of the extremely long exposure necessary, but improvements were rapid, and in March 1841 the first public portrait studio in Europe was opened by Richard Beard on top of the Royal Polytechnic Institution in Regent Street, London. Three months later Claudet set up competition on the roof of the Royal Adelaide Gallery behind St. Martin-in-the-Fields.

Several years passed before Queen Victoria sat for her photograph, and then it was not a daguerreotype but a paper photograph or Calotype—the process invented by W. H. Fox Talbot. Henry Collen, miniature painter and drawing master to the Queen, and Talbot's first licensee, had opened the world's first Calotype studio in Somerset Street near Portman Square in August 1841. His 'Calotype miniatures' were a compromise between the old art of miniature painting and the new art of photography, and being merely over-painted paper photographs, the result was frequently more flattering to the eye than the cold metallic effect of daguerreotypes. The earliest surviving photograph of Queen Victoria, showing her with the little Prince of Wales (Plate 93) was almost certainly taken by Collen in 1844 or 1845.

Meanwhile Prince Albert had been photographed by an unnamed daguerreotypist at Brighton (Plate 62) when he and the Queen were staying at the Royal Pavilion in March 1842. The Queen's diary entry for 6 March merely records the fact that 'Albert sat yesterday to a man who makes photographic likenesses.' The Garter ribbon which the Prince always wore beneath his waistcoat can be seen in this portrait.

According to the Queen's diary, it was not until April 1847 that daguerreotypes were taken of all the royal family. 'We both sat, in the greenhouse, [at Buckingham Palace] to Mr. Killburn [*sic*] for Daguerotypes, [*sic*] which are not much improved to

R

what they were originally. A M. Monsor, a Frenchman, has discovered a process of colouring them, and of producing replicas of the daguerotypes. [*sic*] Mine was really very successful. Those of the children are unfortunately entire failures.' The children were probably too fidgety, for exposures were still about half a minute. Strange to say, the Queen makes no comment on her husband's portrait. These daguerreotypes no longer exist, but those taken by the same photographer nearly five years later in one of the hothouses at Windsor Castle—it was January— are illustrated in Plates 105 and 106. On this occasion the Queen wrote in her journal, 'The day was splendid for it. Mine was unfortunately horrid, but the children's were pretty.'

William Edward Kilburn had opened a studio in Regent Street towards the end of 1846, and was soon counted as one of the three leading daguerreotypists in the country. In acknowledgment of his success with the Queen's and Prince Albert's portraits in 1847, he was immediately appointed 'Photographist to Her Majesty and His Royal Highness Prince Albert'—the first of many photographers to receive this honour. Monsieur Mansion, to give him his correct name, was an old French miniature painter who now made his living by tinting daguerreotypes for several London establishments, and copying them in the form of miniatures.

Soon afterwards, Nicolaas Henneman was appointed 'Her Majesty's photographer on paper'. Originally the valet of Fox Talbot, Henneman had assisted his master in his efforts to commercialize the Calotype, and in September 1847 was set up by him in a studio in Regent Street—the fashionable address for photographic establishments. It was through the influence of Talbot's half-sister the Countess of Mount Edgcumbe, a lady-in-waiting, that Henneman received his appointment. There is no evidence that the Queen was ever photographed by him. Indeed, a high proportion of the early photographs of the royal family were not taken by professionals but by Prince Albert's librarian, Dr. E. Becker, and one of his equerries, Captain Dudley (later Lord) de Ros.

When in May 1853 the Queen and Prince Albert became patrons of the newly formed London Photographic Society, they were said to be 'well skilled and practised in the art of photography'. Unfortunately none of their photographs has been preserved, nor can it be ascertained whether the studio and dark-room used by the Queen's photographers and situated in the Orangery at Windsor Castle was the one originally fitted up for the Queen's and Prince Albert's private use, though its situation close to the Private Apartments lends weight to this theory.

Dr. Becker was a founder member of the Photographic Society and it was probably he who initiated the royal couple into the simple technique of the Calotype or Talbotype, which he was practising at that time. We may also assume that Roger Fenton's connection with the royal family was due to Dr. Becker's introduction. Fenton was the founder and first secretary of the Photographic Society. The many photographs which he took of the royal family and the royal residences in the 'fifties indicate the frequency of his visits (Plates 111, 113–118, 122, 142, 144, 342). The amusing costume pictures of the royal children (Plates 109, 110, 112) were taken by him at the time of the fourteenth wedding anniversary celebration of their parents, when they recited extracts from James Thomson's poem *The Seasons*. The previous month Fenton and Sir Charles Eastlake, President of the Photographic Society, had the honour of conducting Queen Victoria and Prince Albert round the Society's first exhibition, held at the gallery of the Society of British Artists in Suffolk Street. In size alone the exhibition was imposing, for nearly 1,500 photographs were on view. 'It was most interesting', wrote the Queen in her diary. 'There are 3 rooms full of the most beautiful specimens, some from France and Germany, and many by amateurs. Mr. Fenton explained everything, and there were many beautiful photographs done by him. Prof. Wheatstone, the inventor of the stereoscope, was also there. Some of the landscapes were exquisite, and many admirable portraits. A set of photos[1] of the animals at the Zoological Gardens by Don Juan, second son of Don Carlos, are almost the finest of all the specimens.'

To give the new society every possible encourage-

[1] The Queen frequently used this shortened modern form, and as far as we know this is its first use.

ment, Queen Victoria and Prince Albert visited its annual exhibition every year, frequently accompanied by some of their elder children, in whom they wished to instil a similar interest. Convinced that photography was a useful and an elevating art, the Queen presented a photographic outfit to the King of Siam in 1857, after the ratification of the treaty of friendship and commerce between the two countries.

At the suggestion of Prince Albert a committee was formed at the Photographic Society in 1855 to investigate the cause of the fading which was giving rise to much concern, and being a keen collector of photographs, he donated £50 towards the expenses. Hearing that the prints made at Blanquart-Evrard's photographic printing establishment at Lille were permanent, Prince Albert sent Dr. Becker to Lille with the intention of buying the secret of this printing method for the benefit of the photographic world. The French photographer declined to reveal his method, but soon afterwards (July 1855) Thomas Sutton of Jersey published a pamphlet on his method of printing, for which permanency was also claimed. Promising his patronage, Prince Albert encouraged Sutton to open a commercial printing works at St. Brelade's Bay, Jersey, where photographers could send their negatives to be printed. For reasons unknown to us Blanquart-Evrard joined forces with Sutton, and their printing establishment was opened in the late autumn of 1855.

The Queen's and Prince Albert's concern both for the progress of photography and for the dissemination of knowledge through photographs is shown in many ways. Their interest, for instance, in Sir David Brewster's lenticular stereoscope at the Great Exhibition gave the greatest impetus to visual education in the nineteenth century. No English firm had been prepared to risk the commercial manufacture of the stereoscope, considering that (Sir) Charles Wheatstone's earlier instrument (which was not suitable for photographs) had met with no success, and Brewster had to seek an optical-instrument maker in Paris. Realizing the advantages of Brewster's design over Wheatstone's, Jules Duboscq foresaw a great future for it in connection with photography, and constructed a number of stereoscopes for display at the 1851

Advertisement showing Prince Albert's patronage of a photographic printing establishment in Jersey, 1855

Exhibition. At the Crystal Palace the three-dimensional effect of stereoscopic daguerreotypes when viewed in the stereoscope aroused Queen Victoria's admiration. As a result of the interest shown by the Queen, Duboscq was flooded with orders, and English optical-instrument makers then also took up the manufacture of stereoscopes, of which nearly a quarter of a million were sold in London and Paris within three months. When the comparatively expensive stereoscopic daguerreotypes were replaced by glass transparencies, and soon afterwards by paper prints from collodion negatives, the price of stereoscopic slides was brought within reach of everyone. Stereograms of buildings and scenery in all parts of the world were soon available, and by 1858 the London Stereoscopic Company was in a position to advertise the astonishing number of 100,000 different views. By this time the stereoscope had conquered the world, and lending libraries facilitated the exchange of pictures. Men, women and children, rich and poor, gazed into this 'Optical wonder of the age'—the television set of the Victorian era. Like the photograph album soon to come, the stereoscope found a place in every Victorian drawing-room, providing 'refined amusement combined with useful instruction'—the criterion of Victorian recreation.

When cataloguing of the collection of Raphael drawings at Windsor began in 1852, Prince Albert conceived the idea of illustrating Raphael's work by a complete set of photographic reproductions of his entire artistic output. The majority of the photographs were commissioned by the Prince; others were obtained by encouraging owners of Raphael material to have it photographed for his great work.

This enormous *opus* occupied the Prince for the rest of his life, and was privately printed in 1876.[1] The Raphael catalogue is a monument to the Prince Consort's power of organization, and still serves as an important reference work. As far as we know it is the first application of photography to art historical studies, and thus a pioneer work in two fields.

It is doubtful whether without the Queen's and Prince Albert's patronage the monumental publication of Roger Fenton's photographs of the Crimean War—indeed even his expedition to the Crimea—would ever have been possible. In supplying Fenton with letters of introduction to governors and ambassadors on the route and to the commanders in the field, Prince Albert lent all the weight of his position to the undertaking. In consequence Fenton was treated with every consideration and given special facilities denied to the famous *Times* correspondent, (Sir) William Howard Russell. The importance of Fenton's special mission and the high esteem in which his work was held by the Queen and Prince can be gauged from the fact that he was commanded to Osborne for an audience immediately after his return to England in July 1855, and that the royal couple themselves took about twenty of the Crimean photographs to Paris on their State visit in August and showed them to Napoleon III and the Empress Eugénie.

Florence Nightingale, on a visit to Balmoral in October 1856, was shown by the Queen an album of photographs of wounded Crimean heroes who had been decorated by her with the Crimean Medal or the newly instituted Victoria Cross. These photographs by Robert Howlett, and part of Fenton's series, are still in the Royal Collection.

George Washington Wilson of Aberdeen was the first photographer to take the royal family in Scotland. His original commission in September 1854 to photograph old Balmoral Castle (Plate 359) having been performed to Prince Albert's satisfaction, Wilson was sent for the following year to take the historic group reproduced in Plate 135, on the day Prince Frederick William of Prussia proposed to the Princess Royal. On account of dull

weather the exposure was rather long, and on developing the negative in his dark-tent Wilson found that the Queen had moved slightly. She seemed somewhat put out on hearing this, but sat for another picture with better results. A day or two later the Queen and the Prince happened to ride past on their ponies as Wilson was focusing his camera on the mountain Lochnagar. Stopping to enquire whether he had been successful, the Queen jokingly added before Wilson had time to reply, 'If not, you must not blame your sitter this time, for Lochnagar keeps very still and does not fidget.' During the royal family's visits to Balmoral Wilson was frequently in demand, and in 1860 he was appointed Photographer Royal for Scotland (Plates 204, 205, 212, 239, 240, 341, 343, 359, 360, 364, 367, 368).

Visiting the Manchester Art Treasures Exhibition in June 1857 Queen Victoria saw photographs for the first time displayed on equal terms with paintings, drawings, sculpture and engravings. A big allegorical photograph by Oscar Gustaf Rejlander entitled 'The Two Ways of Life'—Industry and Dissipation—took her fancy. It was the most elaborate composition ever produced by photography, having been printed from over thirty separate negatives, an additional novelty being the inclusion of partly nude figures. Greatly impressed by this latest advance in 'art photography', the Queen bought the picture (priced at ten guineas) for Prince Albert, and though Albert the Good hardly needed a reminder of which way of life to take, it hung in his study at Windsor Castle until the accession of Edward VII.

William Lake Price, a former water-colour painter, was another photographer whose imaginative compositions, in the chivalric style of Royal Academicians of the period, won royal approval. Commanded to bring all his exhibition photographs to Windsor Castle, Lake Price was heaped with commissions for portraits, reproductions of Old Master paintings, and views of Osborne House, both exterior and interior. Other leading photographers of the time frequently in demand by the Queen and Prince either for portraits or for photographic surveys of the royal residences were: Bambridge, Antoine Claudet, Caldesi, Disderi, W. & D.

[1] *The Raphael Collection at Windsor Castle formed by H.R.H. the Prince Consort 1853–1861*, with an introduction by C. Ruland.

Downey, Vernon Heath, Hills & Saunders, Hughes & Mullins, J. E. Mayall, Horatio Nelson King and T. R. Williams.

In view of the rapid evolution of photography, Prince Albert, with his methodical mind, soon foresaw the need for building up a photo-historical collection. During his visit to the annual exhibition of the Photographic Society in January 1859 he threw out the suggestion, and in due course a committee was formed to consider ways and means to establish a permanent collection. But as is often the way with committees of this kind, no practical solution was arrived at, and there the matter rested until thirty years later, when much irreplaceable material had already vanished for ever.

The same year, 1859, saw the general introduction of the *carte-de-visite* portrait in France through the immensely popular visiting-card size photographs of Napoleon III by Disderi. Here in England it was also royal patronage that made these portraits fashionable. Seeing Disderi's success, John Edwin Mayall sought permission to take *carte* portraits of the whole royal family, which he did at Buckingham Palace in May and July 1860 (Plates 173, 174, 175). 'He is the oddest man I ever saw', Queen Victoria had commented after her first two-hour sitting with Mayall in July 1855, 'but an excellent photographer. He is an American, and a tremendous enthusiast in his work.' Mayall had first attracted Prince Albert's attention at the Great Exhibition with his pictorial daguerreotypes 'illustrating poetry and sentiment': 'The Lord's Prayer', 'The Soldier's Dream', 'The Venerable Bede blessing an Anglo-Saxon Child', and others of the kind. Though Mayall had stopped producing such trash, finding portraiture far more remunerative, talent once recognized by Prince Albert could always count on royal support—and Mayall almost monopolized portraiture of the royal family for a time (Plates 134, 140, 143, 151, 183, 184, 187, 196, 202, 203, 211).

After the publication of Mayall's *Royal Album* in August 1860, card portraits became the rage, for everyone was eager to possess life-like portraits of the universally-loved Queen and her family. Hundreds of thousands of Mayall's *cartes* were quickly sold. Their unparalleled success gave great impetus to this branch of photography through the understandable desire of every photographer to reap an equally rich harvest with *cartes* of other celebrities, who in their turn were only too glad to follow the example of the royal family, and to have their portraits displayed for sale at printsellers' and stationers' alongside those of their sovereign.

The fashion for collecting *cartes* in albums and exchanging them with friends, like stamps, began with Mayall's publication. One of Queen Victoria's ladies-in-waiting, the Hon. Eleanor Stanley, wrote home on 24 November 1860: 'I have been writing to all the fine ladies in London for their and their husbands' photographs for the Queen. I believe the Queen could be bought and sold, for a photograph.'

Three to four hundred million *cartes* were estimated to be sold annually in England at the height of the craze for them in the early 'sixties, and more than once the Government contemplated following America's example by adding to the national income with a small tax on each photograph. Gladstone considered a penny tax in 1864 and so did Disraeli four years later, when a penny stamp on each of the five million photographs then sold annually would have brought a substantial contribution towards the cost of the Abyssinian War. Ten years later, when war with Russia seemed likely, the imposition of a stamp duty on photographs once more came under consideration. Such a tax, it was argued, would be to a large extent one on vanity and snobbery, and for fiscal purposes these foibles were regarded as fair game. Each time, however, the idea was dropped—quite possibly on the intervention of Queen Victoria, who on other occasions protested against the imposition of a tax on beer and one on matches on the ground that taxing these simple necessities or pleasures would affect the poorest people most—and *carte* portraits were by that time the poor man's picture gallery.

Several of her diary entries show that the Queen derived much pleasure from arranging photographs in her albums. Others were arranged by the Prince Consort, as some inscriptions in the albums bear witness. Photographs were exchanged with related royal families abroad, and others were obtained simply by asking for them. All European dynasties are represented in the Royal Collection, and so is almost anybody with a claim to distinction.

A firm believer in the multiplication of images by photography, Queen Victoria presented photographs on every possible occasion. Anniversaries in particular were always commemorated by photographs. In 1878, on the 'blessed anniversary' of Prince Albert's birth, Princess Beatrice received an enamel photograph of 'our dear Mausoleum'. Photographs figured prominently on the birthday and Christmas present tables of the royal family (Plates 164, 166, 177, 178) and were showered on other relations and on friends. No fewer than twenty copies of the Princess Royal's sixteenth birthday photograph appear on one list in the Queen's handwriting in which she clearly set out whether the recipients—ranging from Prince Albert to Sir Edwin Landseer—should have the photograph penny plain or twopenny coloured, framed or unframed. Gladstone gave vent to his resentment on receiving what he called 'a twopenny-halfpenny scrap' on his retire-

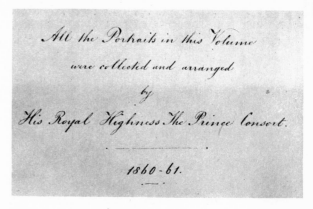

Note in several of Prince Albert's *carte-de-visite* albums.

ment, whereas other Prime Ministers had received the Queen's portrait in oil or bronze.

In February 1859 newspapers and popular magazines went into raptures over 'a new triumph in photography'—microscopically small photographs. The Ten Commandments containing 1,243 letters, the Lord's Prayer, a 'mosaic' of all the kings and queens of England, could be reduced to pinhead size photographs 'so exquisitely minute that their beauty and fidelity are discovered only by the use of a powerful microscope'. Queen Victoria, always eager for photographic novelties, had a signet ring made by the inventor of microphotographs, J. B. Dancer of Manchester. It consisted of a group of five portraits of her family, the whole picture measuring only an eighth of an inch, magnified by a jewel-lens.

Very soon after the Prince Consort's death, Queen Victoria gave some of her ladies gold and drop-pearl pendants containing a tiny photograph 'in remembrance of the best and greatest of Princes, from his broken-hearted widow Victoria R. Dec. 1861'. She herself always wore a bracelet with an enamelled photograph of her husband and some locks of his hair (Plate 297), and the inclusion of his portrait in many of the published photographs of the widowed Queen (Plates 191, 192, 193, 203, 205), showed the people the deep sorrow of their sovereign. Cards were affixed to the doors of the Queen's private apartments in the various royal residences, stating that everything within had been chosen and arranged by the Prince Consort. To ensure that no change should ever be made, every object in all the

Photograph of Leoncavallo bearing his autograph dedication to Queen Victoria.

royal private apartments in every royal residence was photographed and catalogued, a procedure which also made possible the exact replacement of worn-out upholstery.

We have already spoken of Queen Victoria's patronage of Roger Fenton's expedition to the Crimean War. Henceforth albums were arranged for every campaign in which British troops were engaged, for the purpose of commemorating officers and men who distinguished themselves. Collecting these photographs involved her private secretary in lengthy and frequently sad correspondence. (Sir) Frederick Ponsonby recalls that during the Boer War it was decided at first, owing to the very large numbers involved, to collect only photographs of officers killed on active service, to whose portraits he had to append details of service and circumstances of death, but after about a year the Queen came to the conclusion that the album was too sad to be looked at, and ordered that the living should be added to make it less depressing. As it would have proved an impossible task to include all officers serving, Ponsonby limited them to generals.

It was, however, not only officers and men who had distinguished themselves on the battlefield whose memory was thus honoured. The Queen also kept photograph albums of her Household. Any one who was in the service of Queen Victoria for a long period, whether as equerry or lady-in-waiting, as footman or maid, has his or her portrait in the Queen's albums, with details of service. It is touching to come across the portrait of John Meakin 'who has woven her Majesty's hose for sixty years' and his collaborator Anne Birkin 'who embroidered her Majesty's hose for sixty years'.

All centenarians and other people who might be regarded as curiosities are immortalized in the Queen's albums. There is, for example, the photograph of an Eskimo family who visited Windsor in 1854, and of 'General Tom Thumb' who performed before the royal family in 1846. A German pastor ingratiated himself with the Queen by his message of condolence from the people of Lithau in Hesse on the death of Princess Alice. A stage further removed is another photograph showing the members of the deputation from Lithau who had asked the pastor to send the letter of condolence.

Kaiser Wilhelm II gave this portrait to the Queen in August 1889.

Prize bulls and pigs on the royal farms, as well as dogs, cats and horses, have their place in the Queen's albums. Many of Queen Victoria's portraits show her with 'her poor dear friends the dogs'. Half a dozen bronze statues in the private grounds at Windsor testify to the Queen's enduring affection for her favourite dogs. 'Nothing brutalizes human beings more', she protested against vivisection, 'than cruelty to poor dumb animals, whose plaintive looks for help ought to melt the hardest heart.' But this sentiment did not extend to poor wild animals equally dumb, and many a stag shot by Prince Albert has the Queen's proud note of its weight under the photograph.

As indicated, Queen Victoria's huge folio 'Catalogues of Photographs' contain a remarkable mixture of subjects. Every photograph passed through her hands first to be approved before being

List in Queen Victoria's handwriting of intended recipients of the Princess Royal's sixteenth birthday photograph.

had treasured as pictures were burned, but the Queen's albums were apparently not touched. The approximately 100,000 photographs which have survived are contained in 110 albums and these can be roughly classified as follows: four volumes constitute the Queen's catalogue—identification pictures with their negative numbers—and three volumes contain duplicates of the same pictures in carbon printing. There are forty-four volumes of family photographs in chronological order, thirty-six volumes of collected *carte-de-visite* and cabinet photographs. Five albums of reproductions of paintings and engravings relating to the Queen's coronation and marriage, and photographs of christenings, confirmations and weddings of her children. Nine albums contain photographs of military campaigns from the Crimean to the Boer War. Finally, nine volumes are devoted to the royal residences. Once there were also some volumes of the Franco-Prussian War, but these were handed over to the British Museum since this campaign did not concern the British Army.

Considering photography a useful and enjoyable pastime, Queen Victoria gave several of her children photographic outfits and arranged for lessons from well-known professionals. Prince Alfred learned the rudiments of photography in 1860 before going to South Africa, his parents' intention being that he should have something else to occupy him apart from learning navigation during the long voyages which his naval training obliged him to undertake. In order that he should always have someone at hand to help him, the Queen commissioned Frederick York, a professional photographer, to accompany him. Prince Alfred became an enthusiastic amateur, undertaking all the processing work himself (Plate 193). The Prince of Wales, as the royal albums show, also occasionally tried his hand at photography, which he learned from William Ackland and Francis Bedford, but his attempts were few and far between. Francis Bedford was appointed to accompany him on his educational tour of the East in 1862, but the pictures were all taken by Bedford, the Prince confining his interest in photography to a daily enquiry as to results, or occasionally making the actual exposure after Bedford had prepared the plate and focused the view. Prince

pasted in the albums. She was very fond of these albums and few days passed without her sending for one volume or another. Noticing one day in the 'eighties that some of the old prints were fading, the Queen sent for Hughes & Mullins of Ryde, Isle of Wight, and ordered them to reproduce her photographic collection by the permanent process of carbon printing, thus clearly indicating her intention of having it preserved for posterity. In this she showed more foresight than most photographers of the period. Soon after the Queen's death there was a great tidying up under Edward VII and thousands of loose photographs which his parents

Leopold was said to be a better photographer than his brothers. Only Prince Arthur did not attempt it.

The Princess of Wales became a keener photographer than her husband, but by the time she began, about 1890, technique had been greatly simplified by dry plates. Now it was just a matter of pressing the button and leaving the developing and printing to a firm. The Princess of Wales and her children the Duke of Clarence, Princess Louise and Princess Victoria took lessons at the London Stereoscopic School of Photography in Regent Street, and learnt to use a twin-lens reflex camera, a somewhat clumsy forerunner of the present-day Rolleiflex. There was a regular attendance of royalty at this school for several years. Queen Victoria's daughters, Princess Christian of Schleswig-Holstein and Princess Henry of Battenberg, and her granddaughter-in-law the Duchess of York (later Queen Mary) were also initiated there in the technique. Soon they were all happily snapshooting with their Kodaks—the simplest and most popular camera for amateurs—presented by George Eastman, its inventor. In autumn 1897 they participated in an exhibition arranged by the Eastman Company at the New Gallery in Regent Street side by side with the most celebrated pictorial photographers of the day—Henry Peach Robinson, George Davison, Frederick H. Evans, J. Craig Annan, A. Horsley Hinton. As was to be foreseen, 'the royal pictures claimed the first attention of the fashionable visitors, and they were worthy of more attention than they generally received from photographers. As the first general collection shown by a family which has done much good in the encouragement of photography, they are worth careful study. Naturally, as the royal photographers do not produce their work for exhibition and competition, the pictures generally are interesting on account of their subjects rather than from pictorial quality; but apart from the subjects, many of them are very good work; and some show excellent pictorial quality.'[1]

The most enthusiastic and gifted of the royal amateurs was undoubtedly Queen Alexandra, whose interesting Kodak family snapshots taken at Marlborough House, Sandringham, Copenhagen, and on a cruise off the coast of Scotland, were published

[1] *The Photogram*, London. December 1897.

in *The Graphic* in August 1905 and in book form in 1908.

Some time in the 1880s, with relays of grandchildren and great-grandchildren constantly surrounding her, Queen Victoria felt the need for a private photographer and appointed Alexander Lamont Henderson, who also taught Princess Beatrice photography. After Henderson's retirement due to ill-health, this position was held by a Mr. Cleave. Mountains of photographs continued to pile up and—as the *Photographic News* remarked—it almost became necessary to create a new Court position—the Comptroller of Photographs and Keeper of the *Cartes*.

On the last day of the Czar's and Czarina's visit to Balmoral in the autumn of 1896, W. & D. Downey, photographers in Newcastle and London, came to Balmoral to take the first cinematograph pictures of Queen Victoria and her relations. The ciné-camera of the Lumière brothers had only been put on the market a few months earlier. Indeed, the first public showing of ciné-films in Britain had only taken place at the Polytechnic in London on 20 February of the same year. With her usual interest in new inventions, the Queen entered in her diary: 'we were all photographed by Downey by the new cinematograph process, which makes moving pictures by winding off a reel of films. We were walking up and down, and the children jumping about.' Seven weeks later, after the projection of the film in the Red Drawing-room at Windsor Castle, the Queen had a better grasp of the idea: 'It is a very wonderful process, representing people, their movements and actions, as if they were alive.' At the first Royal Command cinema performance, at Windsor Castle, on 23 November of the following year Queen Victoria watched with intense interest Prof. Jolly's film of her Diamond Jubilee procession—the only film presenting the entire procession, and consisting of 22,000 pictures. Fourteen other short films followed, each accompanied by music played by the orchestra of the Empire Theatre, Leicester Square, which was among the earliest theatres to show films in its music-hall programmes.

Queen Victoria's reign was richer in mechanical inventions than any other had been, and anything new had a fascination for her, whether it were learning to photograph, seeing herself on the cinema screen, speaking into the telephone, hearing her voice on the phonograph, or riding a tricycle. The telephone was demonstrated to her by its inventor Alexander Graham Bell in January 1878. At Osborne House the Queen was put into communication with Osborne Cottage and 'talked with Sir Thomas and Mary Biddulph, also heard some singing quite plainly. But it is rather faint and one must hold the tube close to one's ear.' How disappointed she would be, were she to know that after eighty years we still have to do this.

In August 1898 Lord Denbigh demonstrated Edison's phonograph at Osborne and, the wounds of the Abyssinian War healed, Queen Victoria recorded this message of friendship for the Emperor Menelek: 'I, Victoria, Queen of England, hope your Majesty is in good health. I thank you for the kind reception which you have given to my Envoys, Mr. Rodd and Mr. Harrington. I wish your Majesty and the Empress Taitou all prosperity and success, and I hope that the friendship between our two Empires will constantly increase.' In Addis Ababa the Queen's message was accorded a ceremonial reception. An artillery salute was fired when her envoys handed over the cylinder to the Emperor, who received it standing to show his respect. He listened to the message several times and expressed his thanks for the honour paid him by Queen Victoria. Hearing her voice made him feel face to face with her, and he marvelled at her firm and distinct enunciation at the age of seventy-nine. The cylinder was then destroyed as requested by the Queen, who presumably did not fancy her royal message being played again and again as an after-dinner entertainment for the Emperor's guests, or becoming distorted by scratches and heat. The deplorable fact is, however, that a great historic opportunity was missed in failing to record for posterity Queen Victoria's melodious voice, which Fanny Kemble had called in the Queen's youth 'exquisite . . . the enunciation was as perfect as the intonation was melodious, and I think it is impossible to hear a more excellent utterance than that of the Queen's English by the English Queen'.

Queen Victoria's one and only cycling experience is related in *The Rambler*.[1] About 1881 the Queen saw a girl enjoying a morning spin on her tricycle near Osborne House, and asked her to give a demonstration in the grounds. Convinced of its safety, the Queen soon afterwards ordered a tricycle for the use of the Royal Household. When the machine arrived the Queen was unable to resist the temptation of trying it herself, and mounting the saddle in private, took a turn in the grounds. Wisely, perhaps, she had taken the precaution not to be seen cycling by the Household, but she declared that she found the exercise exhilarating. The Queen also gave a tricycle to the Duchess of Albany, and took great interest in her daughter-in-law's cycling lessons in the grounds at Osborne. The Duchess was probably the first royal lady to start the fashion for cycling. The daughters of the Prince and Princess of Wales followed suit in the 'nineties, the only condition Queen Victoria imposed on the new sport being the banning of bloomers. 'Darling Arthur', the Duke of Connaught, was given the command of a bicycle regiment, and learned to cycle in the belief that it would make a good impression to arrive on wheels for the inspection of his troops. But the Duke's good intentions came to a sad end, for in his efforts to return the salute of an N.C.O. he lost control of his machine, and both fell off in an inextricable confusion of legs and wheels.

[1] *The Rambler*, London, Vol. 1, No. 1, 22 May 1897: 'The One and only Cycling Experience of Her Majesty the Queen.'

331   Buckingham Palace, with the Marble Arch (removed in 1851).
*Watercolour by Joseph Nash, June 1846.*

332   Buckingham Palace about 1890, before the alteration of the facade by Sir Aston Webb in 1913.
*Photograph by G. W. Wilson.*

333   The Throne Room at Buckingham Palace.
*Photograph by Hills & Saunders, 1873.*

334   Queen Victoria's sitting-room on the garden side of Buckingham Palace.
*Photograph by Hills & Saunders, 1873.*

335 Queen Victoria's private sitting-room at Buckingham Palace.
*Photograph by Hills & Saunders, 1873.*

336 Queen Victoria's and Prince Albert's bedroom at Buckingham Palace.
*Watercolour by J. Roberts, 1848.*

337 Queen Victoria's dressing-room at Buckingham
Palace.
*Photograph by Horatio Nelson King, c. 1865.*

339 The Prince Consort's dressing-room
at Buckingham Palace.
*Photograph by Hills & Saunders, 1873.*

340 The Prince Consort's sitting-room at
Buckingham Palace.
*Photograph by Hills & Saunders, 1873.*

338 Queen Victoria's dressing-room at Buckingham
Palace. On the wall hang family portraits.
*Photograph by Hills & Saunders, 1873.*

339

340

341 Windsor Castle from the north-west, across the River Thames.
*Photograph by G. W. Wilson, c. 1885.*

342 Windsor Castle: the Round Tower and St. George's Chapel (on the left).
*Photograph by Roger Fenton, c. 1857.*

343   The Throne Room, Windsor Castle.          *Photograph by G. W. Wilson, c. 1885.*

344   The Crimson Drawing-room, Windsor Castle.          *Photograph by Disderi, 1866.*

345 The Green Drawing-room, Windsor Castle.
*Photograph by Disderi, 1866.*

347 The Prince Consort's dressing-room at Windsor Castle. The portrait on the wall is of Queen Victoria as a bride.
*Photograph by H. N. King, c. 1865.*

347

348 The Prince Consort's sitting-room at Windsor Castle.
*Photograph by H. N. King, c. 1865.*

346 Queen Victoria's dressing-room at Windsor Castle.
*Photograph by H. N. King, c. 1865.*

348

349 Osborne House. The Royal apartments from the west.

350 Osborne House. Designed in Italian style by Prince Albert and completed in 1851.

351 One of the corridors at Osborne House.
*Photograph by Disderi, 1866.*

352 The Palladian Colonnade at Osborne House (north wing).
*Photograph by Disderi, 1866.*

353 Queen Victoria's dressing-room at Osborne House. The frame of the looking-glass and the toilet articles are of Minton china. This photograph shows the washstand and footbath, later replaced by an adjoining bathroom.

354 Queen Victoria's sitting-room at Osborne House. The homely interior with its patterned chintz upholstery is crowded with paintings, photographs and bric-à-brac of every description. In the centre stand two tables: at the right-hand one the Queen wrote her letters and studied Government dispatches: Prince Albert sat on her left when submitting memoranda.

355  The drawing-room at Osborne House.                    *Photograph by H. N. King, c. 1885.*

356  Queen Victoria's and Prince Albert's bedroom
at Osborne House. Here the Queen died, surrounded
by her family, on 22 January 1901.

357 The Swiss cottage at Osborne—a genuine châlet brought in sections from Switzerland and erected in 1853–54.

358 The Prince Consort's sitting-room at Osborne House.

359   Old Balmoral Castle, which was demolished and replaced by a larger castle designed by
Prince Albert in 1853.
*Photograph taken by G. W. Wilson in September 1854.*

360   Balmoral Castle in course of construction. View of the north side, September 1855.
*Photograph by G. W. Wilson.*

361  Queen Victoria's Balmoral letter paper with engraving of roebuck designed by
Sir Edwin Landseer, *c.* 1855.

362  Queen Victoria's Balmoral letter paper with engraving of deer designed by
Sir Edwin Landseer, *c.* 1855.

363    The Shiel of Althnaguisach near Balmoral. Queen Victoria and Prince Albert frequently
stayed at this small shooting lodge.
*Pen and wash sketch by W. Wyld, September 1852.*

364    Balmoral Castle from across the River Dee.
*Photograph by G. W. Wilson, September 1857.*

365   The drawing-room at Balmoral Castle.
*Watercolour by J. Roberts, 1857.*

366   Queen Victoria's sitting-room at Balmoral Castle.

367   Queen Victoria's dressing-room at Balmoral Castle.
*Photograph by G. W. Wilson, c. 1875.*

368   Queen Victoria's and the Prince Consort's bedroom at Balmoral Castle. After the Prince's death a photograph of him on his deathbed  and a wreath always hung on the right side of any bed in which the Queen slept.   *Photograph by G. W. Wilson, 1875.*

369  A Balmoral menu card, before 1877.

370  Queen Victoria's and the Prince Consort's bedroom on the royal yacht *Victoria and Albert*, launched at Woolwich on 13 May 1854.

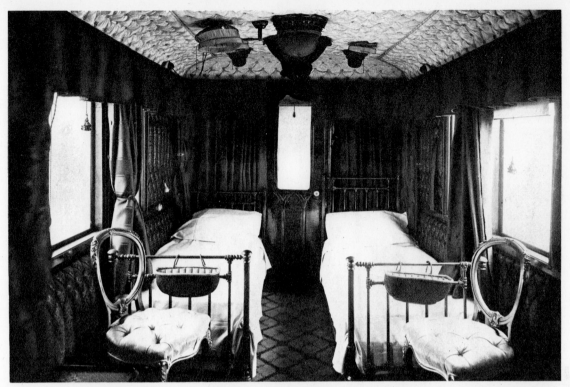

371 The royal railway carriage: the bedroom. Built in 1869 by the London & North Western Railway. It was used by Queen Victoria for thirty years on her journeys to and from Scotland.

372 The royal railway carriage: the day compartment. Built in 1869 and used by Queen Victoria until her death, on her journeys to and from Scotland. In 1895 this compartment (a separate vehicle until then) was joined to the bedroom compartment to make one carriage, 6oft. long and 8ft. wide. The royal train then consisted of fourteen carriages (as against four, fifty years earlier), but still had no through corridor.

373 Gillies and foresters with stag shot by Prince Albert near Balmoral on 5 October 1854.
*Photograph by G. W. Wilson.*

374 Gardeners on the Royal Estate at Windsor, *c.* 1855.

# VI

## QUEEN VICTORIA'S DRAWINGS AND ETCHINGS

ABILITY to sketch was one of the desirable accomplishments of a young lady in the nineteenth century. Princess Victoria's artistic training began at the age of seven or eight, and Richard Westall, R.A., was appointed her drawing master when she was eleven. Under his tuition and that of his successor, William Leitch, who taught her water-colour sketching, she developed apparently such ability that by the time she came to the throne her artistic accomplishments were considered far above those of the average amateur. Leitch relates that he once brought one of the Queen's watercolours to his studio to mount it. Clarkson Stanfield, the marine painter, happened to see the sketch there, and examining it critically asked Leitch who painted it. 'A pupil of mine', came the reply. Stanfield could hardly believe that the picture was not by a fully fledged artist, and was still more mystified when Leitch added that it was 'the work of a lady'. 'If that is so', exclaimed Stanfield, 'she paints too well for an amateur; she will soon be entering our ranks as a professional.'

Landscape sketching was undoubtedly Queen Victoria's *forte*. Her lively pen-and-ink sketches and watercolour drawings, many of them surprisingly free and spirited in style (Plates 386, 389–391), form the bulk of her artistic output. Sometimes tiny sketches of views adorn her letters to relations and close friends. The sketchbook was the Queen's constant companion on her holidays with Prince Albert, frequently helping to pass the time while he was deerstalking. Even after his death, sketching remained a pleasant hobby. Queen Victoria's last picture was a watercolour of one of her Indian attendants, made in 1892 (Plate 392).

Less successful are her portraits. Those made before her marriage have little if any artistic merit, but under the guidance of her portrait-drawing masters Sir George Hayter, Henry Collen and E. T. Parris, her technique made considerable strides. Nevertheless, most of the Queen's portraits from nature are laboured (Plate 388) and only comparatively few, made on the spur of the moment, have a spark of vitality (Plates 159, 380). On the whole she preferred to rely on getting a likeness by copying the portraits of established artists (Plates 376, 392).

Prince Albert, an amateur of greater ability perhaps

than the Queen, did much to encourage her natural inclination towards the graphic arts, and his keen interest in art influenced her more than any of her masters could. Together they began to learn etching in the autumn of 1840 under the tuition of Sir George Hayter (Plate 375) and, in the case of animal studies, Sir Edwin Landseer. Despite the fact that the amount of time they could devote to mastering the technique was necessarily limited, many of their etchings are of surprisingly high quality.

To judge from the numerous proofs of her own and Prince Albert's etchings in the Royal Collection, the Queen took much pleasure in this artistic activity, which continued intermittently until 1849, though the years 1840–3 were the chief period of their productivity. At first, Prince Albert corrected the proofs, and the plate was re-etched, sometimes even a second time, and on occasion a new plate was made. The biting in of the plates with acid was done by the Queen's Wardrobe Woman, Miss Skerritt. The Queen and Prince pulled the proofs on their own press and tried the effect of different papers. Each print bears a note of its state in the Queen's handwriting, and Prince Albert's improvements if any; the authorship of the etching or original drawing appears on the plate with the date of its production, for not infrequently the Queen's etchings are copies from drawings by Prince Albert, Sir Edwin Landseer, Sir William Ross, Sir George Hayter or other artists. Yet, as is to be expected, the Queen's best etchings are those made from her own sketches. The moment she copies, there is something lacking.

The charming double portrait of the little Princess Royal in the eighteenth-century costume in which she appeared on her parents' third wedding anniversary (Plate 383), and the unknown lady (Plate 377) drawn only a few months after the Queen had begun to learn etching, have an admirable clarity of line and neatness of execution.

Some of the etchings, like that of Islay (Plate 378), one of the Queen's pet dogs, are the joint production of the Queen and her husband: drawn by Queen Victoria and etched by Prince Albert, or *vice versa*. Having gained sufficient skill in the technique, the Queen even made some sketches direct on the plate and proudly inscribed them 'Etched at once without a previous sketch.'

More interesting from the artistic point of view are her imaginative pictures of 'Queen Eleanor and Fair Rosamond' and 'Sappho', and her illustrations to Schiller's *Hero and Leander* and *Fiesco* (Plate 387), Goethe's *Goetz von Berlichingen*, *Wilhelm Meister* and others.

Successful etchings were sometimes given to friends, but the royal couple wanted no publicity for their amateur efforts and were furious when in 1848 they were sent *A Descriptive Catalogue of the Royal Victoria and Albert Gallery of Etchings* which had been printed in preparation for a public exhibition of about a hundred of their etchings. Though originally misappropriated, these had been obtained in good faith by the purchaser. However, an expensive lawsuit prevented the exhibition and ruined the owner of the etchings and the publisher of the catalogue.

Early in 1846 Queen Victoria also tried her hand at lithography, but the few productions still in existence lead one to the conclusion that drawing on stone was not her medium. With more practice the Queen might, of course, have achieved far more than she did, but the sparseness of her attempts makes it probable that she did not find lithography congenial. However, it would be unreasonable to expect the Queen to be accomplished in everything she undertook, for even the attempt was, as Prince Albert once explained, 'not with a view of doing anything worth looking at, but simply to enable us to judge and appreciate the work of others'.

375 'Vacation Amusements. Cultivating the Fine Arts—Etching.' *Left*, Lord Melbourne making a study of John Bull; behind Lord Melbourne stands (Sir) George Hayter the artist. *Right*, the Queen and Prince Albert.
*Sketch by John Doyle, October 1840.*

376 Queen Victoria's preliminary sketch for her etching of Prince Albert, copied from Hayter's painting of their marriage, 19 October 1840.

377   Etching of a lady by Queen Victoria,
27 December 1840.

378   The dog Islay drawn by Queen Victoria, etched
by Prince Albert, 11 September 1840.

379 Etching by Queen Victoria of her dachshund
Waldmann, 12 October 1840.

380 Pen and ink sketch by Queen Victoria on her
letter paper with the royal cypher, early 'forties.

T

381  Lithograph by Queen Victoria of the Princess Royal, 6 February 1846.

382  Etching by Queen Victoria of the Princess Royal ('Pussy') going to bed, 9 April 1843.

383 Etching by Queen Victoria of the Princess Royal in eighteenth-century dress and powdered wig, worn on the anniversary of the Queen's wedding day. Etching made on 26 February 1843.

384 Etching by Queen Victoria of Ada (probably Adelaide, daughter of Princess Feodora), 1840.

385 Pen sketch by Queen Victoria of a Highland lassie and laddie, Ardair, 10 September 1847.

386 Sketch by Queen Victoria: Salmon fishing in the Highlands.
*13 September 1850.*

387 Etching by Queen Victoria illustrating the
opening scene of Schiller's *Fiesco*, 7 February 1841.

388 Sketch by Queen Victoria of the Empress
Eugénie, Osborne, August 1857.

389   Watercolour of Glencallater by Queen Victoria, 2 June 1869.

390   Watercolour by Queen Victoria, view from Balmoral Castle, 18 March 1878.

391   Watercolour by Queen Victoria, trees at Balmoral, June 1868.

392   Watercolour by Queen Victoria of one of her Indian attendants, from a painting by Rudolf Svoboda. Made in 1892 at the age of seventy-three, it is the last sketch by Queen Victoria in the Royal Collection.

# BIBLIOGRAPHY

ANDERSON, WILLIAM JAMES, *The Life of F.M., H.R.H. Edward, Duke of Kent*. Ottawa and Toronto, 1870.

BENSON, E. F., *Queen Victoria*. London, 1935.

BESANT, SIR WALTER, *The Queen's Reign 1837–1897*. London, 1897.

BOLITHO, HECTOR (ed.), *The Prince Consort and His Brother. 200 New Letters*. London, 1933.
*Victoria, the Widow and Her Son*. London, 1934.
(ed.), *Further Letters of Queen Victoria from the Archives of the House of Brandenburg-Prussia*. London, 1938.
*The Reign of Queen Victoria*. London, 1949.

BUCHANAN, MERIEL, *Queen Victoria's Relations*. London, 1954.

CRESTON, DORMER, *The Youthful Queen Victoria*. London, 1952.

ERNEST II, *Memoirs of Ernest II, Duke of Saxe-Coburg-Gotha*. 4 vols. London, 1888–90.

(ESHER, LORD), *The Life of Queen Victoria, reproduced from 'The Times'*. London, 1901. (A reprint of Lord Esher's unsigned obituary in *The Times*.)
(ed.), *The Girlhood of Queen Victoria. A selection from Her Majesty's Diaries between the years 1832 and 1840*. 2 vols. London, 1912.

FULFORD, ROGER, *Royal Dukes. The Father and Uncles of Queen Victoria*. London, 1933.
*The Prince Consort*. London, 1949.
*Queen Victoria*. London, 1951.

(GIBBS-SMITH, CHARLES H.), *The Great Exhibition of 1851. A Commemorative Album*. London, 1951.

(GOSSE, SIR EDMUND), Unsigned article *Queen Victoria* in *The Quarterly Review*, Vol. 193, 1901.

GREVILLE, CHARLES F., *The Greville Memoirs. A Journal of the Reigns of King George IV, William IV and Queen Victoria* (up to 1860) edited by Henry Reeve. London, 1875–87.

GREY, GENERAL CHARLES, *The Early Years of the Prince Consort. Compiled under the direction of Her Majesty the Queen*. London, 1867.

GUEDALLA, PHILIP, *Idylls of the Queen*. London, 1937.

HOBHOUSE, CHRISTOPHER, *1851 and the Crystal Palace*. London, 1937.

HOLMES, (SIR) RICHARD R., *Queen Victoria*. London, 1897.
*Edward VII. His Life and Times*, Vol. I. London 1910.

HOUSMAN, LAURENCE, *Victoria Regina. A Dramatic Biography*. London, 1934.

JAGOW, KURT (ed.), *Queen Victoria. Ein Frauenleben unter der Krone. Eigenhändige Briefe und Tagebuchblätter 1834–1901*. Berlin, 1936.
(ed.), *Albert, Prinzgemahl. Ein Leben am Throne. Briefe und Aufzeichnungen 1831–61*. Berlin, 1937.

JERROLD, CLARE, *The Early Court of Queen Victoria*. London, 1912.
*The Married Life of Queen Victoria*. London, 1913.
*The Widowhood of Queen Victoria*. London, 1916.

LEE, SIR SIDNEY, *Queen Victoria. A Biography*. London, 1902.
*King Edward VII. A Biography. Vol. I From Birth to Accession*. London, 1925.

LORNE, THE MARQUESS OF, *V.R.I. Her Life and Empire*. London, 1901.

MARTIN, SIR THEODORE, *The Life of His Royal Highness the Prince Consort*. 5 vols. London, 1874–80.
*Queen Victoria as I Knew Her*. London, 1908.

MAGNUS, SIR PHILIP, *The Life of William Ewart Gladstone*. London, 1954.

MAUROIS, ANDRÉ, *Disraeli. A Picture of the Victorian Age*. London, 1927.

MAXWELL, SIR HERBERT, *Sixty Years a Queen*. London, 1897.

MORSHEAD, SIR OWEN, *Windsor Castle*. London, 1951.

PEACOCKE, MARGUERITE D., *The Story of Buckingham Palace*. London, 1951.

PEARSON, HESKETH, *Dizzy. The Life and Nature of Benjamin Disraeli, Earl of Beaconsfield*. London, 1951.

PONSONBY, ARTHUR (Lord Ponsonby of Shulbrede), *Queen Victoria*. London, 1933.
*Henry Ponsonby, Queen Victoria's Private Secretary. His Life from His Letters*. London, 1942.

PONSONBY, SIR FREDERICK (Lord Sysonby), *Sidelights on Queen Victoria*. London, 1930.
*Recollections of Three Reigns*. London, 1951.

SITWELL, (DAME) EDITH, *Victoria of England.* London, 1936.

SMITH, G. BARNETT, *Life of Her Majesty Queen Victoria. Compiled from all available sources.* London, 1901.

STANLEY, LADY AUGUSTA, *Letters of Lady Augusta Stanley. A Young Lady at Court 1849-1863.* Edited by the Dean of Windsor and Hector Bolitho. London, 1927.

STEEGMAN, JOHN, *Consort of Taste.* London, 1950.

STOCKMAR, BARON, *Memoirs of Baron Stockmar.* London, 1872.

STRACHEY, LYTTON, *Queen Victoria.* London, 1921.

TISDALL, E. E. P., *Unpredictable Queen. The Intimate Life of Queen Alexandra.* London, 1953.

TOOLEY, SARAH, *The Personal Life of Queen Victoria.* London, 1896.

TYTLER, SARAH, *Life of Her Most Gracious Majesty the Queen.* 3 vols. London, 1897.

VICTORIA, QUEEN, *Leaves from a Journal of our Life in the Highlands, from 1848 to 1861.* Edited by Arthur Helps. London, 1868.

*More Leaves from the Journal of a Life in the Highlands, from 1862 to 1882.* London, 1884.

*The Letters of Queen Victoria.* First series: *A selection from Her Majesty's correspondence between the years 1837 and 1861.* Edited by Arthur Christopher Benson and Viscount Esher. 3 vols. London, 1908.

Second series, edited by George Earle Buckle. Vols. 1 and 2, 1862–78, London, 1926; Vol. 3, 1879–85, London, 1928.

Third series, edited by George Earle Buckle. 3 vols., 1886–1901. London, 1930-2.

WATSON, VERA, *A Queen at Home. An intimate account of the social and domestic life of Queen Victoria's Court.* London, 1952.

WILSON, MONA. *Queen Victoria.* London, 1933.

Anon. ONE OF HER MAJESTY'S SERVANTS, *The Private Life of Queen Victoria.* Memorial edition. London, 1901.

# INDEX

Queen Victoria herself is not indexed, as she appears on every page.
The numbers of the pages on which illustrations appear are in italics.

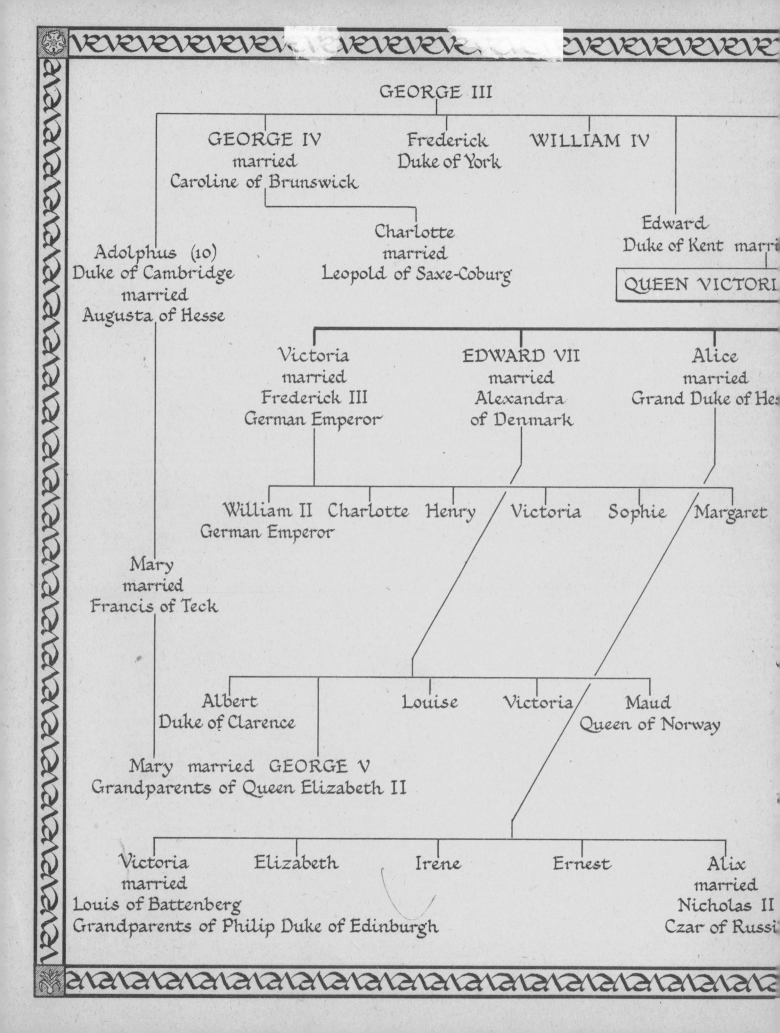

GEORGE III

GEORGE IV
married
Caroline of Brunswick

Frederick
Duke of York

WILLIAM IV

Edward
Duke of Kent marri

QUEEN VICTORI

Adolphus (10)
Duke of Cambridge
married
Augusta of Hesse

Charlotte
married
Leopold of Saxe-Coburg

Victoria
married
Frederick III
German Emperor

EDWARD VII
married
Alexandra
of Denmark

Alice
married
Grand Duke of Hes

William II    Charlotte    Henry      Victoria    Sophie    Margaret
German Emperor

Mary
married
Francis of Teck

Albert
Duke of Clarence

Louise      Victoria      Maud
Queen of Norway

Mary  married  GEORGE V
Grandparents of Queen Elizabeth II

Victoria          Elizabeth          Irene          Ernest          Alix
married                                                             married
Louis of Battenberg                                                Nicholas II
Grandparents of Philip Duke of Edinburgh                           Czar of Russi